D0100288

The Garage Series

Street-smart books about technology

Each author **presents** a unique take on solving problems, using a format designed to replicate the **experience** of Web searching.

Technology presented and **organized** by useful topic—not in a linear tutorial style.

Books that cover **whatever** needs to be covered to get the project done. Period.

Eben Hewitt, *Java Garage.* ISBN: 0321246233.
Tara Calishain, *Web Search Garage.* ISBN: 0131471481.
Kirk McElhearn, *iPod & iTunes Garage.* ISBN: 0131486454.
Marc Campbell, *Web Design Garage.* ISBN: 0131481991.
Don Jones, *PHP-Nuke Garage.* ISBN: 0131855166.
Dan Livingston, *ActionScript 2.0 Garage.* ISBN: 0131484753.

```
<a garage is where you work.
in a garage, you do your  work, not somebody else's.
it's where you experiment and listen to the old ball
                           game. make music.
                                get away.
                                 tinker.
it's where you do projects for passion, make your own
                                 rules, and
              plot like an evil genius./>
```

(Irreverent. **Culturally rooted.**)

Edgy and fun. Lively writing.
(The impersonal voice of an
omniscient narrator is not   **[Eben Hewitt, series editor]**
allowed!)

Check out the series at **www.phptr.com/garageseries**

WEB DESIGN GARAGE

Marc Campbell

Prentice Hall Professional Technical Reference

Upper Saddle River, NJ • Boston • Indianapolis • San Francisco
New York • Toronto • Montreal • London • Munich • Paris • Madrid
Capetown • Sydney • Tokyo • Singapore • Mexico City

PRENTICE
HALL
PTR

The publisher offers excellent discounts on this book when ordered in quantity for bulk purchases or special sales, which may include electronic versions and/or custom covers and content particular to your business, training goals, marketing focus, and branding interests. For more information, please contact:

U. S. Corporate and Government Sales
(800) 382-3419
corpsales@pearsontechgroup.com

For sales outside the U. S., please contact:

International Sales
international@pearsoned.com

Visit us on the Web: www.phptr.com

Library of Congress Cataloging-in-Publication Data

Campbell, Marc.
  Web design garage / Marc Campbell.
    p. cm.
  Includes index.
  ISBN 0-13-148199-1 (pbk. : alk. paper)
    1. Web sites—Design. I. Title.

TK5105.888.C355 2005
006.7—dc22   2004025192

ISBN 0-13-148199-1

Text printed in the United States on recycled paper at Edwards Brothers in Ann Arbor, Michigan.
First printing, January 2005

Contents

x

Preface

sn't it always the way? You take five-hundred-odd manuscript pages, some ninety thousand words, about two hundred thirty figures, and six months of your life trying to explain something, and then some hotshot comes along and sums it all up in a single sentence.

It happened to me when I submitted this humble volume for the approval of Eben Hewitt, series editor of the Garage Series books. He came back with the following—and I quote: "Campbell does a terrific job of illustrating that not only are both design and usability important—they might even be the same thing." When I read that, I nearly fell off my chair. "That's it!" I shouted. "That's what I've been trying to say!"

But then it occurred to me—who else might be reading this? Who at my publisher might be weighing a twenty-word summary against a ream of manuscript and thinking about all the time, effort, and capital that would be saved by putting out a pamphlet or an information sheet or even a clever slogan instead of a full-blown book? How would Hewitt's devastatingly insightful comment affect the terms of my contract? My advance? This especially was a concern, because I had already spent it.

Fortunately for me, the thunder didn't come down. This book quietly went into production, and nobody seemed to notice what Eben Hewitt—a Java programmer, no less—had done. And now, nobody ever will.

Or maybe my saving grace was that, while Hewitt can spout off all the encapsulated central theses that he likes, the book before you, while never achieving the level of clarity of an E. H., provides the details as consolation. It shows by way of many, many examples how design and usability are inexorably intertwined. It even takes a stab at why.

So, if you're an ideas person, a high-concept hierophant with a sixth-level intellect—an Eben Hewitt, if you will— read no further. My series editor just gave you everything that this book has to offer. But if you're like me, more like a fire hydrant than a hierophant with an intellect nowhere near the sixth level, who likes pictures, examples, code snippets, and someone to explain them all: Welcome to *Web Design Garage*.

Perhaps a word or two about the organization of this book is in order. *Web Design Garage* is a bit like object-oriented programming, in that you dip into the library (or the book, as it were); pull out what you need; mix, match, and combine; and get back to work. Instead of traditional chapters, there are topics: eighty-six of them, to be precise. Topics range from short, article-length pieces to chapter-size ruminations, depending on the subject at hand. I put these topics into eight general categories or parts to help you find what you're looking for as quickly as possible.

For best results, don't read this book from cover to cover—you might find that it skips around too much. Occasionally, it repeats itself in the interest of keeping the topics as self-contained as possible.

Your best approach is to refer to the topics that help you to solve specific problems that you're having with your site and to chart your course from there. If any given topic alludes to a design technique like grouping or a technology like Cascading Style Sheets that you aren't as familiar with, you can flip to the topics about these subjects and expand your horizons.

With Web design especially, diverse roads tend to join up, and they all lead to the same place (more or less), so you'll weave your way through the entire book eventually. But you'll do it by following your own path, not the abstruse labyrinth of the author's inner mind. The hope is that you come away from *Web Design Garage* with something approaching a nonlinear experience, much like surfing the Web.

For myself, I like to think that *Web Design Garage* is a kind of fantasy adventure story, one of those choose-your-own-plotline types. You, the hero, are trying to put together the components of a magic spell that will save the kingdom. To do this, you must pore over poorly documented ancient formulae. There's even a recurring villain: the marketing department, who emerges when least expected to hijack your site and use it to brainwash your visitors into buying things. All this technology talk is just a metaphor anyway. Look past it, and you'll find a real page-turner.

If you are reading these words, and if I am right about to whom this book would appeal, then you are a person of obvious taste with some knowledge *a priori* about how to build a Web site. Maybe you're the sole in-house Web designer/developer at your place of employment. Maybe you're self-employed, and you need to build a Web site for your business. Maybe you're an *artiste*, and the medium of the Web intrigues you. Maybe you just enjoy the technology stuff and on the weekends you like tinkering with power beyond human control. Whatever your situation may be, most of the topics assume a baseline familiarity with the essential procedures, like creating HTML documents and working with scripts. If you know a little already, this book helps you to learn a lot more.

But if I am wrong, which is as likely as not, then please begin your *Web Design Garage* journey with *Part VIII: Basic Training Topics*. When I wrote this section, I pretended that I didn't know anything, and I tried to explain the most basic concepts of the craft to myself in the clearest way possible. The idea here is that, even if you have never seen the letters *HTML* arranged in that particular sequence before, you can start with Part VIII and go on to use the rest of the book.

And, what the heck, even if you know a thing or two, you might have a look at Part VIII anyway, just as a refresher. Many Web designers, including this one, are self-taught. We all have these little gaps in our educations. Maybe Part VIII can make a few things clearer for you, just like Barney Marispini and Rob Streeter (the technical editors on this book) helped me to close up some of the potholes in my own education. I owe you one, guys. In fact, I owe you several.

While I'm on the without-whoms, I would be remiss if I did not mention John Neidhart of the Barbs, John Fuller, Raquel Kaplan, Robin O'Brien, Kathleen Addis, Julie Nahil, Dmitri Korzh, and everyone at Prentice Hall PTR who made this book happen. Thanks also to the usual suspects at Studio B, both old and new: Neil Salkind, Lynn Haller, Stacey Barone, Katrina Hillsten, and Jackie Coder.

A special admission of indebtedness emanates directly from me to those persons whom I did not have the pleasure of meeting virtually or physically, whose names I do not know, but whose efforts contributed to the care, feeding, and production of this book and its author, much like a superhero who defends a city anonymously.

PART I:

Design and
Usability Topics

Designing to Aid Navigation

esign on the Web isn't really about giving your visitors something pretty to look at. It plays a more important role: creating a sense of place. A good design unifies the pages of your site by making them look like they belong together. The design gives you the "siteness" of the site, in other words. It draws a border around your particular stake on the Web and says, "This stuff goes together."

You achieve this sense of place by using design elements consistently throughout your site. Things like the layout, color scheme, and text style of your pages should hang together visually. If every page of your site uses different design conventions, no matter how effective these individual designs may be, you create a sense of place akin to a strip mall. Every glaring storefront competes with every other with no discernable intelligence or purpose. It's a visual catastrophe. However, when you apply the same design consistently, page after page after page, you get something like an upscale department store. Your level of class goes way up. You attract a more sophisticated clientele. When your visitors navigate your site, they feel like they're moving from floor to floor and department to department, all under the same roof. Even better, the way you use design can help your visitors figure out what department they're in without searching for those floor plans by the escalators.

Here's how it works. Most sites organize their content according to some type of **hierarchy** or logical structure, which means that the site builders break down the information they're presenting into categories and subcategories, like this:

- Movies
  - Action
  - Comedy
  - Drama
  - Romance
  - Mystery/Suspense
  - Horror
  - Sci-fi
- Music
  - Popular
  - Jazz
  - Classical
- Games
  - PC
  - Console
- About Us

If you're designing this site, the hierarchy does most of the work for you. The top-level items in the list become the choices in the navigation, as in Figure 1.1. These are the floors in your upscale department store. You know right away that you need a page on your site for each of the main categories. What about the subcategories? These are the departments in your department store, with several on each floor of the building. You need a page on your site for each of the subcategories as well. Maybe you need sub-subcategories or sub-sub-subcategories, too, depending on how deep and detailed the hierarchy of the site is. No problem. Count on one page for each item in the list.

The great thing about a hierarchical structure is that it funnels your visitors exactly where they want to go. Your navigation gets them to the right floor, and the subcategories direct them to the right department on that floor. It's quick, easy, and intuitive, just like moving through a physical place. Your task as the designer is to enhance this effect to the utmost. You want your graphical representation of the site to match the organizational structure as closely as possible. The trick is to make the pages for each level of the hierarchy visually distinct while maintaining an overall uniform look and feel.

Look at the designs in Figure 1.2. They're consistent. As a matter of fact, they're exactly the same. But notice that the design on the left is for a top-level

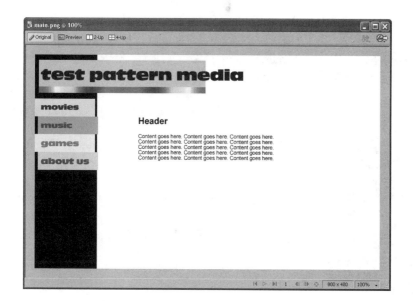

page—a floor of the building—while the design on the right is for a subcategory page—a department on that floor. Nothing about the design suggests the position of the pages in the hierarchy. In one case, the design identifies a main category. In the other, the design identifies a subcategory.

Big deal, right? At least the design is consistent. The navigation is clear and easily accessible. Visitors won't get lost as they browse the site. Well, maybe, maybe not. If your visitors come in through the front door—that is, if they begin at

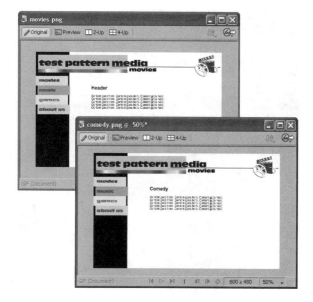

Figure 1.2

The same design appears on two types of pages: a main-category page (left) and a sub-category page (right). The design may be consistent, but it doesn't help your visitors figure out where they are in the site hierarchy.

6

TIP

For every level in your site hierarchy, create a distinct but related page design.

TIP

Don't even think about designing a site without sketching out the site structure first. You don't need to know every single category or subcategory. These will probably change a dozen times during development anyway. However, you should know approximately how deep the hierarchy will go, so you can provide distinct but related designs for each level of page.

the front page of your site and work their way through the categories and subcategories—they'll probably be all right. But a Web site isn't a physical place. It's a virtual one. It has properties that physical places don't. For one, your visitors don't have to come in through the front door. Thanks to search engines, bookmarks, and friends sharing links by email, your visitors can materialize in the deepest recesses of your site without any idea of where they are in relation to everything else. But if your design suggests a specific location and an overall sense of place, you can help your visitors get their bearings, no matter how they arrive.

Compare the previous designs with the ones in Figure 1.3. Here, the designs themselves reinforce the logical structure of the site. The subcategory page on the right takes its visual cues from the main-category page on the left, but the designs are different enough to suggest that the subcategory page is a different type of thing, which it is. Dress all your subcategory pages like this, while using the main-category design for all your main-category pages, and you're home free.

You can go a couple of different ways with distinguishing the designs. The pages in Figure 1.4 get busier and more graphically involved as you go down. This scheme works best when your hierarchy drills down from general categories to increasingly more specific information, such as going from a broad category like a book to a type of book such as fantasy to a specific title in that

Figure 1.3

Two different but related designs—one for the main-category page (left) and another for the subcategory page (right)— help your visitors keep their bearings as they navigate your site.

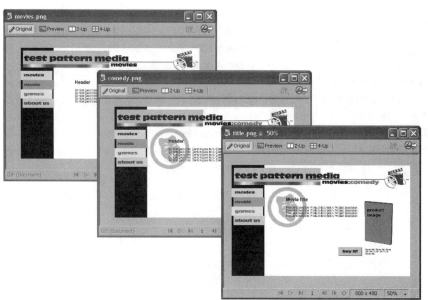

Figure 1.4

In this design, the pages get busier the deeper you go, just as the information on the pages gets more specific.

genre such as *The Lord of the Rings*. The increasingly involved designs suggest to your visitors that they're getting closer and closer to the information they want, which is in the bottom-level pages.

If your site focuses on the information in the top-level pages instead, you might try a design as shown in Figure 1.5. Here, the pages get less involved as they go down. This implies that the lower level pages clarify or expand upon

Figure 1.5

If you want to focus attention on the top-level page, use a less-involved design on the lower level pages.

8

> **TIP**
>
> Use the most design on the pages where you want to focus the most attention. If your bottom-level pages are the most important, as in an ecommerce site, build your design toward the bottom level. However, if your top-level pages are the most important, as in a corporate site, emphasize the top-level pages instead.

the information in the top-level page, but almost as an aside. From your visitor's point of view, the top-level page delivers the goods, while the lower level pages provide secondary information. Corporate sites benefit from this type of structure, since these sites provide general information about a company or organization. This scheme doesn't work as well for ecommerce sites such as bookstores and record stores, which are all about the bottom-level pages—the specific products for sale.

Grouping Similar Functions

rouping is a design technique in which you place similar things next to each other. Take any number of objects, like the set in Figure 2.1. If you arrange them evenly throughout the design space, they look like random objects—nothing less, nothing more. However, if you cluster them, as in Figure 2.2, your eye associates each clump as a unit, and your brain tries to figure out why these particular objects belong to that particular group. Suddenly, where at first you had a bunch of random, meaningless objects, you now have two logical groups: living objects and nonliving objects. The people who come up with I.Q. tests love this sort of thing.

Grouping is easy and intuitive. It works on the principle of guilt by association. It is remarkably effective. And you can use it in Web design.

In fact, a Web site is one of the best places for grouping. Why? Look no further than the humble hyperlink, the basic element of the online computer/human interface. The primary way in which your visitors interact with your site is by clicking on hyperlinks. But hyperlinks themselves have at least three different functions. Clicking often causes a new page to load, but not always. Sometimes, clicking a hyperlink causes an email window to open. Other times, clicking launches a JavaScript or a server-side application. It all depends on how you code the link.

Forget about email and scripts for the moment. Just consider the primary hyperlink function of loading new pages, and you still find plenty of variation. Sometimes the page loads in the current browser window. Sometimes the page

Figure 2.1

Take any set of random, meaningless objects.

loads in a new browser window. Sometimes the visitor goes to another page on the site. Sometimes the visitor winds up on another site entirely. And the trigger that causes all these diverse effects looks exactly the same, as in Figure 2.3. One of these links causes an email window to open, and the only way you can find it is to guess.

Fortunately, you have a design technique that lets you associate objects logically, as in Figure 2.4. Notice how grouping makes picking out the email link so much easier, even though all the hyperlinks say the same thing, and they all require the same kind of interaction—a single mouse click—to oper-

Figure 2.2

Clump the objects into groups, and your brain associates them logically.

ate. When you have objects that look the same and work the same but perform different kinds of functions, grouping is essential for differentiating them.

You can leverage the power of grouping to optimize your Web site's interface. Take a look at the nav bar in Figure 2.5. The labels on the buttons may be clear and easy to understand, but the buttons themselves aren't grouped very effectively. Clicking the first four buttons causes new pages to load, while clicking the fifth opens an email window. This interrupts the logic of your design, because your visitors expect a page to load when they click on Contact Us.

FAQ

Is grouping just a technique for design?
Absolutely not. It's a fundamental psychological principle. Our brains are hard-wired to find meaning in groups.

Early in the 2004 presidential campaign, the Republican Party issued a photograph of a young John Kerry standing a few rows behind the notoriously liberal Jane Fonda during a Vietnam-era peace rally. Mr. Kerry and Ms. Fonda aren't talking in the photo. They aren't conspiring against the government, planning a rendezvous in Cuba, or doing anything that gets conservatives hot under the collar. So why release the photo? Easy. Grouping. Guilt by association. Simply by showing John Kerry in proximity to Jane Fonda, the Republicans hoped to tarnish his image.

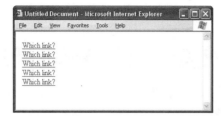

Figure 2.3

Quick! Which of these hyperlinks causes an email window to open? You have no way of knowing without clicking, since hyperlinks always look the same regardless of their function.

Figure 2.4

Apply the technique of grouping to this jumble, and you can probably guess that the link on the right opens the email window.

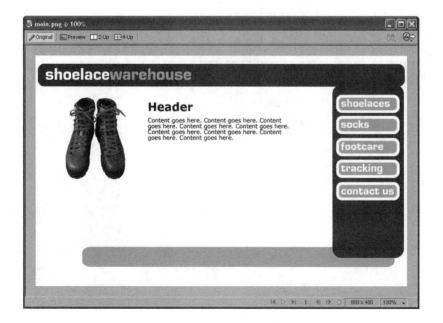

Figure 2.5

Because of grouping, your visitors assume that all five buttons have the same function. However, clicking on Contact Us opens an email window, while the others load new pages.

Figure 2.6

Separate the Contact Us button, and you make it clearer to your visitors that Contact Us doesn't have the same function as the other buttons.

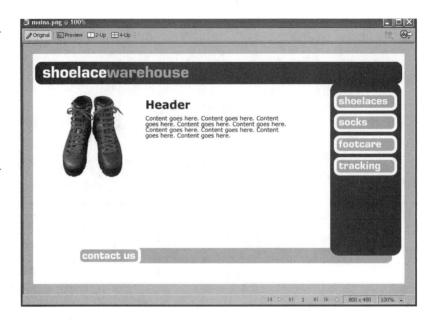

You're better off separating the Contact Us button from the others and moving it somewhere else in the interface, as in Figure 2.6. Better still, change the look of the Contact Us button entirely, as in Figure 2.7. This reinforces the idea that Contact Us has some other function than loading a page.

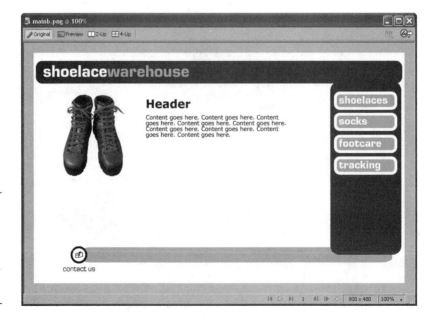

Figure 2.7

By changing the look of the Contact Us button, you reinforce the idea that it's a different kind of thing.

Four buttons remain in the nav bar. What happens if the first three link to pages on the current site, while the fourth opens a new browser window and goes to a different site where your visitors can track their packages? Even though all four buttons load new pages, you probably want to separate the fourth from the other three, simply because it functions slightly differently. But where to put the fourth button? You don't want to group it with the Contact Us button as in Figure 2.8, because your visitors will assume that these buttons have similar functions, which they don't.

Your best bet is to make room for a new group on your interface, as Figure 2.9 shows. Moreover, by changing the button into a regular hyperlink, which usually links to a new page, you give your visitors a hint about its function.

Good grouping doesn't just make life easier for your visitors. It makes life easier for you, the designer. As your site grows, you always know exactly where to add new buttons or links, as in Figure 2.10. This way, your site won't end up looking like Frankenstein's monster. The design itself eliminates the guesswork.

The technique of grouping becomes even more important in apps like shopping carts with lots of clickable controls. Remember, usability is the name of the game on the Web. Try muddling your way through the shopping-cart

TIP

Sometimes, grouping by itself isn't enough. If your interface still feels clunky after separating the controls into distinct function groups, try using different designs for different kinds of buttons or links.

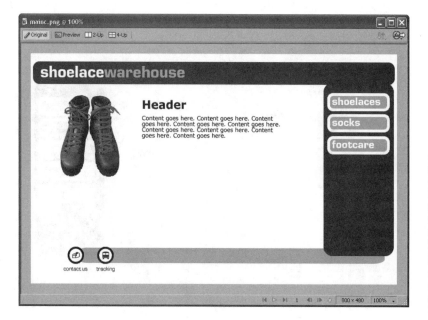

Figure 2.8

Don't add buttons to the new group if they don't have similar functions. The Tracking button links to a page on another Web site.

Figure 2.9

Instead, create separate groups for separate functions.

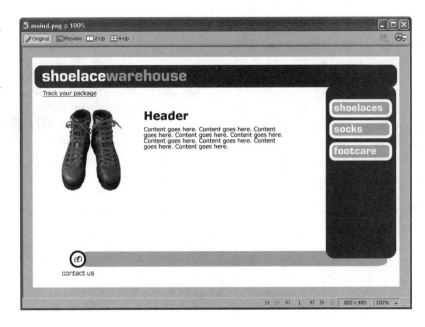

interface in Figure 2.11. The design makes it painful to use. Nothing in the interface is grouped according to function, so your visitors have to read each button to figure out what to do. The more you make them stop and think about what they're doing, the less likely they are to complete the sale.

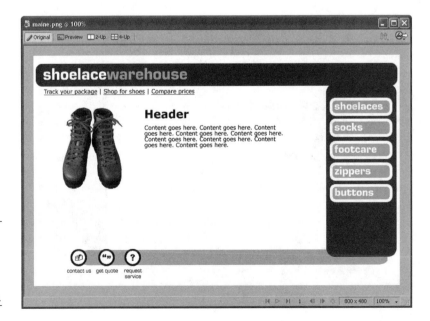

Figure 2.10

Thanks to grouping, you always know exactly where to add new buttons or links.

Figure 2.11

*This shopping
cart is hard for
your visitors to
use; therefore,
they won't use
it. Adios, sales.*

A little grouping improves this interface, as Figure 2.12 shows. Organizing
the buttons according to function makes working with the shopping cart easier
and more intuitive. And tweaking the designs of the buttons to reinforce the
idea of different functions is even better, as in Figure 2.13.

Figure 2.12

*The shopping
cart becomes
more intelligi-
ble when you
organize the
buttons by
function.*

Figure 2.13

Using different designs for different types of buttons is even better.

Designing Graphics for Clicks

aking images into hyperlinks is extremely easy in HTML. Simply nest the image tag between opening and closing anchor tags, like this:

```
<a href="index.htm"><img src="/images/logo.gif"></a>
```

Notice that the browser draws a rectangular border around the hyperlinked image, as in Figure 3.1. The color of the border is the same color as text hyperlinks. Your good old Web browser, always thinking ahead, rightly assumes that you want to give your visitors a visual clue that the image is clickable. The border helps to separate your clickable image from nonclickable images on the page.

But of all the sites you've visited on the Web, how many clickable images have you seen that actually use the built-in border? Not too many. The border is clunky and ugly, and tends to interfere with the visual flow of the page. That's why most Web designers choose to turn off the border, like this:

> **TIP**
>
> A good time to use the default hyperlink border is when you have a clickable thumbnail image that links to a full-sized version of the graphic file.

```
<a href="index.htm"><img src="/images/logo.gif" border="0"></a>
```

Setting the border attribute to 0 solves one problem, but creates another, as Figure 3.2 demonstrates. The hyperlinked image is still clickable, but, without

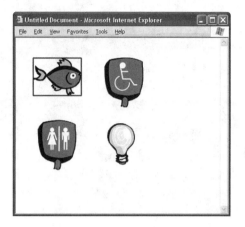

Figure 3.1

When you make an image into a hyperlink, the browser draws a rectangular border around the image, indicating to your visitors that the image is clickable. Notice how the border sets the hyperlinked image apart from the other, nonlinked images on the page.

TIP

You can set the border attribute to any value, not just 0. The higher the value you use, the heavier the border becomes.

the attention-grabbing border, your visitors have no way of knowing which image is clickable without moving the mouse pointer over all the images. Your visitors won't forgive you for this. Anything that requires them to stop and think is an invitation to leave your site.

The trick here is to make your clickable images look clickable without resorting to the ugly hyperlink border. Two techniques serve you well in this regard: context and affordances.

Putting clickable images in the right context on your page goes a long way toward making them stand out as clickable elements. Consider the layout in Figure 3.3. Of these five images, three are clickable, and two aren't. If you take a couple of seconds to think about which are which, you can probably guess, but your visitors won't be nearly as patient with you. To keep them happily immersed in your site, try providing a more intelligent layout, as in Figure 3.4. By separating the clickable images from the nonclickable ones, you create a mini control-panel interface on the page, which suggests the idea of clickability.

TIP

You can also set the border attribute of a nonlinked image. Netscape draws the border in the default text color of the page. Internet Explorer draws the border in black.

Sometimes, the right context isn't enough, especially when you load your design with images. For situations like these, affordances come in handy.

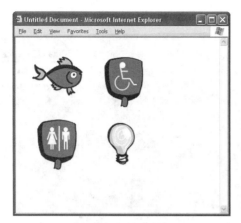

Figure 3.2

You can turn off the built-in hyperlink border, but then the clickable image looks like any other.

Affordances are visual clues in the design element itself that suggest or hint at the element's function. The browser's built-in hyperlink border may not be very pleasing aesthetically, but it makes an excellent affordance, because it visually suggests to your visitors that the image is hyperlinked.

One of the most common affordances on the Web is the button metaphor. It's so common that many designers use the terms **button** and **clickable image** interchangeably. By making clickable images look like buttons—objects that get pressed when they exist in the real world—you associate the act of pressing with your image. Hence, the image attracts mouse clicks.

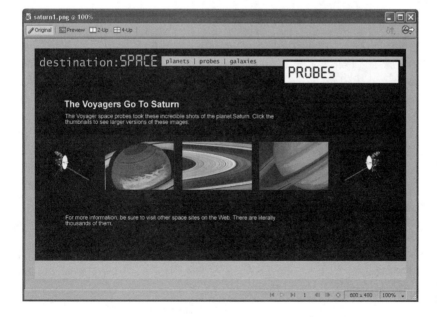

Figure 3.3

This layout needs some work. The three clickable images aren't as easy to distinguish from the two nonclickable images.

Figure 3.4

Ah, much better. The clickable images stand out in this context.

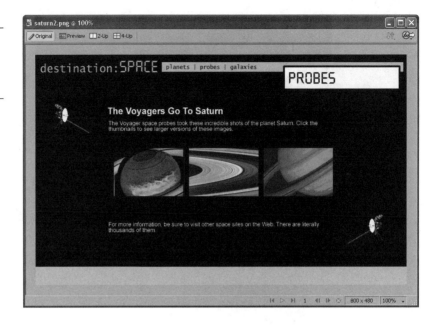

Figure 3.4

Ah, much better. The clickable images stand out in this context.

Watch what happens when you change the thumbnails from the previous example into buttons, as in Figure 3.5. Notice how you effectively remove any lingering doubt about which images are clickable on the page. The design of the buttons helps to set them apart from the nonclickable images, and the telltale button shape encourages clicks.

As powerful as buttons are, be careful not to take them for granted. Buttons don't help you much if your visitors can't find them, as in Figure 3.6. Always try to place your buttons conspicuously, as in Figure 3.7. You want your visitors to feel like your interface is at their disposal.

Figure 3.7 also shows that using icons or symbols as clickable images can be another effective affordance. In this design, the arrow icons are more immediate and intuitive than buttons with Previous and Next labels. You'll notice, though, that the icons have something of a buttonish quality. They're 3D-looking, which helps them to stand out on the page.

Icons and symbols work best when their meaning is obvious and universal. DVD- or CD-style symbols for functions like Play, Fast Forward, Stop, and the rest are generally pretty safe. So is using a trashcan icon for Delete or a piece of paper with a folded corner for

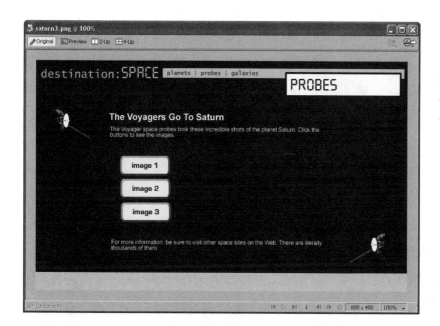

Figure 3.5

Designing clickable images to look like buttons is a sure-fire way to attract clicks.

New Document. However, the other icons in Figure 3.8 are more open to interpretation. A pencil icon might mean Create on some sites and Edit on others. A globe icon might mean Go To The Web, but, then again, it might not. Whether icons are effective on your site depends on how you use them, but a good rule

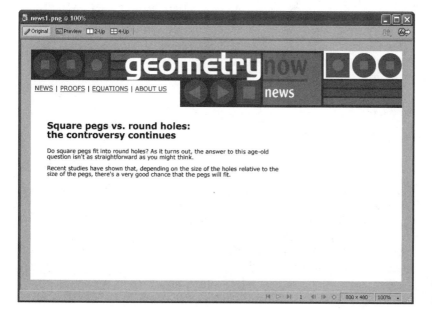

Figure 3.6

The visitors are supposed to step through the news stories using arrow buttons. However, their color, design, and proximity to other design elements make the buttons hard to find.

Figure 3.7

Position your buttons carefully. Context makes all the difference, even when you use a powerful affordance like the button metaphor.

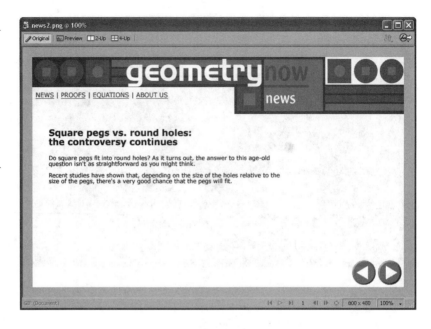

GEEKSPEAK

A *label* is the text on a button.

of thumb is this: If there is any conceivable doubt about what the icon might mean, don't use it.

One way to get around the problem of ambiguity is to include a descriptive text label in the icon graphic, as you see in Figure 3.9. This is the Microsoft Windows approach, and it works pretty well as far as usability goes. Everything in Windows has an icon to click, but every icon comes with a nametag, just in case. Experiment with this approach on your Web site if you like, but if your icons only work when accompanied by labels, you're probably better off just using buttons. Computer users have different expectations of images in a productive environment like Windows and a publishing medium like the Web. What plays well in one doesn't always translate

TIP

It's common practice to make corporate logos clickable, especially when the logo appears in the nav bar or somewhere in the site's main interface. The logo usually links to the front page of the site. You can assume that your visitors know this from experience, so you don't have to go out of your way to make the logo look clickable. That said, adding a rollover effect or something of that nature won't hurt, and it certainly reinforces the idea of clickability.

Figure 3.8

Are the meanings of these icons obvious when you see them out of context? If not, then think twice about using them as clickable images on your site.

Figure 3.9

One way to avoid ambiguity is to include a text label on your icon, but this approach plays better in an OS environment. The Web is more about buttons than icons.

to the other. People expect icons to be clickable on their desktops, because that's how Windows works. They might not be expecting clickable icons on a Web site, where images are often for informational purposes only.

Achieving Balance

alance. It's the Way of Zen. It's also an important design consideration on the Web. If your layout doesn't have balance, it seems off-kilter. It's visually off-putting, as Figure 4.1 shows. However, when you achieve balance, as in Figure 4.2, all the elements in your design look like they belong

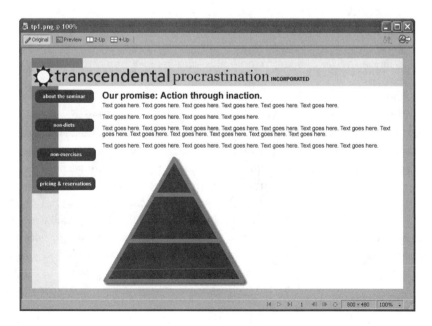

Figure 4.1

This layout doesn't seem very well balanced.

Figure 4.2

A balanced design feels better.

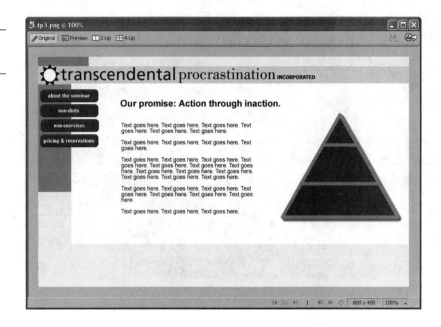

together. They seem to fit. Your Web page finds inner peace and harmony, and that puts your visitors at ease.

Balancing your design isn't just about making your visitors comfortable. A balanced layout is more usable than an unbalanced one. It seems more organized, which helps your visitors find the information they want. Look at the unbalanced columns in Figure 4.3. Because the column on the left is so much shorter than the column on the right, your visitors might not think to scroll down for the buttons at the bottom of the page, as Figure 4.4 shows. Using a Web page shouldn't be like a game of hide-and-seek. When you balance the columns, as in Figure 4.5, the layout itself suggests that the content of the page continues below the fold.

The balancing act is a bit subjective, in that you rely on your designer's instinct to tell you what's working and what isn't. One good trick is to sketch your design using solid shapes for design elements, as in Figure 4.6. Looking at your design in a more abstract way helps you to focus on the balance of the layout instead of the design elements themselves. If part of your design feels heavier than another does, just rearrange the shapes until you get a balanced look. Then, plug the corresponding pieces of content back into their placeholders.

Probably the easiest way to balance a design is to keep all the page elements in the same proportion,

GEEKSPEAK

Content *below the fold* is the stuff that your visitors have to scroll to see.

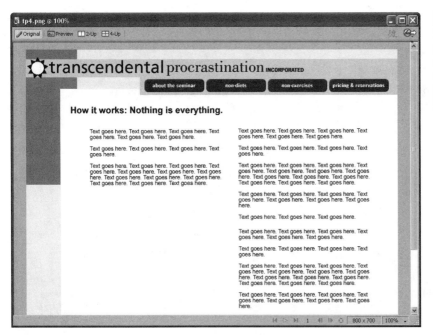

Figure 4.4

If they don't scroll, they miss the goodies at the bottom of the page.

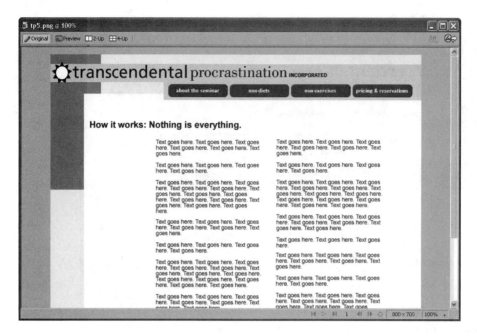

Figure 4.5

Balancing the columns helps to reinforce the idea that the page doesn't end at the bottom of the browser window.

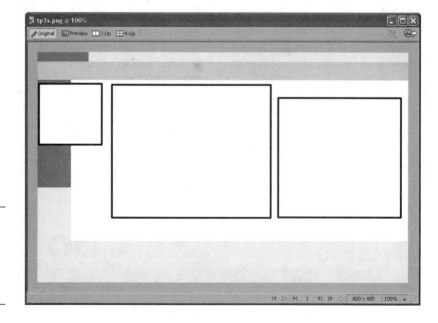

Figure 4.6

Working with your layout in the abstract helps you to focus on balance instead of content.

pretty much as you've seen in the examples so far. You might call this the classical approach. It's a good design choice if you want the overall look and feel of your site to be sober, serious, and informative. Visually, it doesn't exactly grab the attention. Instead, the design recedes into the background, allowing your visitors to focus on the content of the page.

GEEKSPEAK

Visual weight is how heavy a design element appears to be.

The classical approach doesn't play as well if you want your design to create some excitement. For that, you need a more dynamic layout, which makes balancing the layout trickier and more subjective. To help you along, take the visual weight of your design elements into account.

Visual weight is difficult to quantify, but it involves the size and shape of the element in question. It has little to do with the actual weight of the objects if they existed in the real world. As Figure 4.7 shows, larger design elements tend to be heavier than smaller ones, even if the smaller element represents something that weighs more in the physical universe. A square seems heavier than a rectangle, even when they have the same area, as in Figure 4.8. And even washing out or desaturating a larger design element doesn't seem to affect its visual weight.

Once you assess the visual weight of the design elements in play, you can arrange them so that they achieve a kind of harmony or equilibrium. You want

Figure 4.7

The larger image seems visually heavier than the smaller one, even though the smaller image depicts something that is much heavier in the real world.

Figure 4.8

The square and the rectangle may have the same area, but the more solid-looking square feels heavier.

Figure 4.9

*You can desat-
urate a larger
design ele-
ment, but it
doesn't seem to
lose its visual
weight.*

the various weights to cancel out based on where you position them on the page. The lighter and heavier elements seem out of whack in Figure 4.10. However, by repositioning them in the design, as shown in Figure 4.11, you distribute their weights better, which gives you a more balanced, harmonious effect while preserving the sense of motion or excitement that you get when you use elements of differing visual weights.

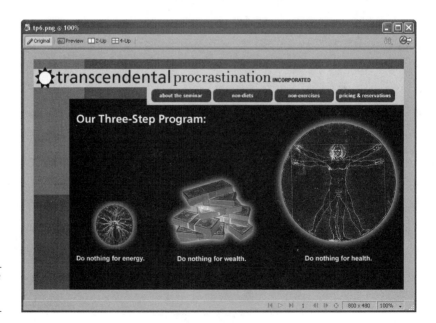

Figure 4.10

*These elements
seem out of
whack.*

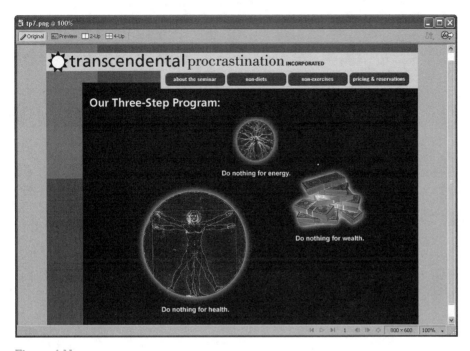

Figure 4.11

Redistributing their weight creates a greater sense of equilibrium without sacrificing the dynamic feel.

Choosing Colors

Choosing an effective color scheme for your Web site is one of the great juggling acts of the designer's role. Every design element on the page—including empty space—has a color, and you want to make sure that all the colors work together to reinforce the mood and purpose of your site.

You can break down the job of color selection into three broad areas: text and background colors, link colors, and interface colors.

TIP

Try this: Keep most of the colors in your site in the same color family: warm and inviting, fun and energetic, or calm and cool. Then, for one or two design elements like links or alert symbols—design elements that really need to stand out—use a color in a completely different family.

Choosing Text and Background Colors

People don't read text on a Web page. They don't have time for it. It slows them down too much. Instead, they like to skim and pick out the bits and pieces of information that interest them. Blame it on the collapse of Western civilization or too much TV and video games if you want, but browsing habits are what they are. As a designer, the best thing you can do for the text of your site is to make it easy to skim.

Contrast is the most important tool in your toolbox in this regard. You want your text to stand out from the background easily, so that roving eyes can skim without having to squint or slow down and read the text word for word. If you don't have enough contrast, as in Figure 5.1, you make it harder for your visitors to skim your text, which makes it harder for them to find what they need.

At the same time, the kind of contrast is important, too. Glaring or gaudy contrast like the kind in Figure 5.2 does two things: It draws too much attention to text, which ought to recede into the background when your visitors don't need it; and it forces your visitors' eyes to work harder than they should, which causes headaches and eyestrain. The ideal text/background contrast is clear in the sense that the text stands out, but it is quiet in the sense that it doesn't overpower the design.

You can't go wrong with black text on a white background, as in Figure 5.3. The contrast is good, and it's easy on the eyes. If you can make this color scheme work in your design, then it's your best bet overall.

Don't feel locked into this scheme, though. There are plenty of good reasons to try different combinations of colors. Washed-out or desaturated tints of colors can be just as effective as white in the background, as in Figure 5.4. You can experiment with light text against a dark background, as in Figure 5.5, although it is generally harder on the eyes. If your site is on the text-heavy side, a scheme like this might not be the best choice.

> **TIP**
>
> To bump up the contrast on your page, you might be tempted to put all the text in boldface. Resist the temptation. Boldface works better in small quantities as a highlight or emphasis. Think of it like this: If you shout all the time, how are you going to up the volume when you need to?

Figure 5.1

Your visitors are skimmers, and low-contrast text is hard to skim.

Figure 5.2

Glaring contrast may be easy to read, but notice how it draws too much attention to itself.

Even if you don't have much text on your site, take care in choosing the background color of the pages. The background should stay in the background as much as possible. You don't want it to siphon away attention from the main

Figure 5.3

When it comes to contrast, nothing beats black text on a white background.

Figure 5.4

Light tints of background color can be effective, at the same time giving your site some character. Notice how well white works as a highlight color in this example.

content of your pages. The background isn't the place for bright or unusual shades. Save those for highlights—elements that you use specifically to draw attention—and let your content be the star of the show.

Figure 5.5

You can also try light text on a dark background, but it isn't as easy on the eyes.

Choosing Link Colors

Over the years, a couple of standards have emerged as far as the colors of hyperlinks go. Table 5.1 summarizes them for you. Go out of your way to use these link colors in your Web design. Your visitors already know from experience that blue stands for an unvisited link, so, if they can fall back on this knowledge when they come to your site, you give them one less usability hurdle.

Of course, it's not always practical or desirable to use the standard hyperlink colors. Maybe you want to key the links to corporate colors, or colors associated with your business or group. Maybe blue and purple don't work in the larger context of your design. Straying from the standards is better in the long run than trying to make the standards work. If you stray, then stray consistently. Use the same colors to represent the same things, page after page after page. Your design motto should be, "Expectations fulfilled." It's the key to educating your visitors about how your site works. If they come to expect red as the color for unvisited links, then deliver red for unvisited links absolutely everywhere on your site.

TIP
Save bright or glaring shades for labels on graphical buttons or hyperlink colors. These elements ought to jump out at your visitors right away, so they're better suited for exotic or unusual color choices.

TIP
You don't have to follow the standards down to the exact hexadecimal color codes. If the recommended shade of blue isn't working for you, try a darker or lighter shade of blue. As long as the color is still recognizably blue to your visitors, your site benefits from the conventional color association.

TIP
As with most other pearls of conventional Web wisdom, hyperlink color standards can backfire on you. If you decide not to follow the standards, then stay away from them entirely. For example, if you don't use blue for unvisited links, don't turn around and use blue for visited links instead. You'll create less confusion if you don't use blue at all.

Table 5.1 Standard Hyperlink Colors

Color	Stands For	Color Code (IE)	Color Code (Netscape)
Blue	Unvisited links	#0000FF	#0000FF
Purple	Visited links	#990099	#663399

Choosing Interface Colors

The graphical dressing of your site gives you the most latitude for color choices. You don't have to think about color usability issues as much. At the same time, this is where you set the visual tone for your site, and color plays no small role in striking the right mood.

Some of the color design work may already be done for you. If you're building a site for a business or organization, your design should use the corporate colors in some meaningful way. Corporate colors are just colors that the marketing department has spent tremendous time and resources trying to associate with the organization. Think of Coca-Cola red or McDonald's golden arches. Guess which colors appear in abundance on which corporate Web sites. Using the corporate colors is a method of **branding**, or bringing the site into the organization's overall corporate image. Just as you want to use the group's logo in your design, you want to incorporate other brand indicators like the corporate colors.

Color also comes with a psychological dimension that's at least worth considering when you're planning your approach. Have you ever wondered why so many Web sites use the color blue in the main interface? A quick look at

GEEKSPEAK

Branding is a way of bringing the site into the organization's overall corporate image by using marketing elements like logos and corporate colors in the design.

FAQ

If I work with the marketing department, will I respect myself in the morning?

Working with the marketing department often leaves a bad taste in your mouth or makes you feel like you need a long shower. But just think of it like this. The advertising budget for your site is probably zero. However, every dollar spent on promoting the company's brand in other media such as TV and print is like a dollar spent on promoting your site—as long as you brand your site effectively. They spend the money, and you reap the benefits. Who says the Web department never has the last laugh?

Table 5.2 Common Psychological Color Associations

Color	Association (Western)	Examples
Red	Passion, intensity, heat, violence, warning	Fire truck, stoplight, Valentine's Day heart
Orange	Warmth, nourishment	Fireplace, interior of fast-food restaurant
Yellow	Playfulness, happiness	Sunlight, flowers
Green	Nature, growth, restfulness, plenty; also jealousy, sickness	Forests, money; also molds, slimes
Blue	Trust, reliability, stability, loyalty	Police and military uniforms
Purple	Luxury, royalty, rarity	King's robes
Brown	Solidity, practicality	Earth, rock
White	Purity, innocence; also coldness, aloofness, rigidity	Ambulances, medical uniforms, wedding dresses; also snow, marble, alabaster
Black	Formality, authority, hipness; also darkness, mourning	Tuxedos, sunglasses; also the Grim Reaper

Table 5.2 tells you that people tend to associate blue with stability and trust—two good virtues to promote if you want to keep your visitors, especially if you're building a site for the financial or medical sectors.

Thankfully, design isn't all about science. You can't simply reduce colors to knee-jerk emotional responses, just as you can't just dress a poorly designed site in blue and hope that it cultivates an air of trust. Color should be one aspect in an overall strategy to convey the mood and purpose of your site. If your goal is to inform, complement a conservative design with soothing colors. If your goal is to entertain, try more dynamic designs, and take some risks with vibrant colors.

Are color associations the same across cultures?

No. Color associations aren't universal. In fact, many cultures have widely different interpretations. You wouldn't expect a bride in the West to wear a fire-engine-red wedding gown without causing some snickers. Yet red is the color of purity in India and China. And just as green might signify wealth in the West, it's a very unlucky color in the East, where it means marital infidelity. If you're designing for an international audience, make sure to do plenty of research into your target cultures.

Designing for Accessibility

You're a designer. A visually oriented person. And the Web is such a graphic medium, it's easy to forget that not everyone browsing the Web uses his or her eyes. However, the Web is a worldwide community of all types of people, including those with disabilities. The visually impaired want to visit your site. So do people with cognitive or learning disabilities. If these people showed up at your front door, you wouldn't dream of insulting them or making their visit unpleasant. Likewise, when you're building your Web site, you should consider their special situations.

Designing for accessibility is about making your Web site's content available to everyone, regardless of disability. The Web isn't the only place where accessibility is important. In fact, the Web is one of the last places to consider accessibility issues. Public buildings need ramps and elevators to provide easy access for the physically impaired. Parking lots set aside the best spots for the handicapped. Movie theaters provide special seats and rows that are easier for wheelchairs. Television goes out with closed captioning for those hard of hearing. It wasn't until the late 1990s that computer people began thinking in the same terms. Now, in the United States and many other countries, accessibility is a matter of law. It's illegal for the U.S. government to award contracts to technology suppliers—including Web builders—whose products don't follow accessibility guidelines. No one's going to drag you off to the Federal penitentiary if you don't build an accessible Web site. You just

> **GEEKSPEAK**
>
> A Web site is *accessible* if it makes its content available to everyone, including those with disabilities.

FAQ

Where can I learn more about accessibility legislation in the United States?
You can find the language for U.S. accessibility legislation in the 1998 Amendment to Section 508 of the Rehabilitation Act, or Section 508 for short. Check out www.section508.gov/.

GEEKSPEAK

Text equivalents are textual descriptions of nontextual content for use in screen readers and other accessibility tools.

won't be able to get on the gravy train and charge the U.S. taxpayers seven thousand dollars per link.

Just mentioning the word **accessibility** in casual conversation is enough to cause some designers distress, but making a Web site accessible isn't really that difficult. You don't have to develop a way to beam images directly into the brains of the visually impaired. You don't have to try to give everyone the exact same experience of your site. You just have to provide an equivalent experience. That is, you provide information on your site in such a way that people with disabilities have the same level of access as people without.

Your disabled visitors will even meet you halfway. They have special software and hardware on their computers such as screen readers, text-to-speech converters, and text-to-Braille converters. All you have to do is present your content so that these devices can find it and work with it.

Plain text is the currency of the realm. It's the raw material that accessibility tools search out and convert. Therefore, in building for accessibility, you want to give corresponding text for every nontextual bit of content on your site. This is the concept of **text equivalents**. The idea behind it is, if you can describe in words the portions of your site that are purely visual (like your images), you give people with disabilities an equivalent experience of your site's content. It's a different experience, yes, but that's all right. The disabled should come away with the same information that everyone else does, whether they get it by looking at a picture or listening to a textual description of that picture.

Making Images Accessible

You probably already know how to provide text equivalents for images, even if you don't realize it. All you need is the alt attribute of the img tag. This attribute is what defines the popup text caption that appears in the browser window when you hover over an image with the mouse pointer. Accessibility tools use the alt attribute to describe the image for the visually impaired.

So, to make an image accessible, simply give it a detailed alternate description, like this:

```
<img src="saturn.jpg" alt="A photograph of the planet Saturn from the Voyager space
probe that shows the planet's giant rings and orange bands of cloud.">
```

Don't cheap out on the text, like this:

```
<img src="saturn.jpg" alt="Saturn">
```

This type of alt label is only useful to people who don't need it. Remember, you want to give your disabled visitors an equivalent experience, so your words should come as close as possible to conveying the essence of the image. Pretend you're back in Lit class writing fiction. Give your audience enough information to form a clear mental picture of what you're describing.

For clickable images, try to put something in the alt text about what happens when your visitors click, like this:

```
<img src="aboutus.jpg" alt="Go to the About Us section of this site.">
```

or this:

```
<img src="macromedia.jpg" alt="Go to macromedia.com.">
```

If your alt text just says "About Us" or "Macromedia," your visually impaired visitors have no context for what the image means or does. By throwing in the action word to describe the result, you render the visual context obsolete. The meaning or function of the image comes through loud and clear in the description alone.

Another accessibility no-no as far as images are concerned: Don't design flashing, blinking, jiggling, strobing, or otherwise visually annoying graphics, like some of your least favorite banner ads. Not only are these images aesthetically ugly, psychologically insulting, and conceptually crass, they

What about images that contain text? Are they accessible?

Not as such. Sometimes, an image contains built-in text; for example, the label on a button or the captions in a diagram. However, a screen reader doesn't perceive the letters and words inside the image, so it can't render this text in a more accessible form. Be sure to provide alt text for these images, too.

also promote eyestrain and headaches for people with sensitive sight, and can actually induce seizures in people with epilepsy. If you're so desperate for click-through that you're willing to create a physical hardship for some of your visitors, perhaps you'd be better suited for a job in the marketing department.

Making Multimedia Accessible

Multimedia like Flash movies, sound files, and QuickTime clips are harder to make accessible, because you aren't just working with a single static image, so you can't just sum up the information in the multimedia file with a simple text description. Moreover, accessibility tools usually can't pick out the text inside a multimedia file for conversion to spoken words or Braille.

Unfortunately, there isn't a quick and easy way to make multimedia accessible. The World Wide Web Consortium, or W3C, offers some solutions, but they're all on the labor-intensive side, and have an unwieldy, counterintuitive feel. For instance, according to the W3C, your multimedia presentation should include a synchronized audio soundtrack that narrates the visuals, much like a play-by-play radio broadcast of a baseball game, along with full text captioning. As a workaround, you could provide a plain-text transcript of the multimedia content or create a separate series of pages that gives the same information in a more accessibility-friendly format.

The truth of the matter is that most of the multimedia on the Web isn't accessible at all. Making an existing presentation accessible often involves starting from scratch and redesigning the thing from the ground up. In addition, you may need to purchase new equipment such as quality microphones and sound-editing software. Of course, all this extra content inside the multimedia file can increase its file size, which makes it less convenient for your visitors to download and enjoy. For these reasons, many accessibility-conscious Web sites prefer to avoid multimedia altogether.

Where can I learn more about accessibility recommendations?

For an exhaustive discussion of accessibility recommendations, see www.w3.org/WAI/.

Software companies are working on the problem. Macromedia in particular distinguishes itself with its Flash MX authoring tool, which just about everyone uses to build Flash movies. Flash MX lets you embed text equivalents, keyboard shortcuts, and other accessibility enhancers into your Flash content. These aren't magic solutions by any stretch, but they're definitely steps in the right direction. Seeing as how Flash is the most popular multimedia format on the planet, any type of progress is encouraging. However, the bottom line is this: No multimedia format is 100% accessible, and don't let anyone tell you differently, especially the Flash people. If you want to include multimedia on your site, get acquainted with the W3C's recommendations, and be prepared to spend the extra effort to do it right.

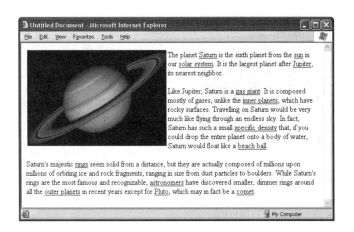

Figure 6.1

Underlines help to call attention to the hyperlinks in a block of text.

Managing Your Use of Color

Color is invaluable as a design tool. You use it to call attention to certain elements on your page. You use it to distinguish one type of content from another type. However, color is just as much a visual element as an image, so, as an accessibility-minded Web builder, you need to be careful about how you use it. After all, many your visitors are colorblind.

Take the example in Figure 6.1. Notice how the underline helps you spot a link in this block of text. However, if you remove the underline, as in Figure 6.2, you have no way of telling where the text ends and the hyperlinks begin.

TIP

Try looking at your site designs in black and white only. If certain elements disappear without color, or if others don't have the proper emphasis, you might want to rethink your strategy.

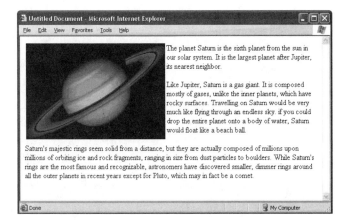

Figure 6.2

Remove the underlines, and someone who can't perceive color has trouble finding the links.

Figure 6.3

You don't need the underline to make hyper-links work without color. Boldface works just as well, and any color-independent visual cue does the job.

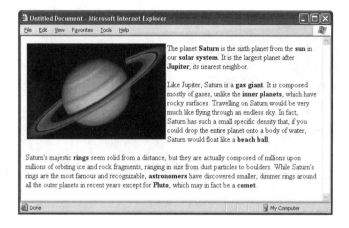

So, while color is an effective visual cue or indicator for an element such as a hyperlink, it shouldn't be the *only* visual cue you provide. By all means, use color to call attention to elements on your page. Just make sure you send the color in with some backup. Use an underline, a solid border, an arrow symbol, boldface, italics—anything that translates to a black-and-white environment, as in Figure 6.3.

Leaving Breadcrumb Trails

olktales and fairy stories have much to teach us. Sure, they might seem like kid's stuff, but, if you examine them closely, you find that they tackle the big questions—evil, justice, virtue, Web design—in deeply symbolic ways.

Take the story of Hansel and Gretel. Hansel leaves a trail of breadcrumbs so that he and his sister Gretel can find their way out of the forest, where their wicked stepmother tries to abandon them. On the surface, the story is just another diatribe against wicked stepmothers, until you realize that the wicked stepmother is you, and your long-suffering visitors are brave Hansel and Gretel, looking for a way out of the gnarled woods of your Web site.

Nobody wants to be the wicked stepmother in anyone's fairy story. Wicked stepmothers all die horribly. Hansel and Gretel's starved to death. However, be comforted, just as Hansel said to his sister. To

GEEKSPEAK

A *breadcrumb trail* is a navigation element that helps your visitors figure out where they are in your site hierarchy by showing the current page's relationship to the rest of the surrounding structure.

FAQ

What is the real story of Hansel and Gretel?

In *Hansel and Gretel* by the Brothers Grimm, the wicked stepmother tries to abandon her kids in the forest twice. The first time, Hansel drops a trail of white pebbles. The second time, he goes with the breadcrumbs, which don't prove to be as useful. The birds of the forest eat up the crumbs before he and Gretel have a chance to follow them. So, even though we call it a breadcrumb trail in Web parlance, what we really mean is a trail of white pebbles.

prevent your Web site from sharing the wicked stepmother's fate, all you have to do is leave a breadcrumb trail for your Hansels and Gretels to follow.

A **breadcrumb trail** is a navigation element that helps your visitors figure out where they are in your site's hierarchy by showing the current page's relationship to the rest of the structure. It's like a mini site map for that particular section of the site.

This is one of those concepts that makes more sense when you see it. Say an arm of your European folklore site goes like this:

Fairy tales

- Brothers Grimm
  - Hansel and Gretel
  - Rapunzel
  - Snow-White and Rose-Red
  - The Elves and the Shoemaker
- Hans Christian Andersen
  - The Ugly Duckling
  - Thumbelina
  - The Emperor's New Clothes
  - The Poor Little Match Girl
- Charles Perrault
  - Little Red Riding Rood
  - Cinderella
  - Sleeping Beauty
  - Bluebeard

The breadcrumb trail on the Brothers Grimm page is:

`Home > Fairy tales > Brothers Grimm`

Moving down to the Rapunzel page, you get:

`Home > Fairy tales > Brothers Grimm > Rapunzel`

But on the Cinderella page under Charles Perrault, the breadcrumb trail is:

`Home > Fairy tales > Charles Perrault > Cinderella`

Notice that the breadcrumb trail doesn't try to give the entire site structure. It just shows your visitors the logical path to the current page—and, more importantly, the path back home.

Typically, all the items in a breadcrumb trail are links, except for the last entry in the list, which represents the current page. Your visitors should be able to click on any of the previous items and work their way back to the home page.

Breadcrumb trails are extremely useful, especially if your site has a complex structure with many levels of pages. These trails help your visitors find their way around, and they give a quick "You are here" to people who arrive on your site from a search engine.

Of course, a breadcrumb trail is only as useful as you make it. Try to position it near the top of the page, right where visitors will see it, as in Figure 7.1. In addition, it's a good idea to distinguish the breadcrumb trail from other types of text navigation. If the breadcrumb trail has the same visual style, as in Figure 7.2, your visitors might not be able to tell what's what. The convention for breadcrumb trails is to use capital and lowercase letters instead of all caps and to separate items with greater-than signs instead of pipes, as Figure 7.3 shows. You're certainly free to experiment with other looks, but keep in mind that your visitors probably already understand this convention.

Finally, breadcrumb trails work best as an alternate method of navigation. All good sites have at least two. Don't try to build your site's main navigation scheme around breadcrumb trails, or you'll have a lot of frustrated visitors

> **TIP**
>
> Just as Hansel started dropping breadcrumbs as soon as he walked out the door of his house, always begin your site's breadcrumb trail with the home page.

> **TIP**
>
> If your site structure doesn't go deeper than, say, two levels of pages (main category and subcategory), you don't need breadcrumb trails.

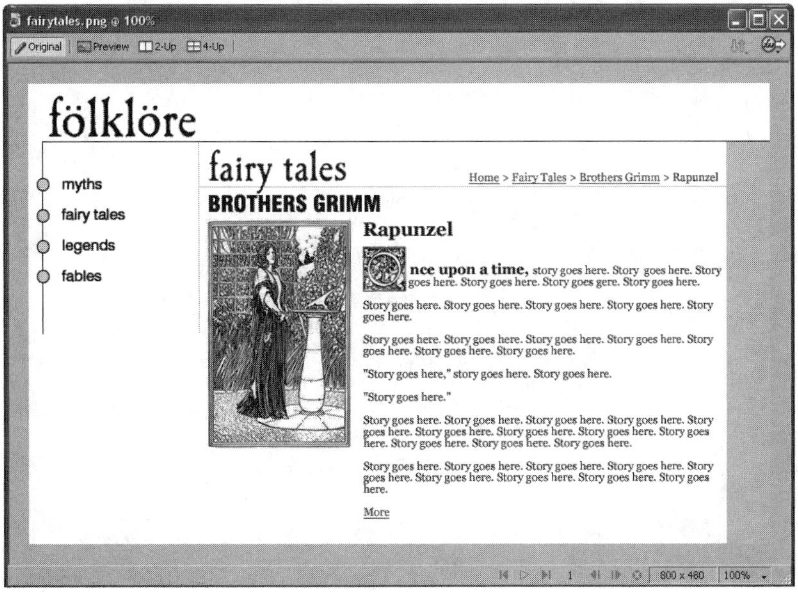

Figure 7.1

Try to position your bread-crumb trail near the top of the page.

Figure 7.2

Don't use the same visual style for breadcrumb trails as you do for other kinds of text navigation. Your visitors might not know which is which.

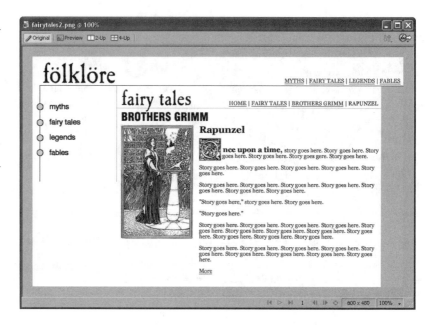

looking for the Hans Christian Andersen link when they're stuck in the recesses of the Brothers Grimm area. However, if you supplement a typical nav-bar scheme with breadcrumb trails, you make it that much easier for your visitors to get around.

Figure 7.3

Stick with cap/lowercase style for the links separated by greater-than signs, and you can't go wrong.

TOOL KIT

Breadcrumb Trail

Add this snippet of code to your page to create a linked breadcrumb trail. Just fill in the placeholders with the correct URLs and page names for your site. If you need fewer than three levels of pages, delete the corresponding lines of code.

```
<p>
  <a href="index.htm">Home</a> &gt;

<!- The code for the greater-than sign is &gt; ->

  <a href="levelone.htm">Level One Page Name</a> &gt;

<!- Copy and paste the following line ad infinitum if you need more
than three levels of pages in your breadcrumb trail. ->

  <a href="leveltwo.htm">Level Two Page Name</a> &gt;

<!- The last item in the list doesn't get a link, because it represents
the current page. ->

     Level Three Page Name
</p>
```

Using Jump Menus

A jump menu is a handy navigation element to use when you have a large site with lots of pages. Essentially, it's a quick index to the most common pages on your site, as Figure 8.1 shows. Your visitors select an item from the menu, and a simple JavaScript function causes that particular page to load. This way, your visitors don't have to navigate your site step by step.

GEEKSPEAK

A *jump menu* is a quick index to the most common pages on your site.

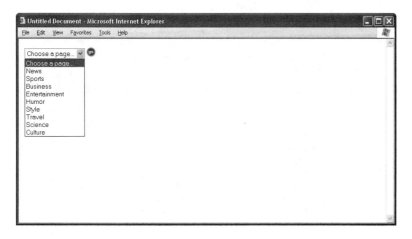

Figure 8.1

Use jump menus like this one to index the most common pages on your site. Your visitor selects a page from the menu, and the page loads.

TIP

A jump menu is a nice extra feature for your site, but don't rely on it for all your navigation. There's no substitute for a good, old-fashioned nav bar.

To build a jump menu, you need two components: an HTML form (which supplies the doohickey that the visitor clicks, otherwise known as the **front end**) and a JavaScript function (the quickie program that makes the jump menu work, also called the **back end**). The toolkits in this topic show you how to create both.

When it comes to jump menus, there are two schools of thought. The first is to include a Go button or something for the visitor to click after selecting a page from the menu. Nothing happens until the visitor clicks the button. The alternative is to make the jump menu self-activating. That is, as soon as the visitor selects a page, the jump menu automatically does its thing.

Which method is better? It's hard to say. If you include a Go button, your visitors are less likely to make mistakes. If they decide they don't want to use the jump menu after they open it (a favorite of the marketing department), or if they second-guess what page they want, the Go button gives them the option of ignoring the jump menu or making another choice before jumping. On the other hand, the Go button requires another click, which slows your visitors down. A self-activating jump menu requires only one click, so it's faster. You might test both types of jump menus on your site to see which works best, but, when in doubt, give yourself some idiot insurance and include the Go button.

TOOL KIT.

Jump Menu with Go Button–Front End

This section of HTML code gives you the front end of your jump menu.

```
<form name="jumpmenu">
 <select name="pages">
```

```
<!- The following line gives the first item in the menu. The selected
attribute in the option tag means that this is the item that appears in
the menu by default when the page loads. ->
```

```
<option selected>Choose a page...</option>
```

```
<!- The next line inserts a division in the list of menu items. You can
delete this line if you want. ->
```

```
<option>First category</option>
```

```
<!- The jump items come next. In the value attribute, give the path to
the page where you want to jump, like aboutus/index.htm or
../products/brochure.htm. It can be an absolute, document-relative, or
root-relative path, just like a hyperlink. ->
```

```
<option value="firstpath">First page name</option>
<option value="secondpath">Second page name</option>
<option value="thirdpath">Third page name</option>
```

```
<!- Repeat lines like the above for as many options as you want in this
division of the list. ->

<!- The next line inserts a new division. Delete at will. ->

   <option>Second category</option>

<!- Here come more jump items. Repeat this line for as many options as
you need, and then close the select element. ->

   <option value="fourthpath">Fourth page name</option>

   </select>

 <!- The next line adds a button to the form. ->

   <input type="button" name="go" value="Go" onClick="doJumpMenu();">

 <!- Now close the form, and you're done. ->

 </form>
```

Self-Activating Jump Menu–Front End

Use this block of HTML to place a self-activating jump menu on the page.

```
<form name="jumpmenu">

<!- The next line adds a select object, a.k.a. a dropdown menu, to the
form, and instructs it to watch for the onChange JavaScript event. When
the visitor changes the form, the jump function launches. ->

   <select name="pages" onChange="doJumpMenu();">

<!- The rest of the form looks and works like the previous one. ->

   <option selected>Choose a page...</option>
   <option>First category</option>
   <option value="firstpath">First page name</option>
   <option value="secondpath">Second page name</option>
   <option value="thirdpath">Third page name</option>
   <option>Second category</option>
   <option value="fourthpath">Fourth page name</option>

<!- Add as many divisions and jump items as you need. ->

   </select>
   </form>
```

TOOL KIT

Jump Menu–Back End

Add this JavaScript function to your site to make your jump menu work. This function is the same for the Go-button and self-activating jump menus.

```
<script language="JavaScript">

/* Use the script tags only if you're embedding this function inside
your HTML page. Omit the script tags if you're adding this function to
an external JavaScript file. */

  function doJumpMenu() {
    var menu = document.jumpmenu.pages;

/* The following line gets the value attribute of the selected menu
item. */

    var menuValue = menu.options[menu.selectedIndex].value;

/* The following if/then block jumps to the selected page as long as
the value attribute isn't empty. */

    if (menuValue != "") {
      location.href = menuValue;
    }
  }
</script>
```

Jump Menu with Graphical Go Button–Front End

If you want to use a graphical Go button instead of the generic gray HTML button, all you have to do is design your button in your favorite graphics program. Then, add the following block of HTML to your page to create the menu:

```
<form name="jumpmenu" onSubmit="return doJumpMenuGraphicButton();">

<!- The form tag above waits for the onSubmit event to launch the jump-
menu script. ->

<!- Below is the menu. It works just like the others. Add as many divi-
sions and jump items as you like. ->

  <select name="pages">
    <option selected>Choose a page...</option>
    <option>First category</option>
    <option value="firstpath">First page name</option>
    <option value="secondpath">Second page name</option>
    <option value="thirdpath">Third page name</option>
    <option>Second category</option>
    <option value="fourthpath">Fourth page name</option>
  </select>
```

```
<!- Here comes the graphical Go button. ->

  <input type="image" name="go" src="imagepath" width="imagewidth"
height="imageheight" border="0">
</form>
```

Jump Menu with Graphical Go Button—Back End

You need a slightly different JavaScript for the jump menu with a graphical Go button. Web browsers such as Internet Explorer and Netscape treat image buttons as
submit buttons—when the visitor clicks, the browser tries to submit the form, which
you don't want or need for a simple jump menu. These little tweaks to the function
prevent the browser from submitting the form.

```
<script language="JavaScript">

/* If you're adding this script to an external JavaScript file, you
don't need the script tags at the beginning and end of this listing. If
you're embedding the page in your HTML document, keep the script tags,
and add the code to the head section of your page. */

  function doJumpMenuGraphicButton() {
    var menu = document.jumpmenu.pages;

/* The following line gets the value attribute of the selected menu
item. */

    var menuValue = menu.options[menu.selectedIndex].value;
    if (menuValue == "") {

/* The following line prevents form submission. */

      return false;
    } else {

/* The following line jumps to the selected page as long as the value
attribute isn't empty. */

      location.href = menuValue;

/* The next line prevents form submission. */

      return false;
    }
  }

</script>
```

Managing Popup Windows

n the feng shui of Web design, popup windows are like the oddly shaped corner cabinet that doesn't quite fit. Some people have never liked them, calling them user-hostile and finding them personally offensive as only people with no other problems can. However, popups used to be a contender. They had their place in Web design. They were great for calling up help screens,

quick definitions, extended descriptions, and other bits of useful but peripheral information that didn't seem to warrant a page of its own. Used properly, popups helped to make a navigation scheme feel more streamlined and focused.

Then, mercenary advertisers like the people in the marketing department co-opted them and turned them into an annoyance of spam caliber. Soon you couldn't go anywhere on the Web without spawning multiple, flashing, slow-loading windows of barely relevant content that you didn't need, ask for, or want. Consequently, popups have taken an all-around credibility hit. Designers don't use them like they used to. It's uncommon to see them pulling actual service on a Web site, while the popup ads keep coming.

If you're willing to reeducate your visitors and deal with the occasional hate email, popups can still be an asset to your site. They're no less helpful for displaying peripheral content than they were at the height of their popularity. They can make an otherwise awkward design like the one in Figure 9.1 feel more intuitive, as Figure 9.2 shows.

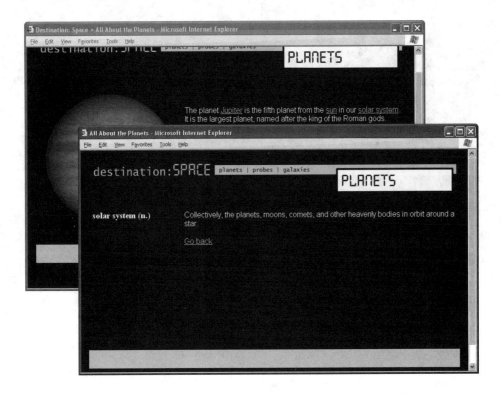

Figure 9.1

In this design, clicking a term causes a definition page to load. Good idea, but clumsy execution. The visitor has to keep jumping back and forth, which interrupts the flow of the main text.

The trick is to use popups effectively. Here are a few guidelines:

- **Keep them small.** That goes for the physical size of the popup window (which you can control) and the amount of content you put in it. Don't try to cram in too much design. Large popups with lots of images and complex layouts can take too long to load, which gives your visitors every reason to assume that a blinking solicitation is on its way.

- **Keep their content focused.** Popups should be short and sweet. If you ramble on enough to create scrollbars in the window, you probably ought to rethink your strategy. Remember, popups work best with quick bursts of peripheral content. Larger chunks of information belong on full-fledged pages of your site.

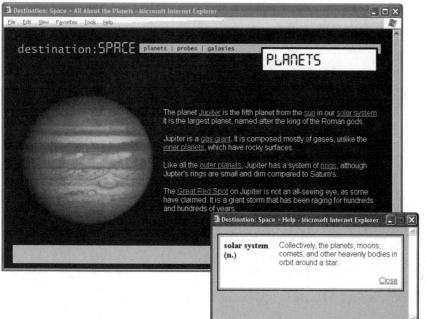

Figure 9.2

By loading the definitions into a popup window instead, your visitors don't have to lose their place in the main text to get the supporting content.

- **Don't rely on them.** Since some people will never bother to look at even the most innocent, thoughtfully-designed popup, don't use popups for mission-critical content. That's the job of your main pages anyway. Popups make more sense in a supporting role; for example, quickie help pages.
- **Give your visitors the control.** Don't cause popups to load automatically! A popup should only open when your visitor expressly clicks a link or button. Likewise, make it easy to close the popup once it has opened.

Making Popups

A popup window is really just a page like any other. You put the content of the popup into an HTML file, just as you would for a normal Web page, and you can link to the popup window anywhere on your site. However, instead of specifying the path to the page as you would for a normal link:

```
<a href="popup.htm">Open the popup window</a>
```

you direct the browser to a simple JavaScript function instead:

```
<a href="javascript:doPopup('popup.htm');">Open the popup window</a>
```

This function instructs the browser to open the page in its own window instead of loading the page in the main window. You can write your own JavaScript to do the job, or you can use this one:

```
<script language="JavaScript">
  function doPopup(popupPath) {
    window.open(popupPath,'name',
      'width=400,height=200,scrollbars=YES');
  }
</script>
```

That's all there is to it. The window.open statement takes care of everything, as long as you send the function the correct path. So, if your popup window's HTML file is in a different directory than the calling page, you'd format your link something like this:

```
<a href="javascript:doPopup('../help/info.htm');">Get help</a>
```

or whatever the correct path might be. Insert the path between the single quotes. If you pass the wrong path to the function, your popup window will load with unexpected content or the famous File Not Found page.

The JavaScript language gives you plenty of control over the size and behavior of the new window. You can give the popup a unique name, which appears right after the path in the window.open statement. Replace the word *name* in the previous script with *popup, help, window, Charlie,* or whatever you like.

After the name comes the properties list, where you define the appearance of the popup window. You can string together as many properties as you want—just separate each with a comma, and don't add a space after the comma. Table 9.1 shows some common options.

So, if you want to add a location field and a status bar to the popup window in the doPopup() function, you simply expand on the set of properties, like this:

```
<script language="JavaScript">
  function doPopup(popupPath) {
    window.open(popupPath,'name',
      'width=300,height=150,scrollbars=YES,location=YES,status=YES');
  }
</script>
```

Figure 9.3 shows the various parts of the browser window, in case you need a refresher.

Table 9.1 **Common Popup Window Properties**

PROPERTY	DESCRIPTION	EXAMPLE
height	Gives the height of the popup window in pixels	height=300
location	Gives the popup window a location field	location=YES
menubar	Gives the popup window a menu bar	menubar=YES
resizable	Allows the visitor to drag the size and shape of the popup window	resizable=YES
scrollbars	Gives the popup window horizontal or vertical scrollbars as needed	scrollbars=YES
status	Gives the popup window a status bar	status=YES
toolbar	Gives the popup window a toolbar	toolbar=YES
width	Gives the width of the popup window in pixels	width=150

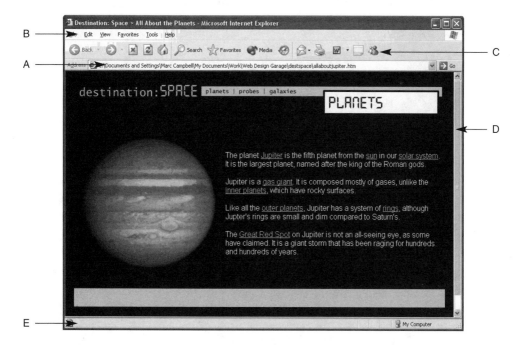

Figure 9.3

Here are the parts of a browser window: (A) Location field, (B)
Menu bar, (C) Toolbar, (D) Scrollbar, (E) Status bar.

> **TIP**
>
> If your site uses different kinds of popups, you probably want to give each type a different name and a different set of properties. To set this up, modify the popup window's link like so (substituting actual values for the placeholders):
>
> ```
> <a href="javascript:doPopup('path','name','properties');">
> ```
>
> As you can see, this code sends three values to the doPopup function, not just one. Now, to use these values, just make a few changes to the JavaScript:
>
> ```
> function doPopup(popupPath, popupName, popupProperties) {
>   window.open(popupPath,popupName,popupProperties);
> }
> ```

Bringing the Popup to the Front

One problem with popup windows is that they tend to sink. They wind up at the bottom of the desktop, along with a small collection of advertisements, hidden under the main browser window. If your site loads another page into the open popup window—a common occurrence when you use a popup to display help tips—the sunken popup window doesn't bob back to the top unless you specifically instruct it.

To do this, add the onLoad event to the body tag of the popup window's HTML file:

```
<body onLoad="window.focus();">
```

The window.focus statement ensures that the popup window gets the top position on the desktop, but only when the page loads. The popup sinks again as soon as your visitor clicks in the main browser window.

If you really want to annoy your visitors and prevent the popup from sinking—ever—try this:

```
<body onBlur="window.focus();">
```

The onBlur event fires whenever the popup window loses its top position, and then the window.focus statement brings the popup back to the front. The only way to get rid of a popup window like this is to close it.

> **TIP**
>
> Never, never, never use unsinkable popups in your design. Your popup window may be tougher than the Titanic, but your site will sink like a stone.

Adding a Close Link

A simple JavaScript trick allows you to add a Close link to the body of your popup, as you saw in Figure 9.2. When your visitors click this link, the popup window closes, saving them the trouble of using the X button along the top of the window.

The code for the link looks like this:

```
<a href="javascript:window.close();">Close</a>
```

You don't even have to create a special function for this job. A single window.close statement is all you need.

10

Creating Popup Menus

opup menus are all the rage these days. Surely, you've seen them on the Web. You hover over a navigation choice, and a menu of related items appears. It's a classy effect, as Figure 10.1 shows.

Figure 10.1

Nothing says class like a popup menu.

68

Popup menus used to be a nightmare to implement. Fortunately, Internet Explorer since version 5 and Netscape since version 6 support a new kind of JavaScript method called getElementById, which simplifies the scripting of all types of interactive features, including popup menus. Browsers capable of understanding getElementId have been available for a couple of years now, and they are now the predominant browsers on the Web by far; so, for most kinds of sites, you can write scripts with this method in good conscience. Older browsers choke, though, so be warned.

Dynamic HTML, or **DHTML**, is the synergy of HTML, JavaScript, and Cascading Style Sheets (CSS), all working together to create an interactive Web experience. The typical popup menu is a perfect example of DHTML in action. You build the layout of the nav bar in HTML. CSS elements called **layers** give you the menus, and a few straightforward JavaScript functions bring the menus to life.

Understanding Layers

CSS **layers** or **div elements** are boxes of content on a Web page. Unlike "flat" elements such as table cells, you can stack layers one atop another and position them anywhere on the screen (see Figure 10.2). In this respect, layers are like the windows on your desktop.

It gets better. With JavaScript, you can do all kinds of things with layers. You can animate them. You can

Figure 10.2

CSS layers are boxes of content. Unlike table cells, you can stack them and position them freely on the page.

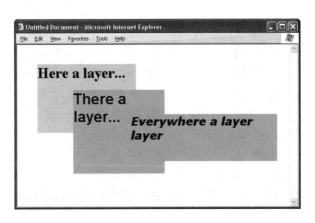

change their size. You can make them draggable. And you can make them disappear and reappear at will, which is how most developers create the popup effect in popup menus.

Each popup menu goes in its own layer, as in Figure 10.3. However, instead of making these layers visible, you specify that they should be hidden or invisible by default. The menus are still there—they're in the code, but the visitor can't see them or interact with them. They're like ghosts: invisible, intangible, and unclickable. That's the way they stay, until the visitor mouses over the predefined hotspot, like the link in a nav bar. Then, a JavaScript function kicks in and changes the visibility property of the layer you want to reveal. The hidden layer appears, and you have a popup menu, as in Figure 10.4. Another script to hide the menu when the visitor is finished with it makes the layer disappear again.

Laying Out Popup Menus

Hopefully, the logic behind popup menus is straightforward. Making popup menus work practically in your layout can take some hard work.

Believe it or not, the best approach is actually a mathematical one, so get out your scratch paper before you start coding and make a few sketches and calculations.

Figure 10.3

Each popup menu goes in its own layer. To create the popup effect, the layers are hidden or invisible by default.

Figure 10.4

Mousing over a nav-bar category makes the corresponding layer appear.

TIP

For these mathematics to add up the same way in Netscape and IE, be sure to set the following spacing attributes to 0: leftmargin, topmargin, marginwidth, and marginheight in the body tag; and border, cellpadding, and cellspacing in each table tag.

Let's say you have a nav bar with five main categories. Let's say that you also know the nav-bar height is 19 pixels, and you want the nav bar to fit across an 800-width screen. Shave off 40 pixels for scrollbars and the like, and you have a nav bar of width 760. Divide it into five equal sections of 152 pixels each, as in Figure 10.5.

Now for the layers. You know how wide each layer has to be: 152 pixels, just like the width of each table cell in the nav bar. You need to calculate the height of each layer, which depends on how many navigation choices you want it to have. Obviously, this number can vary from menu to menu. Since the nav bar is 19 pixels tall, make it easy on yourself and take 19 pixels as your default height per menu choice. A menu with three choices only needs to be 57 pixels tall (19 times 3), while a menu with seven choices needs to be 19 times 7, or 133 pixels tall.

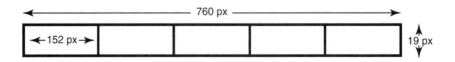

Figure 10.5

Begin by sketching your rough nav-bar design and calculating the size of each table cell.

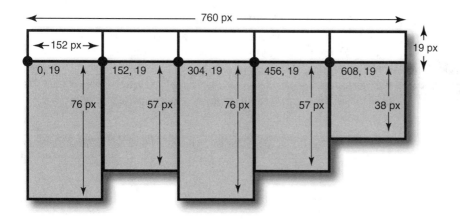

Figure 10.6

Position the layers in offsets from the top and left sides of the browser window.

To line up the layers with the table cells, you express the location of each layer in offsets from the top and left sides of the browser window. Therefore, if your nav bar is 19 pixels tall, you want to position your layers vertically at 19 pixels from the top of the screen. Horizontally, you start at 0 (no offset from the left), and you position each new layer in increments of 152, as Figure 10.6 shows.

Finally, drop a table for the menu into each layer, using one row per menu item, as in Figure 10.7.

TIP

If you use images instead of text links inside your popup menus, be sure to build extra whitespace into the design of your graphics. This helps to make your menus feel less cramped.

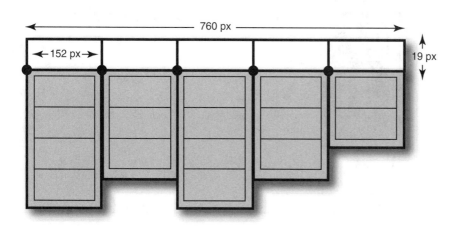

Figure 10.7

Put a table inside each layer for the menus. Each menu item gets its own row in the table.

Creating Popup Menus

This DHTML document shows you how to create a system of popup menus (see Figure 10.8). For simplicity's sake, the nav bar and the menus use text links. With border, cellpadding, and cellspacing at 0, the tables feel compact. Substitute images with plenty of vertical whitespace, and your layout looks better, as in Figure 10.9. You should adjust the heights of the layers, though, to accommodate the taller tables.

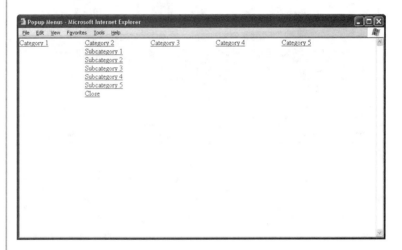

Figure 10.8

This Toolkit creates a system of popup menus.

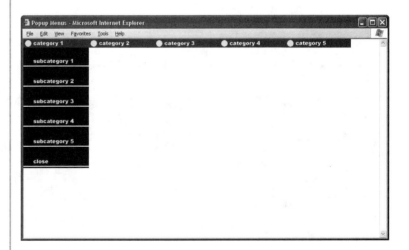

Figure 10.9

Substitute the text links with your own images (adding plenty of vertical whitespace), and the menus don't feel as cramped.

```
<html>
<head>
<title>Popup Menus</title>

<script language="JavaScript">

  function doShowHide(popupMenu) {

/* This function launches when the visitor mouses over the nav-bar
choices. It receives the ID of the corresponding menu and makes this
menu visible while hiding the other four. */

    if (popupMenu == "menu1") {
      document.getElementById("menu1").style.visibility="visible";
        document.getElementById("menu2").style.visibility="hidden";
        document.getElementById("menu3").style.visibility="hidden";
        document.getElementById("menu4").style.visibility="hidden";
        document.getElementById("menu5").style.visibility="hidden";
    }
    if (popupMenu == "menu2") {
      document.getElementById("menu1").style.visibility="hidden";
        document.getElementById("menu2").style.visibility="visible";
        document.getElementById("menu3").style.visibility="hidden";
        document.getElementById("menu4").style.visibility="hidden";
        document.getElementById("menu5").style.visibility="hidden";
    }
    if (popupMenu == "menu3") {
      document.getElementById("menu1").style.visibility="hidden";
        document.getElementById("menu2").style.visibility="hidden";
        document.getElementById("menu3").style.visibility="visible";
        document.getElementById("menu4").style.visibility="hidden";
        document.getElementById("menu5").style.visibility="hidden";
    }
    if (popupMenu == "menu4") {
      document.getElementById("menu1").style.visibility="hidden";
        document.getElementById("menu2").style.visibility="hidden";
        document.getElementById("menu3").style.visibility="hidden";
        document.getElementById("menu4").style.visibility="visible";
        document.getElementById("menu5").style.visibility="hidden";
    }
    if (popupMenu == "menu5") {
      document.getElementById("menu1").style.visibility="hidden";
        document.getElementById("menu2").style.visibility="hidden";
        document.getElementById("menu3").style.visibility="hidden";
        document.getElementById("menu4").style.visibility="hidden";
        document.getElementById("menu5").style.visibility="visible";
    }
  }

  function doHide(popupMenu) {

/* This function launches when the visitor clicks the Close button at
the bottom of the menu. It receives the ID of the current menu and then
hides that menu. Easy as pie. */
```

```
        document.getElementById(popupMenu).style.visibility="hidden";
    }
</script>

</head>

<body leftmargin="0" topmargin="0" marginwidth="0" marginheight="0">

<!- First thing's first. Create the code for the popup menus. The menu
itself is a table with six rows: one for each of the five choices in
the menu, plus a row for the Close link. If you need fewer choices,
delete table rows. If you need more choices, add more table rows. Just
be sure to put the table between div tags, which nests the element in a
layer.

Looking at the div tag, the id property gives the ID of the layer,
which is absolutely essential for the JavaScript functions above. In
the style attribute, notice the position of the layer appears as the
offset from the top and left margins.

The width and height give the physical dimensions of the layer. The
width of 152 comes from the width of the nav bar (760 pixels) divided
by the number of main categories, five. The height of 114 is the height
per menu choice (19 pixels) times the number of choices in the menu,
six (including the Close link). The height of the layer changes depend-
ing on how tall each menu choice should be as well as how many choices
total appear in the menu. The number 19 as the height of each menu
choice isn't written in stone. As you tinker with the size and format
of each menu to fit your site, be sure to adjust the height values
accordingly.

Notice that the visibility is set to hidden, which makes the layer
invisible by default. ->

<div id="menu1" style="position: absolute; left: 0px; top: 19px; width:
152px; height: 114px; visibility: hidden;">
  <table width="152" border="0" cellpadding="0" cellspacing="0">
    <tr>
      <td><a href="path01">Subcategory 1</a></td>
    </tr>
    <tr>
      <td><a href="path02">Subcategory 2</a></td>
    </tr>
    <tr>
      <td><a href="path03">Subcategory 3</a></td>
    </tr>
    <tr>
      <td><a href="path04">Subcategory 4</a></td>
    </tr>
    <tr>
      <td><a href="path05">Subcategory 5</a></td>
    </tr>

<!- This row contains the Close option at the bottom of the menu.
Clicking this link launches the doHide function. The link passes along
the ID of the menu to close. ->
```

```
        <tr>
          <td><a href="javascript:doHide('menu1');">Close</a></td>
        </tr>
      </table>
    </div>

    <!- This div element contains the second popup menu. It works just like
    first. ->

    <div id="menu2" style="position: absolute; left: 152px; top: 19px;
    width: 152px; height: 114px; visibility: hidden;">
      <table width="152" border="0" cellpadding="0" cellspacing="0">
        <tr>
          <td><a href="path06">Subcategory 1</a></td>
        </tr>
        <tr>
          <td><a href="path07">Subcategory 2</a></td>
        </tr>
        <tr>
          <td><a href="path08">Subcategory 3</a></td>
        </tr>
        <tr>
          <td><a href="path09">Subcategory 4</a></td>
        </tr>
        <tr>
          <td><a href="path10">Subcategory 5</a></td>
        </tr>
        <tr>
          <td><a href="javascript:doHide('menu2');">Close</a></td>
        </tr>
      </table>
    </div>

    <!- This div element contains the third popup menu. ->

    <div id="menu3" style="position: absolute; left: 304px; top: 19px;
    width: 152px; height: 114px; visibility: hidden;">
      <table width="152" border="0" cellpadding="0" cellspacing="0">
        <tr>
          <td><a href="path11">Subcategory 1</a></td>
        </tr>
        <tr>
          <td><a href="path12">Subcategory 2</a></td>
        </tr>
        <tr>
          <td><a href="path13">Subcategory 3</a></td>
        </tr>
        <tr>
          <td><a href="path14">Subcategory 4</a></td>
        </tr>
        <tr>
          <td><a href="path15">Subcategory 5</a></td>
        </tr>
        <tr>
          <td><a href="javascript:doHide('menu3');">Close</a></td>
        </tr>
```

```
      </table>
</div>

<!- This div element contains the fourth popup menu. ->

<div id="menu4" style="position: absolute; left: 456px; top: 19px;
width: 152px; height: 114px; visibility: hidden;">
  <table width="152" border="0" cellpadding="0" cellspacing="0">
    <tr>
      <td><a href="path16">Subcategory 1</a></td>
    </tr>
    <tr>
      <td><a href="path17">Subcategory 2</a></td>
    </tr>
    <tr>
      <td><a href="path18">Subcategory 3</a></td>
    </tr>
    <tr>
      <td><a href="path19">Subcategory 4</a></td>
    </tr>
    <tr>
      <td><a href="path20">Subcategory 5</a></td>
    </tr>
    <tr>
      <td><a href="javascript:doHide('menu4');">Close</a></td>
    </tr>
  </table>
</div>

<!- This div element contains the fifth popup menu. ->

<div id="menu5" style="position: absolute; left: 608px; top: 19px;
width: 152px; height: 114px; visibility: hidden;">
  <table width="152" border="0" cellpadding="0" cellspacing="0">
    <tr>
      <td><a href="path21">Subcategory 1</a></td>
    </tr>
    <tr>
      <td><a href="path22">Subcategory 2</a></td>
    </tr>
    <tr>
      <td><a href="path23">Subcategory 3</a></td>
    </tr>
    <tr>
      <td><a href="path24">Subcategory 4</a></td>
    </tr>
    <tr>
      <td><a href="path25">Subcategory 5</a></td>
    </tr>
    <tr>
      <td><a href="javascript:doHide('menu5');">Close</a></td>
    </tr>
  </table>
</div>
```

```
<!- Here at last is the table that creates the nav bar. It's the first
(and only) visible element on the page. The rest of the content is hid-
den in the invisible layers. ->

<table width="760" border="0" cellspacing="0" cellpadding="0">
  <tr>
    <td width="152">

<!- The onMouseOver event fires when the visitor moves the mouse over
the hotspot. In this case, the hotspot is the link for Category 1. The
visitor mouses over the link, and the browser launches doShowHide,
sending along the ID of the corresponding menu. ->

        <a href="path26" onMouseOver="doShowHide('menu1');">
          Category 1
        </a>
    </td>
    <td width="152">
      <a href="path27" onMouseOver="doShowHide('menu2');">
        Category 2
      </a>
    </td>
    <td width="152">
      <a href="path28" onMouseOver="doShowHide('menu3');">
        Category 3
      </a>
    </td>
    <td width="152">
      <a href="path29" onMouseOver="doShowHide('menu4');">
        Category 4
      </a>
    </td>
    <td width="152">
      <a href="path30" onMouseOver="doShowHide('menu5');">
        Category 5
      </a>
    </td>
  </tr>
</table>

</body>
</html>
```

Providing a Way Back

magine that you walk through a door into a room, but when you turn around to leave, the doorway isn't there. You wouldn't design a house this way unless you worked for the carnival. However, there are plenty of fun-house sites on the Web that do essentially the same thing—stranding their visitors on a page without providing a way back.

Designing good navigation helps to prevent the funhouse effect. Take the diagram in Figure 11.1. In this navigation scheme, the visitors go from the top-level page to the lower-level pages in a nice, clear, linear fashion, step by step by step. Providing a way back is as easy as including a link on each lower level page to the next page up in the site structure, just as you include a link from each upper level page to the next page down.

Many Web sites aren't strictly linear like this. In fact, a good Web site is usually nonlinear, allowing the visitor to make huge leaps across the site structure in the interest of speed. Diagrams like the one in Figure 11.2 aren't uncommon at all. Here, the visitor can arrive on a product page several different ways: by browsing step by step through the hierarchy, by going through the Specials section, or jumping directly to the product from the featured items on the home page.

In this scenario, providing a way back isn't as straightforward as linking both ways. You'd clutter up the

> **TIP**
> When the visitor drills down through several levels of pages, it's common to link from each of the lower level pages directly to the top-level page. This is a great convenience, as it allows the visitor to take a couple of steps at once. But don't forget to include the single-step moves, too. Always give your visitors the option of going back to the page immediately above the current one.

Figure 11.1
When a site unfolds in a linear fashion, make sure the links go both ways: higher level page to lower level page, and lower level page to higher level page.

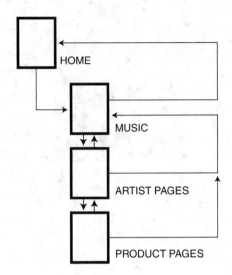

screen with links to all the possible referring pages. At the same time, in a non-linear site, it's more important to provide a way back because of the sheer number of possibilities. You don't want your visitors to feel lost at sea.

If your visitors get lost, they'll go for the Back button on their browser, which does the job. It also breaks their focus on your site and your content, which isn't

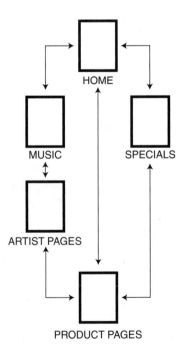

Figure 11.2
A nonlinear site offers many avenues of getting to the same page. Providing a way back isn't as straightforward as linking both ways.

good for you. It isn't good for them, either, because it slows them down. A simple JavaScript link solves this problem entirely:

```
<a href="javascript:history.back();">Go back</a>
```

The history.back method works exactly like the Back button. It loads the previous page. No matter which door your visitors end up using, a Go Back link leaves the same door open.

History.back isn't the only method in JavaScript's history object. Table 11.1 lists some of the others for your information, but don't go crazy with history methods. A Go Back link is very useful indeed, but a Go Forward link or a Go Two Steps Back link is clutter.

Table 11.1 **JavaScript History Methods**

Method	Description	Example
back()	Goes one step back	history.back()
forward()	Goes one step forward	history.forward()
go(**x**)	Goes **x** steps forward (positive value) or **x** steps back (negative value)	history.go(3), history.go(−2)

12

Working with Scripts and Style Sheets

he Web isn't all about HTML anymore. It hasn't been for years now. Even if you leave out technologies like database connectivity and server-side programming languages like PHP and Cold Fusion, Web builders rely on the interactive power of scripting and the stylistic control of Cascading Style Sheets (CSS) to make their sites more interactive and aesthetic. If you've already tried some of the Toolkits in this book, you know that they use JavaScript and CSS extensively.

GEEKSPEAK

Embedding material such as JavaScript or CSS code means including it in the HTML document. *Attaching* it means saving it in a separate file and then pointing to the file from the HTML.

With so much additional material going into your Web site, it's a good idea to look at how you get it in there. For JavaScript and CSS, you have two choices: embedding and attaching. Embedding the material means putting it in the same document as the HTML, while attaching it is to create a separate file containing the scripts or CSS code and then point to it in the HTML.

Embedding Scripts

Browser software is dumb in the sense that it thinks everything is HTML. Feed it a Web page, and everything is fine. But feed it a text document or a JavaScript, and the browser tries to interpret it as HTML, and you get something like

Figure 12.1

If you embed a
script without
enclosing it
in script tags,
the browser
assumes it's
HTML and dis-
plays it on the
page.

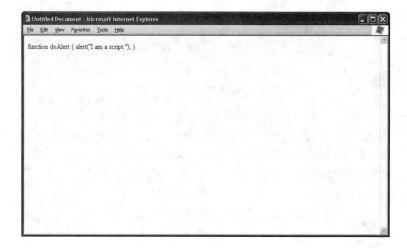

Figure 12.1. Instead of executing the embedded script, the browser treats it as HTML and displays the code on the page.

To avoid this problem, you have to tell the browser exactly where the script begins and ends. Hence, the script tag. Enclose your script between a pair of script tags, like this:

```
<script language="JavaScript">
  function doAlert() {
    alert("I am a script.");
  }
</script>
```

This way, when the browser translates the HTML, it knows to skip over whatever appears between the script tags.

That's the first step to embedding a script. The second is figuring out where to place the embedded script in the HTML code. The answer depends on what type of script it is. Scripts with repeatable or interactive functions—functions that can be called more than once per page or functions that change the appearance of the page after the browser builds it—belong near the top of the HTML code, between the head tags and after the title tag:

```
<html>
  <head>
    <title>Page Title</title>
    <script language="JavaScript">
      /* The JavaScript goes here. */
    </script>
  </head>
  <body>
```

```
  <!-- The content of the page goes here. -->
  </body>
</html>
```

Scripts for image rollovers or popup menus fall into this category, as do scripts that verify form input.

However, if you have a script that executes once when the browser initially builds the page, as in the case of custom text or a timestamp, embed the script exactly where you want the results to appear:

```
<html>
  <head>
    <title>Page Title</title>
  </head>
  <body>
    <!-- Insert a dateline at the top of the page. -->
    <script language="JavaScript">
      /* Dateline script goes here. */
    </script>
    <!-- The rest of the page goes here. -->
  </body>
</html>
```

Embedding Style Sheets

As with JavaScript, the browser interprets CSS as HTML unless you tell it otherwise. Style tags do for CSS what the script tags do for JavaScript. They tell the browser to treat everything between them as CSS, not HTML:

```
<html>
  <head>
    <title>Page Title</title>
    <style type="text/css">
      /* The CSS code goes here. */
    </style>
  </head>
  <body>
    <!-- The content of the page goes here. -->
  </body>
</html>
```

Also as with JavaScript, place embedded style sheets in the head section of the code.

TIP

Some ancient browsers don't understand script and style tags. These browsers render everything between them as text anyway. While it's difficult to imagine any visitor having anything like an enjoyable modern Web experience when browsing with these antiques, you might want to put HTML comment tags before and after the script or style tags, like this:

```
<script language="JavaScript">
  <!-


  ->
</script>
```

Adding comment tags prevents older browsers from displaying the script or code as HTML.

Attaching Scripts

The alternative to embedding is attaching, where you put the JavaScript in a separate file. However, for a Web page to use the external script, you have to tell the browser where to find it.

To do this, you use the src attribute of the script tag, like so:

```
<html>
  <head>
    <title>Page Title</title>
    <script language="JavaScript" src="../scripts/myscript.js">
    </script>
  </head>
  <body>
    <!-- The content of the page goes here. -->
  </body>
</html>
```

The src attribute gives the path from the current page to the script file that you want to attach, just like a hyperlink.

Attaching Style Sheets

Here it gets a little tricky. The style tag doesn't have a src attribute, so you can't use the style tag to attach an external style sheet. Instead, use the link tag:

```
<html>
  <head>
    <title>Page Title</title>
    <link href="css/mystyles.css" rel="stylesheet" type="text/css">
  </head>
  <body>
    <!-- The content of the page goes here. -->
  </body>
</html>
```

TIP

Another alternative is to import the external style sheet. See Topic 42 for details.

You'll note a couple things about the link tag here. It doesn't have an src attribute, either, but it does have an href attribute, which works exactly the same way. The path from the current page to the external style sheet goes in there. The rel attribute describes the relation of the linked document, and the type attribute tells what kind of style sheet the linked document is. The last two attributes aren't mission critical, in that all you really need is the href attribute to attach the style sheet, but they can be useful to the software or hardware that reads the Web page, so you should try to include them.

TIP

The link tag must always appear in the head section of the HTML document. You can't put it anywhere else.

Another thing about the link tag is that it doesn't require a closing version of itself, </link>. The link tag is self-contained, while the script tag isn't. That means, when you open a script tag, always try to close it, even if you don't have any embedded JavaScript between the tags. But with a link tag, you don't have to go to the trouble.

BLOG:
Embedding or Attaching?

You have two methods: embedding and attaching. Which is better?

The answer is, attaching. By far.

I like attaching scripts and style sheets. It allows me to use the same script file or style sheet on as many Web pages as I want, which is invaluable for frequently used functions like rollovers or popup menus and sitewide styles. If I tried to embed these things, I'd have to copy and paste the same blocks of code over and over again onto each and every page that requires them. This seems to me like a waste of time, not to mention bandwidth. The visitor's browser has to load the embedded stuff again and again, while the browser caches attached files.

Even more importantly, if I want to change something late in the process, I only have to fix it once, in the attached script or style sheet. When you embed everything, you have to go through every instance of the code and make the same corrections over and over again. Another needless waste of time.

Besides, for those who strive for per-spec implementation, the W3C recommends that you attach rather than embed.

Bottom line: Embedding is fine for quick, one-shot functions and styles. For anything you might want to reuse, attaching is the only way to fly.

Launching Scripts with Links

n the good old days, the humble hyperlink had a very specific job: navigation. The visitor clicked a link and went somewhere. It was as simple as that.

Even today, navigation remains the hyperlink's prime directive. However, your visitors want to do more on the Web than move from page to page. They want functionality. They want scripts and other interactive goodies. They want mini software solutions.

When you sit down to design these types of interfaces, you soon realize that something on the page has to trigger all those custom-built functions. Something clickable becomes the logical choice. HTML form buttons are an option. So are images that look like buttons. And so are hyperlinks. When you surf the Web, clicking what looks like a hyperlink might not have anything to do with navigation. It could launch a script instead.

From a usability standpoint, launching scripts with hyperlinks is a risky proposition because of the potential problems the practice creates. If you aren't careful about distinguishing script hyperlinks from navigation hyperlinks, you could very easily confuse your visitors and confound their expectations about what happens when they click. On the other hand, text hyperlinks are more graceful and unassuming than most graphical buttons, and they

> **TIP**
> Since navigation hyperlinks and script hyperlinks look exactly the same on the page, you can't rely on their appearance to distinguish them. Instead, use other tricks to convey the link's function to your visitors. Factors like the wording of the link and its placement in relation to other page elements help your visitors to figure out what happens when they click.

are nowhere near as clumsy and ugly as HTML form buttons. When used in the right context, script-launching hyperlinks improve the overall look and impression of your interface, which is never bad.

One way of launching a script with a link is to create a link that goes nowhere while assigning a result to the link's onClick event, like this:

```
<a href="#" onClick="doScript();">Launch the script</a>
```

Okay, okay. Technically, this link goes somewhere. The number sign in the href attribute refers to the current page, so clicking this link is like clicking the Refresh button on the browser.

Why the self-referential link? Plain HTML text doesn't respond to the onClick event, but a hyperlink does. You need to give the visitor something to click, so you specify a link, but you don't want the hyperlink to go anywhere. A link that essentially refreshes the page seems like a harmless compromise.

This strategy works well enough, but it can lead to annoyances, particularly when the visitor has to scroll the page to get to the link. Clicking a self-referential hyperlink causes the browser to jump back to the top of the page, so your visitors lose their place in your text.

A better alternative is to specify a script in the href attribute itself, like so:

```
<a href="javascript:doScript();">Launch the script</a>
```

Doing it like this, you don't have a self-referential link, so the browser doesn't jump around the page when the visitor clicks. It's better for everyone this way. Just make sure you preface the JavaScript code in the href attribute with **javascript:**. Otherwise, the browser assumes that the href value is the path to a page.

BLOG: JavaScript Links or onClick Links?

avaScript links, or links with *javascript* in the href attribute, cause problems for visitors who either turn off or don't have JavaScript support in their browsers. Not to be callous, but, in almost all cases, this percentage of your audience is small.

As a compromise, you can always use self-referential links that respond to onClick events. These links are easier for non-JavaScript browsers to handle, but then you have the problem of the browser jumping back to the top of the page. This inconveniences a larger cross-section of your audience than it helps.

If you really want to court the HTML purists, don't use JavaScript on your site, period. However, if you want or need the extra functionality, JavaScript links work better than onClick links for the majority of your visitors.

PART II:
Layout Topics

14

Creating Fixed-Width Layouts with Tables

Fixed-width layouts use absolute pixel measurements to determine the width of the page. The opposite of fixed width is **liquid** or **expando**, which automatically resizes itself to fit the width of the visitor's browser window.

Fixed-width layouts are the only choice for pages that require precise control over graphic design. You can't expect to place visual elements with any accuracy when a liquid layout keeps changing the width of the page to match the width of the browser window. At the same time, fixed width means fixed width, whether the size of the browser window matches the actual width of the page or greatly exceeds it. As Figure 14.1 shows, fixed-width layouts can feel simultaneously cramped and lost in interstellar space when the browser window is too large for the page. Centering the fixed-width layout cuts down on this phenomenon, as in Figure 14.2.

All good Web layouts start with a sketch like the one in Figure 14.3, where you mark out the main areas of your page. Don't get too clever with the layout here. HTML's colspan and rowspan attributes let you build incredibly complex tables, but do everything in your power to avoid

GEEKSPEAK

Fixed-width layouts use absolute pixel measurements to determine the width of the page.

Where can I find a fixed-width site?

Famous fixed-width sites include nytimes.com and yahoo.com. Both sites pack a tremendous amount of content into carefully designed layouts, which require the precision of fixed widths.

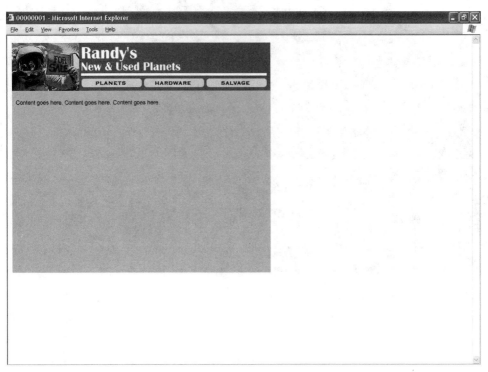

Figure 14.1

A fixed-width page can feel cramped when you look at it in a much wider browser window.

them. Colspans and rowspans are fine for **data tables**, or tables that present rows and columns of data according to HTML spec. Layout tables like the kind you're building here are against spec, and browsers tend to do unfriendly things to your colspanned or rowspanned design.

If you want a more adventurous design, try **nested tables** instead. A nested table is a table that appears inside the cell of another table. The design in Figure 14.3 isn't adventurous by any stretch of the imagination, but it nests a table in the bottom cell of the main table to avoid a colspan in the top cell.

Once you sketch your design, you should start to think about pixel measurements. The pixel is the basic unit of measurement in HTML tables. Conveniently enough, computer operating systems measure screen

GEEKSPEAK

A **data table** is a table that presents rows and columns of data. This is the only type of table that HTML officially supports. Using tables to create layouts, while exceedingly common, is against the rules.

GEEKSPEAK

A **nested table** is a table that appears inside the cell of another table.

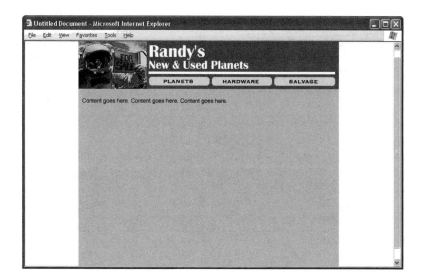

Figure 14.2

Centering the fixed-width layout improves matters.

widths in pixels, too, which makes sizing your layout for a particular screen setting a painless operation. You simply pick a screen width that makes sense for your visitors, and then you custom-build your layout to fit in a similarly sized table.

Table 14.1 gives you the numbers. As you can see, it isn't quite as easy as building a 640-pixel-wide table to match a 640-pixel-wide screen. You have to factor in browser interface elements such as scrollbars, so you

TIP

When you build your design, set the valign attribute of the cells to "top." This instructs the browser to align the content vertically along the top of the cells. Otherwise, the browser centers the content vertically.

Logo	
Nav	Main Content Area

Figure 14.3

Begin by sketching the layout you want to build and labeling the areas.

Table 14.1 **Common Screen Widths and Corresponding Table Widths**

SCREEN WIDTH	TABLE WIDTH	COMMENTS
544 pixels	544 pixels	WebTV/MSNTV
640 pixels	600 pixels	Absolute minimum for most applications
800 pixels	760 pixels	The safe default size
1024 pixels	955 pixels	The emerging default size
1280 pixels	1210 pixels	Not recommended for general-purpose sites
1600 pixels	1530 pixels	Not recommended for general-purpose sites

TIP

While it's true that many people are surfing the Web with desktop and laptop monitors set to 1024-width screens, don't forget that there are other types of browsing devices on the Web, too, such as PDAs, TVs, telephones, video game consoles, kitchen appliances, wristwatches, and who knows what else. If your site appeals to the wireless crowd, stay away from the larger screen sizes.

subtract a couple of pixels from your table, just to be on the safe side. The exception is MSNTV, still occasionally known as WebTV, which doesn't have scrollbars or other interface elements to eat into your design space.

For the purposes of this example, play it safe and go with an 800-width screen, which calls for a table width of 760 pixels. Now that you know this, figuring out the widths of the areas inside the table isn't hard. Eyeball it. Make your best guess. You can adjust the values later if need be. Just make sure the individual widths don't add up to more (or less) than the total width of the table.

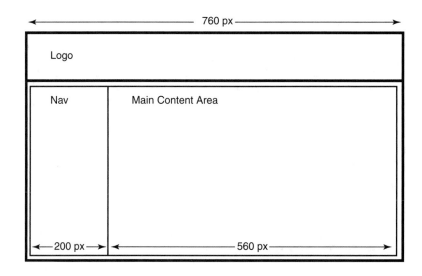

Figure 14.4

After you determine the width of the table, the rest of the numbers fall into place.

Record the numbers on your sketch as in Figure 14.4, and the table code practically writes itself. Replace the labels in the HTML with your site's content—using nested tables if you need extra design— and you have a fixed-width layout.

Listing 14.1 **View Source for Figure 14.4.**

```
<div align="center">

<!-- If you don't want to center the layout table, delete the div tag  here and at
the end of the listing. -->

  <table width="760" border="0" cellpadding="0" cellspacing="0">
    <tr>
      <td width="760" valign="top">Logo</td>
    </tr>
    <tr>
      <td width="760" valign="top">

<!-- The nested table begins here. -->

        <table width="760" border="0" cellpadding="0" cellspacing="0">
          <tr>
            <td width="200" valign="top">Nav</td>
            <td width="560" valign="top">Content</td>
          </tr>
        </table>

<!-- The nested table ends here. -->

      </td>
    </tr>
  </table>

</div>
```

Notice in this example that you don't worry about the heights of the table cells. This is actually one of the advantages of building layouts with tables. The browser automatically adjusts the heights of the table cells to match whatever content sits inside them. While you can certainly specify precise height measurements if you know them, you can also just let nature take its course and rely on the browser to calculate the correct heights.

Here's what the listing might look like with some height values thrown in:

```html
<div align="center">

  <table width="760" border="0" cellpadding="0" cellspacing="0">
    <tr>
      <td width="760" height="100" valign="top">Logo</td>
    </tr>
    <tr>
      <td width="760" height="400" valign="top">

<!-- The nested table begins here. -->

        <table width="760" border="0" cellpadding="0" cellspacing="0">
          <tr>
            <td width="200" height="400" valign="top">Nav</td>
            <td width="560" height="400" valign="top">Content</td>
          </tr>
        </table>

<!-- The nested table ends here. -->

      </td>
    </tr>
  </table>

</div>
```

The downside to omitting the heights is that your table looks completely collapsed in a browser window until you start adding content to the cells. If this bugs you, just give your table cells arbitrary height values while you're building it, but then don't forget to remove the heights once the content is in the cells.

TIP

If a cell in your table is the same width as the table itself, you can omit the table cell's width attribute. This way, if you change your mind about the width of the table, you only have one width attribute to update.

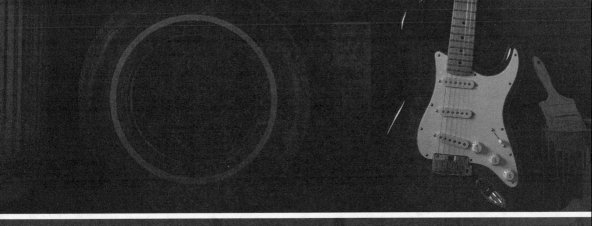

BLOG: HTML or CSS for Layout?

here are two general approaches to creating layouts on a Web page: HTML tables or Cascading Style Sheets (CSS). The tables method is the classic approach. It's easy to do, and it works reliably across many different types of browsers. However, using HTML tables for layout gets the standards police all in an uproar. Groups like the World Wide Web Consortium (W3C) hate it when you use tables this way, because HTML's table tags are supposed to be for rows and columns of data. Using tables for graphic design is like using a hammer to pound in a screw—it gets the job done, but not the job that the hammer or screw had in mind. This type of argument isn't entirely nitpicking. Accessibility devices like text-to-speech converters and screen readers rely on strict interpretations of HTML standards, so your tables-based layout could very easily play tricks on the visually impaired. In spite of these limitations, tables-based layout dominates the Web.

The CSS alternative follows spec to the letter, satisfying even the most fastidious members of the W3C. CSS has been around for a while, but it is still very much a maturing technology. Style sheets wouldn't be so bad if browsers would get their collective acts together with regard to them. The latest versions of Internet Explorer, Netscape, and Opera support CSS reasonably well, but none of them supports it entirely and not without significant inconsistencies. Building a CSS layout requires more effort and more testing time, and it seems to work best with straightforward designs. Still,

CSS-based layout or something very much like it is the future of graphic design on the Web.

If you're trying to reach the largest audience possible, your choice is easy: Go with tables. However, if you're mindful of standards and accessibility concerns and have an eye to the future, CSS is the choice for you.

15

Creating Fixed-Width Layouts with CSS

or those just joining us, a fixed-width layout uses absolute measurements to determine the width of the page, which gives you a higher degree of control over the graphic design. Topic 14 discusses how to create fixed-width layouts using tables. This topic shows you how to achieve the same effect with Cascading Style Sheets (CSS).

If you look at any topic on tables-based layouts in this book, you read over and over again about how you should always build your design with nested tables. You find no such advice in this topic, because you don't need nested tables in CSS. Instead, you divide your layout into a series of rectangular areas called **divs** or divisions. You construct each area of the design separately using HTML's div tags, and then you lay these elements out on the Web page like the pieces of a puzzle. In this sense, CSS is more graphically oriented than HTML tables. Thinking in terms of rectangles is completely natural for visual people, who tend to see the world in shapes anyway.

As with table layouts, CSS layouts begin life as sketches (see Figure 15.1). Note again that you don't have to worry about nested tables when you work in CSS. You just need to define the different rectangular areas that make up the page.

TIP

This procedure gives you a fixed-width layout that sits on the left side of the browser window. If you want to center your CSS-based layout instead, skip ahead to Topic 16.

GEEKSPEAK

The **div tag** in HTML stands for **division**. It marks off an area or division of a Web page. Each division can have its own CSS style properties.

Figure 15.1

Don't call these rectangles table cells. They're divs.

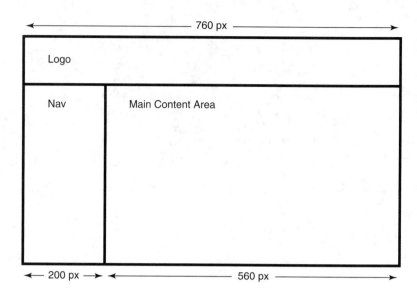

To create this layout, you need three rectangles:

1. One for the Logo area with a width of 760 pixels
2. One for the Nav area with a width of 200 pixels
3. One for the Content area with a width of 560 pixels

Three rectangles mean three div elements. Here they are:

```
<div id="logo" style="position: absolute; width: 760px;">
  Logo
</div>

<div id="nav" style="position: absolute; width: 200px;">
  Nav
</div>

<div id="content" style="position: absolute; width: 560px;">
  Content
</div>
```

The style attributes of these tags give the width in CSS format, not **width="760"** like you might use if you were building a table. It's important to remember to use CSS format instead of HTML format for everything inside the style attribute. That means a couple of things:

- Use the colon character (:) instead of the equals sign (=) to give attribute/value pairs.

- Separate compound attribute names with a hyphen, as in **background-color**, not **backgroundcolor** or **back-ground_color**.

- Always specify the unit of measurement after a numerical value, and don't put a space between the number and the unit, as in **560px**, not **560** or **560 px**.

- Separate attribute/value pairs with the semicolon character (;).

TIP
Before figuring out the top and left offsets for your divs, do yourself a favor and set the leftmargin, topmargin, marginwidth, and marginheight attributes to 0. These attributes are in the body tag. Making this change improves the consistency of your design across different browsers, which add different amounts of margin space to the page by default.

As you recall, the div tags give you the divisions or areas of the page. The next step is to position them on the page. To do this, you express their location as offsets from the top and left side of the browser window. The first div element is easy: It starts in the upper-left corner, so there is no top or left offset:

```
<div id="logo" style="position: absolute; width: 760px; top: 0px; left: 0px;">
  Logo
</div>
```

The second div element starts at the left, so there is no left offset, but what about the top offset? You need to specify something here. Otherwise, the second div overlaps the first, which isn't what your design calls for. Let's say you plan to insert a graphical logo in the first div, and you know that the image has a height of 100 pixels. If the second div starts directly under the logo, the offset is 100 pixels, as in Figure 15.2. Therefore, the code is:

```
<div id="nav" style="position: absolute; width: 200px; top: 100px; left: 0px;">
  Nav
</div>
```

For consistency's sake and to spell everything out very clearly for CSS-challenged browsers, you should go back to the Logo div and hard-code the height value:

```
<div id="logo" style="position: absolute; width: 760px; height: 100px; top: 0px;
left: 0px;">
  Logo
</div>
```

The third div element needs a top offset of 100 pixels to clear the Logo area and a left offset of 200 pixels to clear the Nav area:

Figure 15.2

Since you position each div element according to offsets from the top and left, you need to figure out how tall the Logo element is. You can always pick an arbitrary value and refine it later.

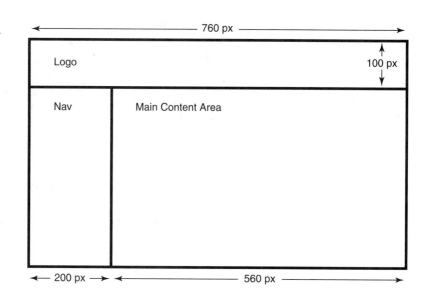

```
<div id="content" style="position: absolute; width: 560px; top: 100px; left:
200px;">
  Content
</div>
```

TOOL KIT.

Fixed-Width Layout in CSS

This Toolkit gives you a fixed-width layout in CSS with any combination of the following elements: a banner, a left column, a middle column, and a right column.

```
<body leftmargin="0" topmargin="0" marginwidth="0" marginheight="0">

<!- Add the following div if you want a banner to appear across the top
of the layout. ->

  <div id="banner" style="position: absolute; width: designwidthpx;
height: bannerheightpx; top: 0px; left: 0px;">
    Content goes here
  </div>

<!- End of banner div ->

<!- Add the following div if you want a left column. If you aren't
using a banner, give 0 for bannerheight below. ->

  <div id="leftcol" style="position: absolute; width: leftwidthpx; top:
bannerheightpx; left: 0px;">
    Content goes here
  </div>
```

```
<!- End of left-column div ->

<!- Add the following div if you want a right column. Again, give 0 for
bannerheight if you aren't using a banner. ->

<div id="rightcol" style="position: absolute; width: rightwidthpx; top:
bannerheightpx; right: 0px;">
   Content goes here
  </div>

<!- End of right-column div ->

<!- The following div is for the main content area of the page. Give
zeroes for values that you don't need. ->

  <div id="middlecol" style="position: absolute; width: middlewidthpx;
top: bannerheightpx; left: leftwidthpx; right: rightwidthpx;">
     Content goes here
  </div>

<!- End of middle-column div ->

</body>
```

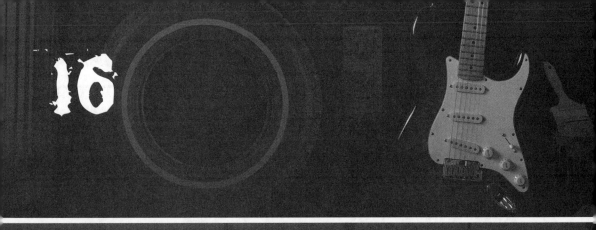

16

Centering Fixed-Width CSS Layouts

ne good technique for centering a fixed-with CSS layout is to use nested layers, a.k.a. nested divs. A **nested layer** is a div element inside another div, just as nested tables are tables within tables. In this scenario, the main div is a container. This is the div that you actually center. The nested layers inside provide the site content. Figure 16.1 shows a typical CSS layout with nested layers.

This layout calls for four nested divs:

1. One for the Logo area with a width of 760 pixels
2. One for the Nav area with a width of 200 pixels
3. One for the Content area with a width of 400 pixels
4. One for the Links area with a width of 160 pixels

You also need a container div to hold these four.

The trick with this technique is to set the left margin of the page to the center point of the browser window, which you achieve by adding the style attribute to the body tag of the page:

```
<body style="margin-left: 50%;">
```

GEEKSPEAK

A **nested layer** or **nested div** is a div element that appears inside another div.

Figure 16.1

To build a centered CSS layout, use a container div to hold nested content divs, and then center the container.

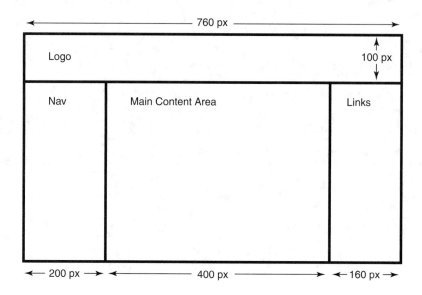

Notice the percentage value instead of an absolute, pixel-based measurement. Using a percentage here is wise, since you don't know for sure the width of your visitor's browser window.

Now, because the left margin of the page begins in the middle of the browser window, you need to express the position of the container div in relation to that margin. Use this code:

```
<div id="container" style="position: relative; width: 760px; left: -380px;">
```

The left offset is a negative number here, and for good reason. Since the position of the container div is relative instead of absolute, the browser uses the left offset a little differently, subtracting 380 pixels from the position of the left margin. Why 380 pixels? Because 380 is half of 760, which is the width of the entire layout. What you're doing, in essence, is finding the center of the page and then moving half of the layout to one side. The result is a perfectly centered container div.

When you use this technique, the left offset of the container div is always one-half of its width. However, if you have no time for math, Table 16.1 provides a quick reference.

The nested divs look just like the divs from Topic 15. Their position is absolute, but, because they are nested, the browser uses their parent element—in this case the container div—as the reference point for counting top and left offsets, not the upper-left corner of the browser window.

Here's the code for the entire layout:

Table 16.1 Common Container-Div Widths and Corresponding Left Offsets

Screen Width	Container Div Width	Left Offset for Centering
640 pixels	600 pixels	–300 pixels
800 pixels	760 pixels	–380 pixels
1024 pixels	954 pixels	–477 pixels
1280 pixels	1210 pixels	–605 pixels
1600 pixels	1530 pixels	–765 pixels

```
<body style="margin-left: 50%;">

<!-- The style attribute moves the left margin of the page to the center of the
browser window. -->

<!-- Here is the container div. Its negative left offset is relative to the left
margin of the page as defined in the body tag, and its value comes from half of its
width. -->

  <div id="container" style="position: relative; width: 760px; left: -380px;">

<!-- Here come the nested divs. -->

    <div id="logo" style="position: absolute; width: 760px; top: 0px; left: 0px;">
      Logo
    </div>

    <div id="nav" style="position: absolute; width: 200px; top: 100px; left: 0px;">
      Nav
    </div>

    <div id="content" style="position: absolute; width: 400px; top: 100px; left:
200px;">
      Content
    </div>

    <div id="links" style="position: absolute; width: 160px; top: 100px; left:
600px;">
```

```html
<!-- That's it for the nested divs. -->

  </div>

<!-- The line above closes the container div. -->

</body>
```

Creating Liquid Layouts with Tables

Liquid or **expando** layouts are layouts that automatically resize themselves to fit the visitor's browser window. Compare liquid layouts with their fixed-width counterparts, which use absolute measurements like 600 pixels or 760 pixels, no matter what size browser window the visitor prefers.

The obvious benefit to liquid layouts is that they take advantage of all available screen real estate, which makes them look classier. Liquid layouts don't seem too compact when you view them in very wide browser windows, as fixed-width layouts sometimes do. Moreover, visitors with huge monitors and professional video cards can maximize their browsers and see more of your site before having to scroll, and visitors with special requirements are less likely to break your layout by setting their browser's font size to Largest. Controlling graphic design in liquid layouts is much more challenging. You don't have the benefit of knowing at exactly which pixel a certain element appears, since the width of the design space changes with the browser window.

Liquid layouts begin life as fixed-width layouts. That is, when you build a liquid layout, you design the table that controls the

GEEKSPEAK

Liquid or expando layouts are layouts that automatically resize themselves to fit the visitor's browser window.

FAQ

Where can I find a liquid site?
Famous liquid sites include Amazon and most of eBay. Both have an abundance of content and straightforward (some might say uninspiring) graphic design.

116

Figure 17.1

*Start with an
initial, fixed-
width design—
and keep it
simple. Never
use colspans or
rowspans to
achieve a com-
plex design.
Use nested
tables instead.*

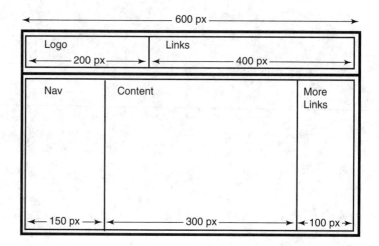

layout to fit into a certain minimum-width browser window, say 600 pixels.
Visitors who show up with browser windows smaller than the minimum width
get the horribly unattractive horizontal scrollbars, even in a liquid layout.

If you wanted nothing more than a fixed-width layout, you'd stop there. For
a liquid layout, however, you're not quite done. To create the liquid effect, you
very carefully set the width of certain table cells to the asterisk value (*), which
is HTML shorthand for **whatever**. Using this generic width instead of a fixed
pixel value forces the browser to calculate the width of the design in terms of
the width of the browser window. Hence, liquefaction.

So, which table cells get the width value of **whatever**? Here is where a
plan and a sketch or two come in handy.

Start with your initial, fixed-width design, like the one in Figure 17.1. Notice
the simplicity of the layout, which is critical. This particular layout calls for two
nested tables inside a two-cell container table. You could achieve the same
effect with a single table that uses the colspan attribute, but you don't want to
do that here. Never, under any circumstances, use rowspan or colspan attributes in liquid designs. If you do, as the table expands, your visitor's browser
takes the liberty of inserting whitespace everywhere, especially where you
don't want it.

Listing 17.1 View Source for Figure 17.1.

```
<table width="600" border="0" cellpadding="0" cellspacing="0">
  <tr>
    <td>

<!-- The first nested table begins here. -->
```

```
        <table width="600" border="0" cellpadding="0" cellspacing="0">
          <tr>
            <td width="200">Logo</td>
            <td width="400">Links</td>
          </tr>
        </table>

<!-- The first nested table ends here. -->

      </td>
    </tr>
    <tr>
      <td>

<!-- The second nested table begins here. -->

        <table width="600" border="0" cellpadding="0" cellspacing="0">
          <tr>
            <td width="150">Nav</td>
            <td width="350">Content</td>
            <td width="100">More links</td>
          </tr>
        </table>

<!-- The second nested table ends here. -->

      </td>
    </tr>
</table>
```

This table has a width of 600 pixels, so it fits comfortably in a maximized browser window on a 640-width screen. However, it looks too compact in larger browser windows on wider screens. To make this table expand, you need to decide which table cells to switch from absolute, pixel-based width attributes to relative, percentage-based ones.

In the first nested table, the Links cell makes a good choice, so you set its width attribute to the asterisk value, as in Figure 17.2. (You also set the width of the table to 100%. If you don't, the table remains fixed at 600 pixels, even with the liquid cell.) With this code, the Logo cell grows no wider than 200 pixels, but

TIP

When you use this method of liquefaction, choose one and only one cell per table row to be the variable-width cell. Don't try to make two liquid cells in the same row. In addition, if your table has more than one row, the same cell in each row has to be the liquid one.

118

Figure 17.2

In the first nested table, the Links cell is the better choice for variable width.

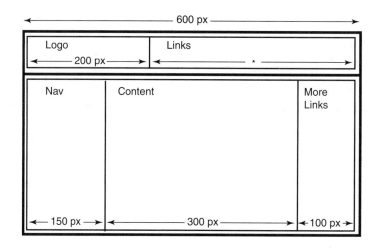

the Links cell expands and contracts with the width of the browser window. If the logo cell expands instead, the browser keeps the Links cell at 400 pixels and puts the extra whitespace inside the Logo cell, which could throw your layout off-balance.

Listing 17.2 **View Source for Figure 17.2.**

```
<table width="100%" border="0" cellpadding="0" cellspacing="0">
    <tr>
        <td width="200">Logo</td>
        <td width="*">Links</td>
    </tr>
</table>
```

TIP

A good rule of thumb is to pick the cell with the most content to be the liquid cell.

In the second nested table, the Content cell is the best choice for relative width (see Figure 17.3). This keeps the cells on either side at controlled widths while allowing the content of the page to fill the browser window naturally. So set the width of the Content cell to **whatever**, and set the width of the nested table to 100%.

Now, just set the width of the container table to 100% to make it expand with the browser window, and you're done. Figure 17.4 shows the finished layout sketch.

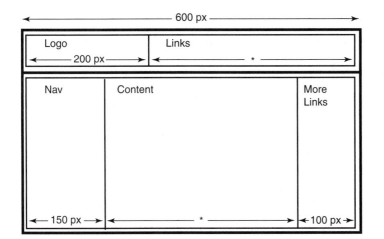

Figure 17.3

In the second nested table, choose the Content cell as the one for variable width.

Listing 17.3 **View Source for Figure 17.3.**

```
<table width="100%" border="0" cellpadding="0" cellspacing="0">
    <tr>
      <td width="150">Nav</td>
      <td width="*">Content</td>
      <td width="100">More links</td>
    </tr>
</table>
```

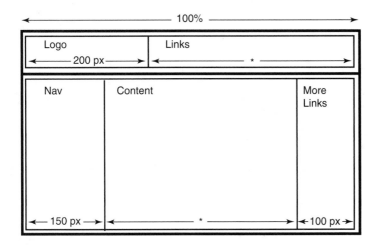

Figure 17.4

Set the width of the container table to 100%, and your layout is liquefied.

Listing 17.4 **View Source for Figure 17.4.**

```
<table width="100%" border="0" cellpadding="0" cellspacing="0">
  <tr>
    <td>

<!-- The first nested table begins here. -->

      <table width="100%" border="0" cellpadding="0" cellspacing="0">
        <tr>
          <td width="200">Logo</td>
          <td width="*">Links</td>
        </tr>
      </table>

<!-- The first nested table ends here. -->

    </td>
  </tr>
  <tr>
    <td>

<!-- The second nested table begins here. -->

      <table width="100%" border="0" cellpadding="0" cellspacing="0">
        <tr>
          <td width="150">Nav</td>
          <td width="*">Content</td>
          <td width="100">More links</td>
        </tr>
      </table>

<!-- The second nested table ends here. -->

    </td>
  </tr>
</table>
```

Creating Liquid Layouts with CSS

irect from Topic 17, **liquid** or **expando** layouts are layouts that automatically resize themselves to fit the visitor's browser window. However, while the previous topic covered tables-based liquid layouts, this topic shows you how to build liquid layouts with Cascading Style Sheets (CSS).

TIP

As with fixed-width CSS layouts, you'll want to set the leftmargin, topmargin, marginheight, and marginwidth attributes to 0 in the body tag so that your mathematics add up correctly across browsers.

Start with a sketch of the layout, like the one in Figure 18.1. CSS layouts don't require nested tables, so you don't have to worry about those. Just break down the design into rectangular areas. Each of these becomes a div element in the HTML code.

The next step is to decide which divs should be liquid. Let's say you want the Content div to expand and contract, but you want to keep the left and right sidebars at a fixed width, say 200 pixels for the Nav div and 150 pixels for the Links div. The Content div needs to be liquid, clearly, but what about the Logo div? If you were building this layout as a table, you wouldn't necessarily have to specify the width of the top cell as 100%, because the table itself would have a width of 100%, and the browser would resize the Logo cell to match the width of the table perfectly.

You get no such shortcut in CSS. If you want the Logo div to stretch across the full width of the browser window, you have to put it in the CSS code explicitly. So

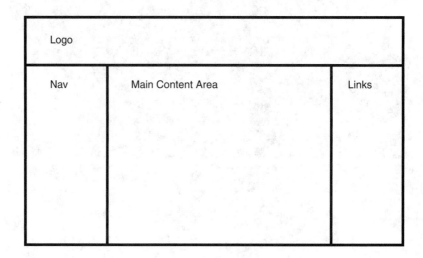

add the Logo div to your still-short list of liquid elements, and mark up your sketch as in Figure 18.2.

One of the less desirable features of CSS layout is that there isn't one single solution for creating the liquid effect. You have to use different methods depending on the position of the div in the layout:

- If the div stretches across the entire width of the browser window, create the liquid effect by setting the div's width to 100%.

- If other elements appear to the left or right of the div—if it doesn't stretch across the entire browser window—you don't give the div a width value.

Figure 18.2

Since you're dealing with CSS, you have to define the Logo div as being liquid in this layout. If you were building a table, you wouldn't nec-essarily need to do this.

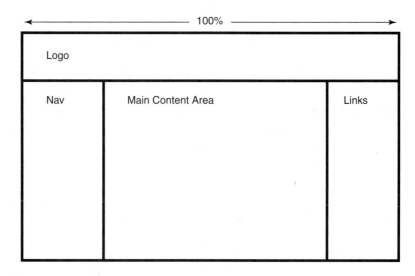

The Logo div stretches across the browser window from left to right, so this element falls into the first category. Its code looks like this:

```
<div id="logo" style="position: absolute; width: 100%; height: 100px; top: 0px;
left: 0px;">
  Logo
</div>
```

The divs for the nav bar and links section are regular fixed-width elements:

```
<div id="nav" style="position: absolute; width: 200px; top: 100px; left: 0px;">
  Nav
</div>
```

```
<div id="links" style="position: absolute; width: 150px; top: 100px; right: 0px;">
  Links
</div>
```

The Links style description says, among other things, **right: 0px**. This particular bit of code places the element against the right side of the screen. It's necessary to define the style this way, since you don't know how wide the content area will be, which is the whole point of liquid layouts in the first place.

Now for the Content div:

```
<div id="content" style="position: absolute; top: 100px; left: 200px; right:
150px;">
  Content
</div>
```

Since this div appears between the left and right sidebars, it falls into the second category. You don't give it a width value, but you do position it 200 pixels from the left side of the browser window and 150 pixels from the right side. Why? To make sure it doesn't overlap the nav-bar and links areas.

There you have it: a liquid layout in CSS. Figure 18.3 shows the finished layout sketch.

TIP

If you assign background colors to your divs, you should make the main content area the same background color as the page. Doing this prevents the browser from displaying the seams of your design, so to speak. The Content div might not fit snugly against the right column depending on what you have in the main content area, and you don't want the background color of the page poking through the space between the divs.

Figure 18.3

Figure 18.3

*The finished
sketch for your
liquid layout
with CSS.*

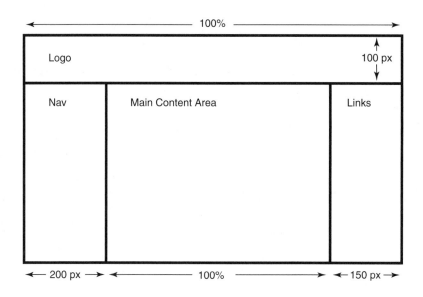

Liquid Layout with CSS

This Toolkit shows you how to make a liquid CSS layout with any combination of the
following elements: a banner, a left column, a middle column, and a right column.

```
<body leftmargin="0" topmargin="0" marginheight="0" marginwidth="0">
```

```
<!- Add the following div if you want a banner to appear across the top
of the layout. ->
```

```
  <div id="banner" style="position: absolute; width: 100%; height: ban-
nerheightpx; top: 0px; left: 0px;">
    Content goes here
  </div>
```

```
<!- End of banner div ->
```

```
<!- Add the following div if you want a left column. Use a pixel value
for the width if you want a fixed-size column, or give a percentage for
a liquid column. If you aren't using a banner across the top of the
page, insert 0 for bannerheight below. ->
```

```
  <div id="leftcol" style="position: absolute; width: leftwidth; top:
bannerheightpx; left: 0px;">
    Content goes here
  </div>
```

```
<!- End of left-column div ->
```

```
<!- Add the following div if you want a right column. Like with the
left-column div, you can use an absolute pixel value or a percentage. A
percentage makes the right column liquid. ->

   <div id="rightcol" style="position: absolute; width: rightwidth; top:
bannerheightpx; right: 0px;">
      Content goes here
   </div>

<!- End of right-column div ->

<!- The following div is a liquid column for the main content of the
page. Supply zeroes for values that you don't need. ->

   <div id="middlecol" style="position: absolute; top: bannerheightpx;
left: leftwidth; right: rightwidth;">
      Content goes here
   </div>

<!- End of middle-column div ->

</body>
```

Slicing Images for Layout Tables

ne popular technique for creating Web layouts is **slicing.** In slicing, you design the layout as a graphic file in an application such as Macromedia Fireworks, Adobe Photoshop, or Adobe ImageReady. Then, you literally slice the file into pieces for the different sections of the page as in Figure 19.1, and your graphics software gives you an HTML table that reassembles the pieces in a Web browser. This is the perfect solution for people trained as graphic designers: You get to design in a completely visual environment, and you don't have to do any of the coding yourself.

That's the theory, at least. To make slicing work in a practical sense, you need to know something about creating layout tables the hard way, from the HTML up instead of from the graphics down. This book has made a habit of warning you against the evils of colspans and rowspans in your layout tables, and layout tables that come from sliced graphic files are no exception. If your slices result in a layout table that uses colspans or rowspans (like the slicing job in Figure 19.1, incidentally), you will almost certainly run into problems when you try to add content to the layout in your site editor. Content that pushes against the boundaries of the table causes your layout to break in unattractive ways, as in Figure 19.2.

Avoiding colspans and rowspans is pretty easy if you slice each area of your page separately. Divide the initial slices from Figure 19.1 into separate

GEEKSPEAK

Slicing is a technique for creating layout tables in applications such as Fireworks and Photoshop. First, you design the layout in the graphics editor, and then you cut the layout into divisions or slices based on the different sections of the page. When you export the slices as individual graphics files, you also get an HTML table that reassembles the pieces in a Web browser.

Figure 19.1

Figure 19.1

Slicing a layout in software such as Macromedia Fireworks gives you individual graphics files and an HTML table that reassembles them in a Web browser.

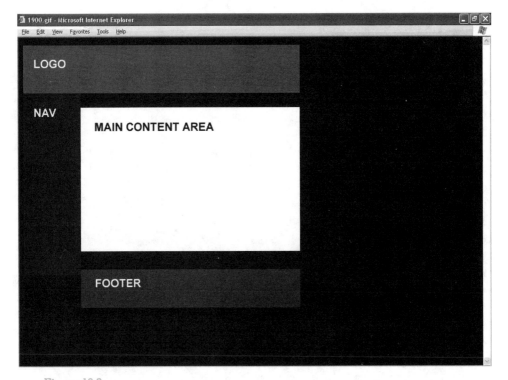

Figure 19.2

Problem. Your layout table uses colspans and rowspans, so it breaks easily when you fiddle with it.

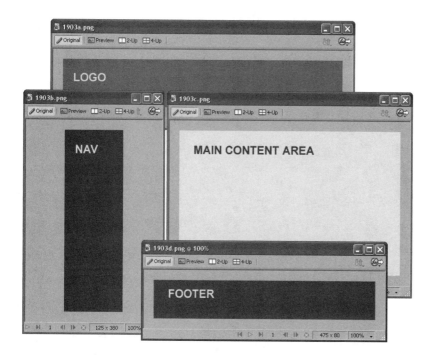

Figure 19.3

To avoid colspans and rowspans, divide the areas of your layout into separate graphics, and slice each graphic individually.

graphics files, as in Figure 19.3, and slice and export these layouts individually. In this case, you get four separate layout tables for the four areas of the page.

Now, how to put the areas back together? The best way is to roll up your sleeves, fire up your HTML editor, and build the container table by hand. Make a sketch of the overall layout, as in Figure 19.4. Notice that the bottom cell of the

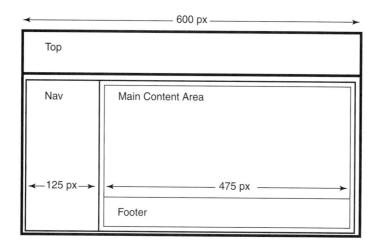

Figure 19.4

Sketch the container table, using multiple nested tables to avoid colspans and rowspans, and build this table in your site editor.

container table requires a nested table to avoid a colspan, and the right cell of the nested table needs another nested table to avoid a rowspan.

Listing 19.1 **View Source for Figure 19.4.**

```
<table width="600" border="0" cellpadding="0" cellspacing="0">
  <tr>
    <td>Top</td>
  </tr>
  <tr>
    <td>

<!-- First nested table begins. -->

        <table width="125" border="0" cellpadding="0" cellspacing="0">
          <tr>
            <td>Nav</td>
            <td>

<!-- Second nested table begins. -->

            <table width="475" border="0" cellpadding="0" cellspacing="0">
              <tr>
                <td>Main Content Area</td>
              </tr>
              <tr>
                <td>Footer</td>
              </tr>
            </table>

<!-- Second nested table ends. -->

            </td>
          </tr>
        </table>

<!-- First nested table ends. -->

      </td>
    </tr>
  </table>
```

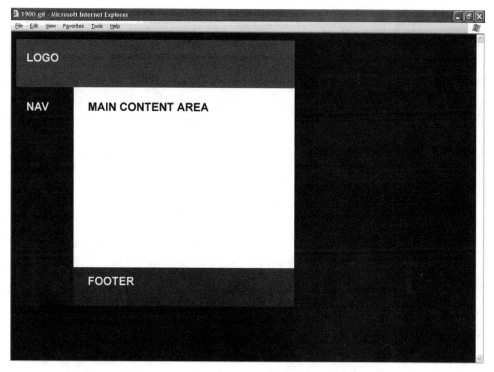

Figure 19.5

Insert the HTML from the sliced graphics into the container table.
When the dimensions of the table change, your layout doesn't break.

Now, just paste the HTML code from the four sliced graphics into their corresponding cells in the container table, and you have a table-based layout
built to last, as in Figure 19.5.

TIP

Your graphics software may have an option for exporting your sliced layout in nested
tables instead of as a single table with colspans and rowspans. You might give this
method a try, although you're often better off building the container table from
scratch. Homemade tables are generally sturdier than the ones that a software application spits out.

Creating Multicolumn Layouts with Tables

The best way to get multiple columns of text in your table-based design is to drop a nested table into the main content cell, as in Figure 20.1. The nested table can have as many columns as you need, although you probably don't want to use more than two or maybe three.

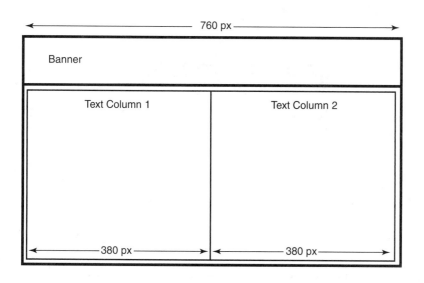

Figure 20.1

Use a nested table in the main content cell of your layout to create multiple columns for text.

134

TIP

You don't want to use more than two or three columns in a multicolumn layout, and three columns is pushing it. Think of the visitors to your site who don't have giant monitors with ultrahigh-resolution displays. When you try to squeeze too many columns into the content cell, you get columns that are too narrow to read or the dreaded horizontal scrollbars.

Normally, when you nest a layout table inside another layout table, you set the border, cellpadding, and cellspacing attributes of the nested table to 0. Doing this makes sure the nested table fits snugly inside its container cell. However, when the layout table holds multiple columns of text, you don't want this effect. Try reading two columns of text sitting next to each other without sufficient whitespace separating them, as in Figure 20.2, and you'll see exactly why.

The cellspacing attribute of the table tag can help you here. Cellspacing controls the amount of space between adjacent cells. Just set the cellspacing

TIP

Cellspacing also affects the space around the table cells, not just between them. Consequently, your columns of text won't fit snugly against the sides of the container cell. If this throws off the look you're trying to achieve, you can keep the cellspacing of the nested table at 0 and add a separate column for whitespace between the columns of text. Set the width of this column to the amount of whitespace you want, like this:

```
<table width="412" border="0" cellpadding="0" cellspacing="0">
<tr>
<td width="200" valign="top">First column of text</td>
<td width="12"><!– White space –></td>
<td width="200" valign="top">Second column of text</td>
</tr>
</table>
```

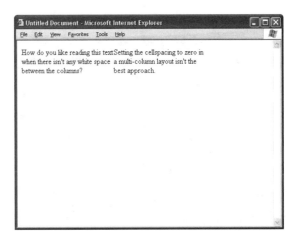

Figure 20.2

You have to plan for white-space between the columns, or you get some-thing like this.

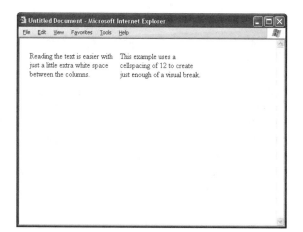

Figure 20.3

Setting the cellspacing of the table to a value like 12 gives you automatic white-space.

attribute to something other than 0, and you get instant whitespace. The exact value depends on the look you're going for, but 12 to 16 pixels are generally sufficient. The layout in Figure 20.3 uses a cellpadding of 12.

Listing 20.1 **View Source for Figure 20.3.**

```
<table width="400" border="0" cellpadding="0" cellspacing="12">
  <tr>
    <td width="50%" valign="top">
      <p>Reading the text is easier with just a little extra white space between the
columns.</p>
    </td>
    <td width="50%" valign="top">
      <p>This example uses a cellspacing of 12 to create just enough of a visual
break.</p>
    </td>
  </tr>
</table>
```

You want to be sure to do a couple of other things, too:

- **Give equal widths for each column.** This forces the browser to make them the same size. If you don't do this, the browser adjusts the widths of the columns to fit the amount of text you put in them.
- **Set the valign attribute of each table cell to top.** This makes sure your columns of text line up along the top. Otherwise, the browser centers them vertically.

- **Balance the columns of text so they're roughly the same height.** The browser won't do this for you, so you have to do it by hand. Make sure you have about the same amount of text in each column, or you'll throw off your layout.

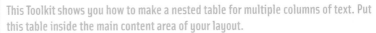
Multicolumn Layout with Tables

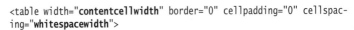
This Toolkit shows you how to make a nested table for multiple columns of text. Put this table inside the main content area of your layout.

```html
<table width="contentcellwidth" border="0" cellpadding="0" cellspac-
ing="whitespacewidth">

<!-- In the table tag above, insert the width of your layout table's
content cell. Also give the amount of white space you need between the
columns, generally between 12 and 16 pixels. -->

  <tr>

<!-- This block of code creates a single column. Copy and paste this
section for as many columns as you need. Be sure to specify the width
of each column. In a two-column layout, make the width 50%. In a three-
column layout, make the width 33%. In a four-column layout, make the
width 25%, and so on. -->

    <td width="columnwidth" valign="top">
      Content goes here
    </td>

<!-- End of column code. -->

  </tr>
</table>
```

21

Creating Multicolumn Layouts with CSS

Just as you used a nested table to create a multicolumn layout for table-based designs in Topic 20, you use nested div elements to create a multi-column layout in CSS. Drop the nested divs into the main content div of your layout, as in Figure 21.1, and you're golden. The only catch is, your main content div has to be fixed-width. It can't be liquid, or certain browsers choke when you apply the technique given here.

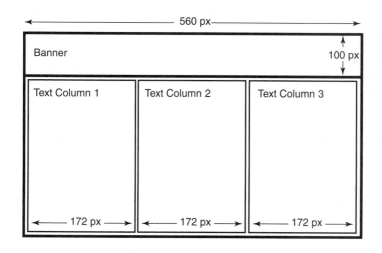

←──────── 560 px ────────→		
Banner		100 px ↕
Text Column 1	Text Column 2	Text Column 3
←── 172 px ──→	←── 172 px ──→	←── 172 px ──→

Figure 21.1

The main content div of this layout has a nested div for each of the columns of text.

Listing 21.1 **View Source for Figure 21.1.**

```
<div id="logo" style="position: relative; width: 560px; height: 100px;">
  Banner
</div>

<div id="container" style="position: relative; width: 560px;">

<!-- Nested divs start here -->

  <div id="leftcolumn" style="position: absolute; width: 172px; left: 0px;">
    Text Column 1
  </div>

  <div id="middlecolumn" style="position: absolute; width: 172px; left: 186px;">
    Text Column 2
  </div>

  <div id="rightcolumn" style="position: absolute; width: 172px; left: 372px;">
    Text Column 3
  </div>

<!--Nested divs end -->

</div>
```

TIP

One way to work around the fixed-width limitation is to use a layout table for the multicolumn structure inside the main content div. Mixing tables and CSS for layout is perfectly workable, although proponents of CSS usually cringe at the mere mention of the idea. The fact remains that tables give you more reliable layout overall. See Topic 20 for how to create multicolumn layouts with tables, and then drop that table into the main content div of your CSS layout.

Follow these steps to create the nested divs:

1. Take the width of the main content div, and divide by the number of columns you want to create. In Figure 21.1, the main content div is 560 pixels wide, so 560 divided by three columns is roughly 186 pixels. This is the unadjusted width of each column.

2. You need whitespace between the columns, so knock a few pixels off the width you calculated in Step 1. Fourteen pixels is a good amount of whitespace, so 186 minus 14 gives you a width of 172 pixels per column.

3. You need the horizontal position of each column as expressed as an offset from the left side of the parent div—in this case, the main content holder. The first column is always 0 pixels from the left. The next one falls at the original width you calculated in Step 1, or 186 pixels from the left. The next one falls at twice that width, or 372 pixels from the left, and so on and so on, depending on how many columns you have.

4. Write the code for the nested divs using the values from the previous steps. The Toolkit that follows gives you a template.

TIP

As with tables, don't try to fit more than two or three CSS columns in your layout.

Why are the positions of the columns relative to the position of the main content div, not the browser window?

Because the column divs are nested, they inherit their baseline position from the parent div. The same code in unnested divs would give you columns that begin at the extreme left of the browser window.

TOOL KIT

Multicolumn Layout with CSS

This Toolkit gives you the code for multicolumn divs. Nest these inside the main content div of your layout. Remember, the main content div has to be fixed-width—it has to have an absolute pixel measurement for its width, not a percentage.

```
<!-- Each column gets its own div. Number the columns from left to
right starting with 0, not 1, or the formula in the code won't work
right.

Replace columnwidth with the value you calculated in Step 2 above.

Replace columnposition with the value you calculated in Step 1 above. -->

<div id="columncolumnnumber" style="position: absolute; width:
columwidthpx; left: (columnposition * columnnumber)px;">
   Content goes here
</div>

<!-- Repeat this block of code for each column in your layout. For most
sites, don't try to squeeze more than two or three columns into the
main content div. -->
```

22

Preventing a Nav Bar from Breaking

When you're designing a layout table, it's only natural to think in terms of the fewest number of cells. It's easier on the design software, it's easier on your coders, and, most importantly, it's easier on you.

Depending on what element of the page goes where, you might be able to get away with a layout like the one in Figure 22.1. Just fill the cells with the

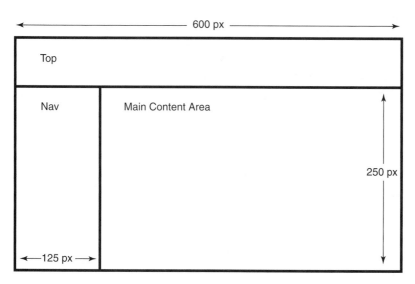

Figure 22.1

A simple layout like this can save you time and effort.

appropriate content, let the table expand vertically to infinity, upload to the Web, and call it a day.

Listing 22.1 **View Source for Figure 22.1.**

```
<table width="600">
  <tr>
    <td colspan="2">Top</td>
  </tr>
  <tr>
    <td width="125">Nav</td>
    <td height="250">Main Content Area</td>
  </tr>
</table>
```

In the spirit of simplicity, you might be tempted to break the cell on the left into discrete rows for nav-bar buttons using the rowspan attribute, as in Figure 22.2.

The layout in Figure 22.2 works as long as you know beforehand the height of the main content area. (In this case, the height is 250 pixels.) This height value isn't always easy to guess. Maybe your design needs to service a number of different pages, each having a different amount of content. Maybe your site will change in the future, and the design needs to be flexible enough to deal with variable amounts of content.

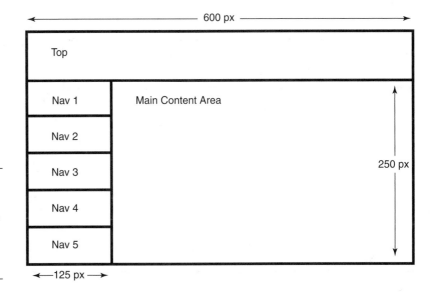

Figure 22.2

To keep things nice and simple, you might try to break the cell on the left into rows for nav-bar buttons.

Listing 22.2 **View Source for Figure 22.2.**

```
<table width="600">
  <tr>
    <td colspan="2">Top</td>
  </tr>
  <tr>
    <td width="125">Nav 1</td>

<!-- Here comes the cell with the rowspan -->

    <td height="250" rowspan="5">Main Content Area</td>
  </tr>
  <tr>
    <td>Nav 2</td>
  </tr>
  <tr>
    <td>Nav 3</td>
  </tr>
  <tr>
    <td>Nav 4</td>
  </tr>
  <tr>
    <td>Nav 5</td>
  </tr>
</table>
```

Even if you have this all figured out, remember the old saying about the best laid plans. A user will probably come along with his browser's default text option cranked up to Largest. Better yet, he'll use his own style sheet with some obscure font. Someone out there will find some way to push the borders of the layout beyond the height you specified in the design.

Figure 22.3 shows you what happens. As the height of the main content area increases, the heights of all the nav-bar cells increase to keep step.

It might not seem like too big of a deal in the abstract, but look at Figure 22.4. Notice how the buttons of the nav bar spread out when the main content area pushes past the maximum height. The white background of the page shows through the gaps in the design, giving you an unsightly mess.

This is a problem for at least two reasons. First, it ruins the consistency of your site's design. Your users are impatient people, and they don't want to have to search each new page for the location of the right nav button. They want it to stay in the exact same place from page to page. Second, your bottommost nav-bar

144

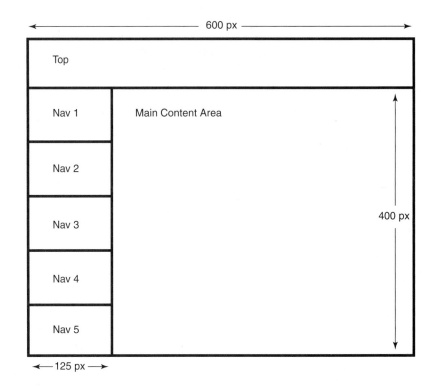

Figure 22.3

As the height of the main content area increases, the heights of the nav-bar cells keep pace.

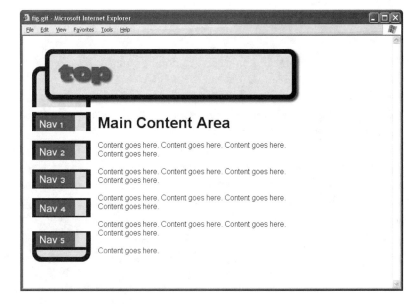

Figure 22.4

Too much content causes the nav bar to break.

buttons might disappear below the fold. Users don't want to have to scroll to find the main navigation of your page. Your navigation should be clear and immediately accessible throughout your site.

Why does the nav bar break? Blame it on the rowspan. Check out Listing 22.2, and notice that the td tag of the main content area is the one that gets the attribute **rowspan="5"**. In other words, the main content area spans the five nav-button cells in the layout table, which means that the heights of the nav-button cells depend entirely on the height of the main content area. Naturally, as the content area changes size, the rows that span it—your nav-bar cells— change size proportionately.

So that's the problem. You might try fixing it by specifying heights for each of the five nav-bar cells, but, alas, that approach doesn't work. The browser automatically pads the nav-bar cells to force them to span the content area, no matter what height values you give. As soon as the main content area exceeds your predetermined height, the browser ignores the height value of this cell and the heights of the spanned rows, and your nav bar breaks anyway.

> **TIP**
> Once you add content to the Main Content Area cell, get rid of the height attribute, since the browser makes the table cell precisely as tall as it needs to be.

The easiest way to make this layout work is to use nested tables, or tables within tables. Go back to the original layout, the one in Figure 21.1. That commodious table cell on the left can hold any type of content: text, an image, a media file, or even another table, as Figure 22.5 shows.

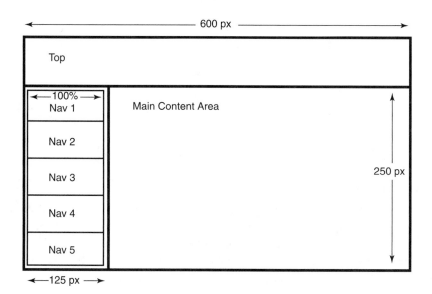

Figure 22.5

Create a nested table for the nav bar in the cell on the left.

146

Listing 22.3 **View Source for Figure 22.5.**

```
<table width="600">
  <tr>
    <td colspan="2">Top</td>
  </tr>
  <tr>
    <td width="125" valign="top">

<!-- Begin nested table. -->

      <table width="100%">
        <tr>
          <td>Nav 1</td>
        </tr>
        <tr>
          <td>Nav 2</td>
        </tr>
        <tr>
          <td>Nav 3</td>
        </tr>
        <tr>
          <td>Nav 4</td>
        </tr>
        <tr>
          <td>Nav 5</td>
        </tr>
      </table>

<!-- End nested table. -->

    </td>
    <td height="250" valign="top">Main Content Area</td>
  </tr>
</table>
```

Notice that you set the width attribute of the nested table to 100%. This forces the table to expand to fill the width of its cell. Notice also that the cell with the nested table has the attribute **valign="top"**. This forces the browser to top-align the content of the cell, which keeps your nested table against the upper-most edge of the cell at all times, right where your visitors expect to find it.

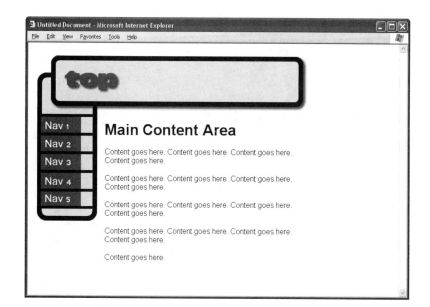

Figure 22.6

The nested table eliminates the rowspan, which keeps your nav bar intact no matter how much content you add.

TIP

If your nav bar still seems to break after you put it in a nested table, check the attributes of the nested table's table tag. You probably need to set the cellpadding, cellspacing, and border attributes to 0, like this:

```
<table width="100%" cellpadding="0" cellspacing="0" border="0">
```

Now, you can add as much content to the main cell as you like. Since you didn't use a rowspan to create the nav-bar cells, you can add as much content to the main cell as you like, and the nav bar doesn't break. Figure 22.6 proves it. The cell that contains the nested table grows, but the nested table itself won't change size unless you change the contents of the nested table's cells.

TIP

If you use software such as Macromedia Fireworks, Adobe Photoshop, or Adobe ImageReady to slice your design, unexpected nav-bar breakage is never far away. To avoid this, consider slicing each of the main areas of your design separately. See Topic 19 for more information.

23

Coloring Table Cells

able cells in HTML have the bgcolor attribute, which controls the background color of the cell. Specifying background colors for certain cells in your layout gives your design a more graphical feel without the use of image files. Compare the layout in Figure 23.1 with the one in Figure 23.2, and you'll agree.

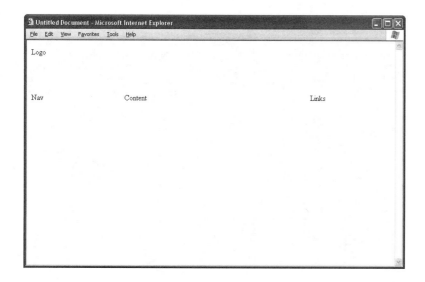

Figure 23.1

The table cells in this layout don't use background colors.

150

Listing 23.1 **View Source for Figure 23.1.**

```
<table width="760" border="0" cellpadding="0" cellspacing="0">
  <tr>
    <td width="760" valign="top">Logo</td>
  </tr>
  <tr>
    <td width="760" valign="top">
      <table width="760" border="0" cellpadding="0" cellspacing="0">
        <tr>
          <td width="200" valign="top">Nav</td>
          <td width="400" valign="top">Content</td>
          <td width="160" valign="top">Links</td>
        </tr>
      </table>
    </td>
  </tr>
</table>
```

TIP

Use background colors instead of image files whenever possible. Since you define the colors in the HTML, your visitors don't have to download separate image files to see the colors.

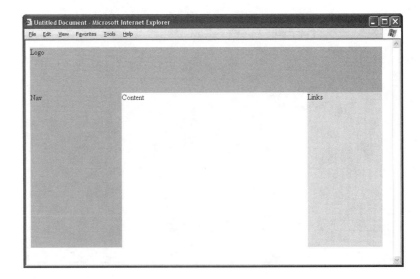

Figure 23.2

By specifying background colors for the Logo, Nav, and Links areas, you create a more graphical page without using image files.

Listing 23.2 **View Source for Figure 23.2.**

```
<table width="760" border="0" cellpadding="0" cellspacing="0">
  <tr>
    <td width="760" valign="top" bgcolor="#99CCFF">Logo</td>
  </tr>
  <tr>
    <td width="760" valign="top">
      <table width="760" border="0" cellpadding="0" cellspacing="0">
        <tr>
          <td width="200" valign="top" bgcolor="#99CCFF">Nav</td>
          <td width="400" valign="top">Content</td>
          <td width="160" valign="top" bgcolor="#99FF99">Links</td>
        </tr>
      </table>
    </td>
  </tr>
</table>
```

Notice in Listing 23.2 that you specify the desired color with a string of characters called a **hexadecimal color code**. The code begins with a number sign (#), followed by a six-digit hexadecimal number. The hexadecimal number system is base 16 instead of base 10 like our common, everyday decimal number system, as the math geeks among us already know. The first ten digits in the hexadecimal system are the regular decimal digits 0 through 9. The six remaining digits are the letters A through F, since we don't have number symbols to represent them. So when you see a hexadecimal value like FC or FF, don't think these are letters. They're actually numbers.

A hexadecimal color code contains three sets of hexadecimal numbers with two digits each. The first two-digit set controls the amount of red in the color. The second set controls the amount of green, and the third controls the amount of blue. Mixing different levels of red, green, and blue creates every single color you see on screen. The higher the value of a particular two-digit set, the more prominent the component color is in the final shade.

Take the hexadecimal code for red, which is #FF0000. If you break it down, you get a value of FF for the red component, 00 for the green component, and 00 for the blue component. That's full-on red, with FF in the red slot—the highest

GEEKSPEAK

The hexadecimal number system is base 16 instead of base 10. It represents numerical values with the symbols 0 through 9 for the first ten digits and A through F for the last six digits.

TIP

Make sure your text is legible against the background color of the table cell. If the contrast looks like it could go either way, err on the side of caution.

possible two-digit hexadecimal number. In this particular shade, there are no green or blue components to dilute the purity of the red. Likewise, the code for green is #00FF00 (zero red, full-on green, and zero blue), while the code for blue is #0000FF (zero red, zero green, and full-on blue).

> **TIP**
>
> The digits in each slot of a hexadecimal color code don't need to match. #FC02D5 is a perfectly good hexadecimal color, with FC in the red slot, 02 in the green slot, and D5 in the blue slot. However, for best results on the Web, stick to matching digits in multiples of three: 0, 3, 6, 9, C, and F. So the closest Web equivalent of #FC02D5 is #FF00CC.

To create a color like violet, you mix a couple of components together. Red and blue make violet, so one possibility is to mix full-on red with full-on blue, as in #FF00FF, which gives you a very bright and pure shade. But maybe you want a redder-looking violet. Just turn down the blue component by giving it a smaller value, as in #FF0099 or #FF0066. For a bluer-looking violet, do the opposite. Keep blue full-on, and reduce the amount of red, as in #9900FF or #6600FF.

> **TIP**
>
> If you truly hate hexadecimal codes, you can always specify the color name instead, as in bgcolor="lightgreen", but you're better off using the closest Web hexadecimal value, which is less open to interpretation by the visitor's browser. Further, the names can be misleading. The color named **darkgray** actually corresponds to a lighter shade of gray than the color named **gray**.

With a little practice, you can learn to mix whatever color you need without having to memorize something like Table 23.1, which gives the names and hexadecimal color codes for common shades.

Table 23.1 **Common Colors and Their Codes**

Color	Name	Hexadecimal Code	Closest Web Equivalent
Aqua	aqua	#00FFFF	#00FFFF
Black	black	#000000	#000000
Blue	blue	#0000FF	#0000FF
Blue, dark	darkblue	#00008B	#000099
Blue, light	lightblue	#ADD8E6	#CCCCFF
Blue, sky	skyblue	#87CEEB	#99CCFF
Gold	gold	#FFD700	#FFCC00
Gray	gray	#808080	#999999
Gray, dark	dimgray*	#696969	#666666
Green	green	#008000	#009900
Green, dark	darkgreen	#006400	#006600
Green, light	lightgreen	#90EE90	#99FF99
Green, sea	seagreen	#2E8B57	#339966
Indigo	indigo	#4B0082	#330099
Orange	orange	#FFA500	#FF9900
Pink	pink	#FFC0CB	#FFCCCC
Purple	purple	#800080	#990099
Red	red	#FF0000	#FF0000
Red, dark	darkred	#8B0000	#990000
Silver	silver	#C0C0C0	#CCCCCC
Violet	violet	#EE82EE	#FF99FF
White	white	#FFFFFF	#FFFFFF
Yellow	yellow	#FFFF00	#FFFF00

* The color called **darkgray** is actually lighter than the color called **gray**. Use **dimgray** instead.

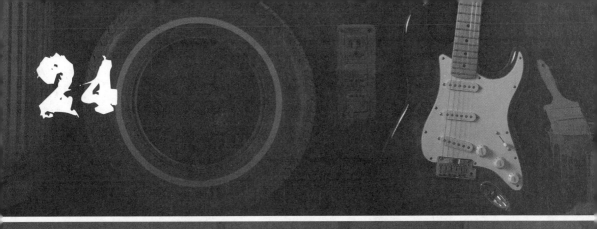

Coloring and Formatting CSS Divs

opic 23 showed you how to color the cells of a table. You can specify background colors for divs, too, along with a couple of other appearance attributes that HTML tables just don't support. Once again, as with all things CSS, make sure you test your design in a number of browsers before you upload to the Web. Who knows how your target browsers will garble your perfectly legitimate CSS markup this time.

If the layout in Figure 24.1 looks familiar, that's because you've seen something like it before, in Topic 18, to be exact. No background colors appear in the code, as the View Source bears out. As you can see in Figure 24.2, adding the background-color attribute to the style definition creates a more graphical effect.

View Source for Figure 24.1.

```
<div id="logo" style="position: absolute; width: 100%; height: 100px; top: 0px;
left: 0px;">
   Logo
</div>

<div id="nav" style="position: absolute; width: 200px; top: 100px; left: 0px;">
   Nav
</div>
```

```
<div id="links" style="position: absolute; width: 175px; top: 100px; right: 0px;">
  Links
</div>

<div id="content" style="position: absolute; top: 100px; left: 200px; right:
175px;">
  Content
</div>
```

Figure 24.1
This CSS layout doesn't specify background colors for any of the divs.

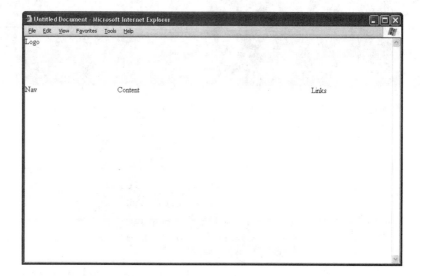

Figure 24.2
This CSS layout creates a more graphical effect by specifying background colors in the Logo, Nav, and Links divs.

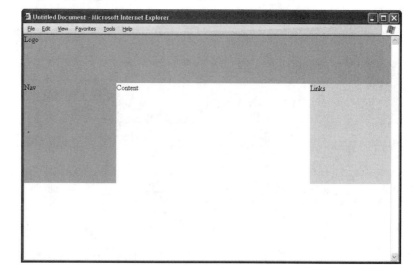

Listing 24.2 **View Source for Figure 24.2.**

```
<div id="logo" style="position: absolute; width: 100%; height: 100px; top: 0px;
left: 0px; background-color: #99CCFF;">
  Logo
</div>

<div id="nav" style="position: absolute; width: 200px; top: 100px; left: 0px; back-
ground-color: #99CCFF;">
  Nav
</div>

<div id="links" style="position: absolute; width: 175px; top: 100px; right: 0px;
background-color: #99FF99;">
  Links
</div>

<div id="content" style="position: absolute; top: 100px; left: 200px; right:
175px;">
  Content
</div>
```

As with table cells, the background color is a hexadecimal color code. See Topic 23 for a list of common colors and their hexadecimal values.

Since you're working with CSS, you don't have to stop at coloring the background. For instance, you could add a solid black border around the Links div, as in Figure 24.3.

To create the border, you add three new attributes to the div's style definition:

```
<div id="links" style="position: absolute; width: 175px; top: 100px; right: 0px;
background-color: #99FF99; border-width: 4px; border-style: solid; border-color:
#000000;">
  Links
</div>
```

Maybe you want a coupon-style dashed line instead of a solid line, and maybe you want a blue border instead of a black one, and maybe you want a lighter border weight, as in Figure 24.4.

Maybe you don't like the way the text fits snugly against the corner of the div. Just give the div some interior whitespace with the padding attribute, as in Figure 24.5.

TIP

You can define different appearances for the top, left, right, and bottom segments of the border. See Table 24.1 at the end of this topic for details.

158

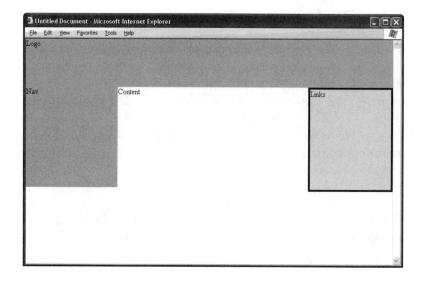

Figure 24.3

Nothing but your own design sensibilities and the CSS capabilities of your target browser prevent you from adding a border around the Links div.

Listing 24.3 **View Source for Figure 24.4.**

```
<div id="links" style="position: absolute; width: 175px; top: 100px; right: 0px;
background-color: #99FF99; border-width: 2px; border-style: dashed; border-color:
#0000FF;">
   Links
</div>
```

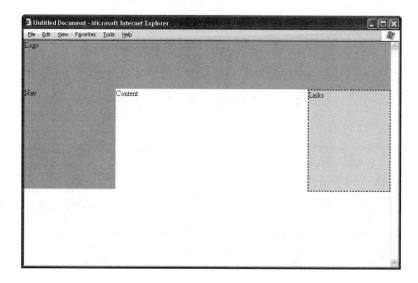

Figure 24.4

Choose a different border style, and the border changes.

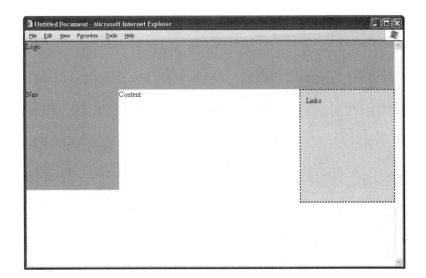

Figure 24.5

Introduce extra whitespace with the padding attribute.

TIP

As with border styles, you can go crazy with padding and define different amounts of it for the top, left, right, and bottom sides of the div. It's all in Table 24.1.

Listing 24.4 **View Source for Figure 24.5.**

```
<div id="links" style="position: absolute; width: 175px; top: 100px; right: 0px;
background-color: #99FF99; border-width: 2px; border-style: dashed; border-color:
#0000FF; padding: 12px;">
  Links
</div>
```

And, as you saw (or didn't see) in Topic 10, you can actually make div elements disappear without deleting their code, as in Figure 24.6.

Listing 24.5 **View Source for Figure 24.6.**

```
<div id="links" style="position: absolute; width: 175px; top: 100px; right: 0px;
background-color: #99FF99; border-width: 2px; border-style: dashed; border-color:
#0000FF; padding: 12px; visibility: hidden;">
  Links
</div>
```

Figure 24.6

Where did the div go? It's still in the code, but its visibility attribute is set to hidden.

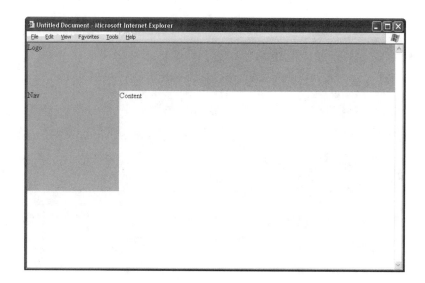

FAQ

I hate CSS. Can't I get extra whitespace with the cellpadding attribute?

Sort of. HTML tables have the cellpadding attribute, which works much like the padding attribute of CSS. However, in an HTML table, the same cellpadding value applies to all the cells in the table. If you want padding in one cell but not in another, you're out of luck. In CSS, each div can have its own padding value.

Table 24.1 lists common CSS attributes for formatting the divs of your layout. Remember, each div can have its own custom style, so CSS provides a much larger range of options than HTML tables ever could. Then again, HTML tables are more stable, so you sacrifice broad browser compatibility when you start tinkering with CSS.

Table 24.1 **Common CSS Attributes for Formatting Layout Divs**

ATTRIBUTE	CONTROLS	POSSIBLE VALUES*	EXAMPLE
background-color	The background color of the div	Hexadecimal color code	background-color: #FFCC00;
border-color	The color of all four sides of the border	Hexadecimal color code	border-color: #000000;
border-color-bottom	The color of the bottom side of the border	Hexadecimal color code	border-color-bottom: #000000;
border-color-left	The color of the left side of the border	Hexadecimal color code	border-color-left: #000000;
border-color-right	The color of the right side of the border	Hexadecimal color code	border-color-right: #000000;
border-color-top	The color of the top side of the border	Hexadecimal color code	border-color-top: #000000;
border-style	The type of border on all four sides	dashed, dotted, double, groove, inset,outset, ridge, solid	border-style: dashed;
border-style-bottom	The type of border along the bottom	dashed, dotted, double, groove, inset, outset, ridge, solid	border-style-bottom: dotted;
border-style-left	The type of border on the left side	dashed, dotted, double, groove, inset, outset, ridge, solid	border-style-left: double;
border-style-right	The type of border on the right side	dashed, dotted, double, groove, inset, outset, ridge, solid	border-style-right: groove;
border-style-top	The type of border along the top	dashed, dotted, double, groove, inset, outset, ridge, solid	border-style-top: inset;
border-width	The weight (thickness) of all four sides of the border	Any CSS-supported measurement, such as px, cm, or in	border-width: 4px;

Table 24.1 Common CSS Attributes for Formatting Layout Divs *(Continued)*

ATTRIBUTE	CONTROLS	POSSIBLE VALUES*	EXAMPLE
border-width-bottom	The weight of the bottom side of the border	Any CSS-supported measurement, such as px, cm, or in	border-width-bottom: 0.03cm;
border-width-left	The weight of the left side of the border	Any CSS-supported measurement, such as px, cm, or in	border-width-left: 0.03in;
border-width-right	The weight of the right side of the border	Any CSS-supported measurement, such as px, cm, or in	border-width-right: 4px;
border-width-top	The weight of the top side of the border	Any CSS-supported measurement, such as px, cm, or in	border-width-top: 0.03in;
padding	The amount of white space around all four sides of the div's	Any CSS-supported measurement, such as px, cm, or in interior	padding: 12px;
padding-bottom	The amount of white space at the bottom of the div	Any CSS-supported measurement, such as px, cm, or in	padding-bottom: 0.33cm;
padding-left	The amount of white space on the left side of the div	Any CSS-supported measurement, such as px, cm, or in	padding-left: 0.33in;
padding-right	The amount of whitespace on the right side of the div	Any CSS-supported measurement, such as px, cm, or in	padding-right: 12px;
padding-top	The amount of whitespace at the top of the div	Any CSS-supported measurement, such as px, cm, or in	padding-top: 0.33cm;
visibility	The appearance or disappearance of the div	hidden, visible	visibility: hidden;

* Some browsers may support other values besides those listed, and some browsers may not support the given values.

Controlling Design Space with HTML

By default, Web browsers put some extra whitespace between the browser interface and the start of the page. This comes in handy when you have a text-only Web page, but many types of designs—especially liquid layouts—don't feel right with the extra padding.

You can turn off the extra padding by setting a couple of attributes in the body tag to 0. Which attributes you use depends on the browser. In Internet Explorer, the appropriate attributes are leftmargin and topmargin:

```
<body leftmargin="0" topmargin="0">
```

In Netscape browsers, the attributes are marginwidth and marginheight:

```
<body marginwidth="0" marginheight="0">
```

If you're smart, you'll use all four:

```
<body leftmargin="0" topmargin="0" marginwidth="0" marginheight="0">
```

 FAQ

What happens to the values that the browser doesn't understand?

IE and Netscape ignore the attributes that they don't understand, so you aren't really creating compatibility problems by setting all four attributes.

163

Conversely, you can create extra padding by setting these attributes to nonzero values. The leftmargin and topmargin attributes in IE control the amount of spacing along the left and top of the browser window, respectively, but do nothing to the right and bottom, while the Netscape attributes supply spacing equally to the left and right with marginwidth and to the top and bottom with marginheight.

Remember, IE doesn't understand the Netscape attributes and vice versa, so you can't get extra right-margin padding by setting marginwidth in IE. Likewise, you can't affect the left side of the browser window only by setting leftmargin in Netscape.

For a better level of margin control overall, try using CSS instead of HTML (see Topic 26).

26

Controlling Design Space with CSS

As you saw in Topic 25, HTML provides a few body-tag attributes to control the default amount of whitespace in the browser window, but these attributes are proprietary—they only work in certain browsers. Browsers that don't understand the attributes ignore them completely.

You get better margin control with Cascading Style Sheets (CSS). Just define a style for the body tag of the page, like this:

```
<body style="margin: 0px;">
```

This line of code sets all four margins—top, left, right, and bottom—to 0 pixels, thereby eliminating any default whitespace on the page.

CSS doesn't stop there. You can easily define different amounts of whitespace for the different margins with the margin-top, margin-left, margin-right, and margin-bottom attributes. The layout in Figure 26.1 has a top margin of 200 pixels, a left margin of 300 pixels, a right margin of 400 pixels, and a bottom margin of 100 pixels.

TIP

Ironically, you want to watch your use of CSS margin control when your page features CSS layouts. Getting fancy with margin spacing can throw off the positions of your divs. You may need to adjust their position values (left, top, right, and bottom) after you set the margins.

166

Figure 26.1

This page uses CSS to control the amount of whitespace on all four margins.

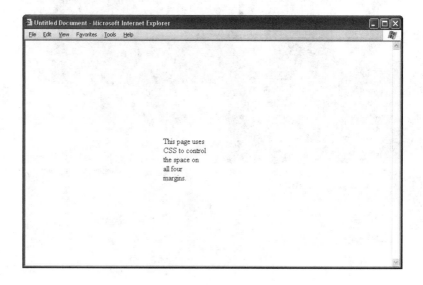

Listing 26.1 **View Source for Figure 26.1.**

```
<body style="margin-top: 200px; margin-left: 300px; margin-right: 400px; margin-bot-
tom: 100px;">
```

> **TIP**
>
> As a shortcut, you can give the size of all four margins in the margin attribute, going in clockwise order (top, right, bottom, and left), like this:
>
> ```
> <body style="margin: 200 400 100 300px;">
> ```

PART III:

Image Topics

Choosing the Right Image File Type

Image files come in many different formats, but only a few of these work well on the Web. Browsers that display graphics tend to cluster their support around the most common file types, but, as you might expect, browsers don't agree on exactly which types of graphics files to display. The Microsoft browser, for instance, supports Windows bitmap files (BMP), but the Netscape browser does not.

To decide which image formats to use on your site, ask yourself two questions:

1. Which file types work in all the major browsers?
2. Of those file types, which one creates the lightest file size without sacrificing image quality?

The answer to the first question is straightforward. All the major browsers display GIF, JPEG, and PNG images, so you want to limit your Web graphics to these three formats.

The answer to the second question is the dreaded, "It depends." Generally speaking, photographs and other images with a large amount of color information work best in the JPEG format, while line art and images with large areas of flat color work better as GIFs or PNGs. Why? JPEGs don't have a built-in **palette** or color chart, while GIFs and PNGs do. The palette of a GIF or PNG

TIP

The GIF and PNG file types are very similar. You use them for the same types of images, and they give you about the same file weight. Once upon a time, the main difference was that the GIF format was the property of CompuServe, while PNG has always been nonproprietary. However, the patent on GIFs has since expired worldwide, and the format now belongs to the world.

determines which colors appear in the image, up to a maximum of 256 different shades. As you add more colors to the palette, the heavier the image becomes overall. Since photos usually have lots of subtle shading and gradation, the 256 color slots in a GIF or PNG go pretty quickly. You end up with a GIF or PNG that looks grainy, yet its file size is heavier than a JPEG because of its fully loaded palette.

However, if your image has fewer than 256 colors, the GIF and PNG formats typically give you lighter file sizes while maintaining overall image quality.

Even so, the number of colors isn't the only consideration, because the various formats offer different features, too. GIFs and PNGs allow you to define transparent colors, and GIFs allow animation. JPEGs have neither, as you can see in Table 27.1. And some photos look fine in GIF or PNG format, even with the loss of color information. It behooves you to test your images in all three formats to get the best possible Web file.

Table 27.1 **Common Web Image File Types**

FILE TYPE	PRONOUNCED	STANDS FOR	PALETTE?	TRANSPARENCY?	ANIMATION?
GIF	jiff or giff	Graphics Interchange Format	Yes; up to 256 colors	Yes; one level of transparency	Yes
JPEG	jaypeg	Joint Photography Experts Group	No; no color limit	No	No
PNG	ping	Portable Network Graphics	Yes; up to 256 colors	Yes; multiple levels of transparency	No

Optimizing Web Images

Optimizing a graphics file for the Web means reducing the weight of the file as much as possible while maintaining image quality. This is an important step in creating Web graphics, since you should always be mindful of the download time of the pages on your site. Even though more and more people connect to the Web over high-speed DSL and cable lines, regular old dial-up modems aren't anywhere near obsolete, and graphics are still the number-one bandwidth bottleneck. No matter how many images you use on your site, you will see an improvement in performance by optimizing your images specifically for the Web.

At the same time, you don't want to reduce file weights so much that image quality deteriorates. Fast-loading graphics that don't look good are worse than beautiful graphics that take too long to download. Make no mistake: Your visitors want graphics. Sit them down in front of anything that looks like a TV, and they expect to see pictures. Remember that the Web didn't explode into the mainstream until it shifted from pages and pages of pedantic HTML text to graphic designs with full-color images. If your graphics look blocky, cheesy, grainy, or muddy, your visitors will draw similar conclusions about the quality of the information on your site.

This topic suggests several ways to optimize your image files for the Web using all but the most rudimentary graphics-editing applications. If your graphics software

GEEKSPEAK

Optimizing an image file for the Web means reducing its weight for faster downloading while maintaining image quality.

TIP

More advanced graphics software gives you a number of other techniques for Web optimization than the ones described here. Check your manual or the online help system for more information.

doesn't allow you to perform these operations, it's time to think about an upgrade. You don't have to break the bank here. Adobe Photoshop Elements, a scaled-down version of granddaddy Photoshop, is an excellent Web-graphics tool for about $100 U.S. Another good one is Jasc Paint Shop Pro, which costs about the same. If designing Web sites is your profession, try to get your employer to spring for the full version of Photoshop or Macromedia Fireworks. These apps cost more, but they're worth it.

Optimizing Resolution

An image file's **resolution** determines the size of its pixels: the higher the resolution, the smaller the pixels and therefore the sharper the image. The more pixels you have, however, the heavier the image becomes, and the longer it takes to download.

In the world of print graphics, higher resolution is almost always better than lower resolution. But in Web graphics, the display capability of monitor screens puts a tight constraint on image resolution. Windows monitors display at 96 ppi (pixels per inch), which is actually fairly low-res. Macintosh monitors

GEEKSPEAK

The **resolution** of an image file determines the size of its pixels: the higher the resolution, the smaller the pixels and the sharper the image.

are even lower, at 72 ppi. In the spirit of cross-platform compatibility, the resolution of 72 ppi has emerged as the standard for Web images, even though the vast majority of monitors can display at the slightly higher benchmark of 96 ppi.

What that means is this: Higher-resolution images look no better on screen than 72- or 96-ppi images. If your Web images are print-quality, say 300

Why do optimized Web images look grainy when I print them out?

On screen, 72 ppi looks crisp and clear, but that's because monitors are fairly low-res output devices. Good old low-tech paper is actually a much higher-res output device. You can cram more dots into the same amount of space on the printed page, so lower-res images show their graininess more readily.

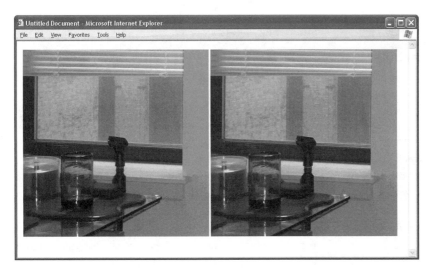

Figure 28.1

The image on the left has a resolution of 600 ppi, while the image on the right has a resolution of 72 ppi—more than eight times lower. However, both look exactly the same on screen, since monitors are relatively low-res output devices.

or 600 ppi, all that additional clarity is dead weight. Your visitors see no difference whatsoever on screen, as Figure 28.1 shows. Why force them to download high-res images when faster-loading, low-res images work just as well?

> **TIP**
>
> Images that you specifically intend for your visitors to print out should be optimized for print instead of the screen. But not everyone who visits your site will print out these images. To improve the performance of your site, don't build the high-res images into your pages. Use low-res, screen-optimized images instead, and include links to high-res, print-quality images for those who want them. The high-res images won't look any different on screen, but they'll translate much better to print than their low-res counterparts will.

In your graphics software, reduce all Web images to the standard resolution of 72 ppi. This is the easiest and most effective technique for optimizing images for monitor output.

Optimizing Image Size

Screen real estate is like physical real estate in midtown Manhattan—absurdly expensive. You get a lot more mileage out of your Web site if you use images with smaller physical dimensions (that is, smaller width and height values).

Smaller images download faster than larger ones. Plus, by using smaller images, you can fit more information on the screen before your visitors have to scroll, and your site looks better on the compact displays of portable devices.

While smaller is better, avoid using the browser to resize images for you. It's perfectly doable in HTML to turn a 300-by-150 image into, say, a 60-by-30 image by tweaking the width and height attributes of the img tag (see Topic 29). But if you want to display an image at 60 by 30, fire up your graphics software and create a copy of the image at those precise dimensions. Otherwise, the browser still has to download the larger 300-by-150 file, and you don't shave off any download time.

Along similar lines, don't build excessive amounts of whitespace into your image file. Instead, crop the image to the size of whatever you want to display, and incorporate the whitespace into the design of the page.

Optimizing the Palette in GIFs and PNGs

As you know from Topic 27, GIF and PNG files have a built-in palette of up to 256 colors. The more colors in the palette, the heavier the image file. If your GIF or PNG image needs all 256 colors, then so be it. However, most GIFs and PNGs can stand to lose some color slots without affecting image quality too noticeably.

Watch out for images that contain round or curved shapes. These images often make use of a technique called **antialiasing**, which creates the illusion of smoothness by inserting subtly blended pixels along the curved edge. Antialiasing minimizes the naturally blocky appearance of pixels, which are square-shaped, and tricks the eye into seeing graceful, flowing curves. Each blended shade requires a slot in the palette of a GIF or PNG. Cutting too many colors from the palette reduces the effectiveness of antialiasing.

Optimizing the Compression in JPEGs

JPEG images don't have palettes as GIFs and PNGs do. Instead, the JPEG format **compresses** the visual information in an image by making it more efficient and tossing out information that the human eye isn't likely to miss. Too much compression gets rid of too much information, and image quality deteriorates noticeably.

Good graphics software allows you to specify the amount of compression in a JPEG file by adjusting its quality. There's no hard-and-fast rule for the best quality setting. It all depends on the amount of information in the JPEG.

To optimize a JPEG, play around with the level of compression and see which quality setting works the best. There's usually a point at which the image quality degrades significantly. When you reach this point, just go back to the previous level of compression.

GEEKSPEAK

Compression in a graphics format such as JPEG makes a lighter image file by losing a portion of the visual information. Too much compression gets rid of too much information, and image quality deteriorates noticeably.

29

Transforming Images with HTML Attributes

rowsers that support images can do more than display graphics. They can also resize their physical dimensions.

When you add an image to your page, you generally specify the exact dimensions of the graphic with the width and height attributes of the img tag, as in Figure 29.1.

Listing 29.1 **View Source for Figure 29.1.**

```
<img src="logo.jpg" width="150" height="75">
```

Figure 29.1

Give the exact dimensions of the image in its image tag, and the image appears on the page exactly as you designed it in your graphics software.

178

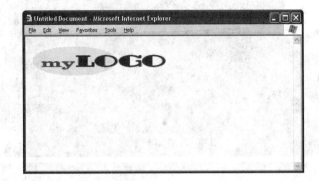

But who says you have to give the image's actual dimensions? You can transform the image by stretching its width or height, as in Figure 29.2.

Listing 29.2 **View Source for Figure 29.2.**

```
<img src="logo.jpg" width="300" height="35">
```

And by increasing or decreasing the width and height values proportionately, you can resize the image, as in Figure 29.3.

Listing 29.3 **View Source for Figure 29.3.**

```
<img src="logo.jpg" width="300" height="150">
```

Use these tricks judiciously, though. HTML is the poor person's Photoshop, and you definitely get what you pay for. Transforming an image in dedicated graphics software gives you better-looking results as a rule. And making an

image smaller in HTML doesn't change its download time, just as making an image larger doesn't increase download time. The browser always downloads the source file at its normal dimensions, no matter how you transform the image in the HTML.

TIP
For extreme transformations like the kind in Figures 29.2 and 29.3, it's better to edit your images in graphics software. However, for subtle changes here and there, HTML transformations generally work fine.

30

Positioning Inline Images with HTML

nline images are images that appear inside a block of text. These are typically content images, such as charts, graphs, or photos, as opposed to logos, navbar buttons, and other graphical interface elements, which usually have their own table cells or CSS divs in the page layout.

The simplest way to add an inline image in HTML is to insert the img tag into the text exactly where you want the image to appear, as in Figure 30.1. As you can see, this method is serviceable but not very aesthetically pleasing. If the image is taller than the point size of the surrounding text, the browser splits the lines of type in the most unattractive way imaginable.

Listing 30.1 View Source for Figure 30.1.

```
<h2>A complete brain-trust solution</h2>

<p>When you consult with us, you'll be amazed at the results. We offer the most
interesting, creative, out-of-the-box, and forward-thinking ideas <img
src="images/bulb.gif" width="47" height="84"> in the industry. You won't believe
what we'll come up with next. We have won several international awards for our ideas
alone, including the prestigious Nobel Prize. You simply won't find better ideas
anywhere.</p>
```

Figure 30.1

Dropping the img tag into a block of text creates an inline image, but the browser splits the lines of type without much artful subtlety.

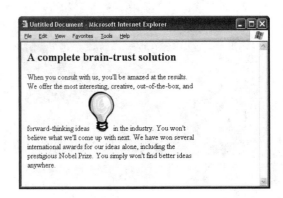

GEEKSPEAK

Floating an inline image means pushing it to the left or right of a block of text so that the text wraps around it.

The align attribute of the img tag helps you to place the image more effectively, as in Figure 30.2. Just choose a value for the align attribute from Table 30.1. You can **float** the image to the left or right of the entire block of text, or you can align the image vertically to the top, middle, or bottom of the line of text in which the inline image appears.

Listing 30.2 **View Source for Figure 30.2.**

```
<h2>A complete brain-trust solution</h2>

<p><img src="images/bulb.gif" width="47" height="84" align="left"> When you consult
with us, you'll be amazed at the results. We offer the most interesting, creative,
out-of-the-box, and forward-thinking ideas in the industry. You won't believe what
we'll come up with next. We have won several international awards for our ideas
alone, including the prestigious Nobel Prize. You simply won't find better ideas
anywhere.</p>
```

Figure 30.2

Use the align attribute of the image tag to tell the browser how to place the image in relation to the surrounding text.

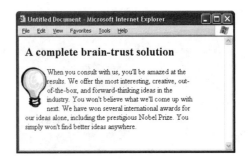

Table 30.1 **Align Attribute Values for the img Tag**

VALUE	EFFECT
bottom	Vertically aligns the bottom of the image with the bottom or baseline of the line of text
left	Floats the image to the left of the block of text
middle	Vertically aligns the image with the middle of the line of text
right	Floats the image to the right of the block of text
top	Vertically aligns the top of the image with the top of the line of text

TIP

To float an inline image to the right or left of a block of text, move the img tag to the beginning of the block of text, as in the View Source of Figure 30.2.

Floating Inline Images with CSS

31

As with all design and formatting issues these days, the politically correct method for floating inline images is not by setting the align attribute of the img tag to **left** or **right** (see Topic 30), but by using Cascading Style Sheets (CSS). On the plus side, CSS gives you more options than the align attribute does. On the minus side, browsers regularly flake out on CSS wherever they find it, so you need to test your CSS styling in a variety of browsers.

The first step is to float the inline image against a block of text, as in Figure 31.1. As you might guess, the CSS style definition **float: left;** pushes the image to the left of the text block, while **float: right;** pushes the image to the right.

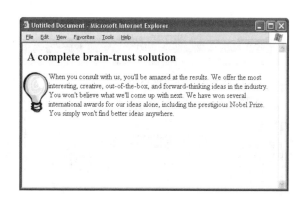

Figure 31.1

Floating an inline image with CSS is pretty straightforward.

Listing 31.1 **View Source for Figure 31.1.**

```
<h2>A complete brain-trust solution</h2>

<p><img src="images/bulb.gif" width="47" height="84" style="float: left;">When you
consult with us, you'll be amazed at the results. We offer the most interesting,
creative, out-of-the-box, and forward-thinking ideas in the industry. You won't
believe what we'll come up with next. We have won several international awards for
our ideas alone, including the prestigious Nobel Prize. You simply won't find better
ideas anywhere.</p>
```

So far, so good, but CSS hasn't given you anything that you can't get with
the align attribute of the img tag. The fun begins when you break a single block
of text into two or more pieces, as in Figure 31.2. You can then change the way
the additional text blocks flow around the floating image.

Listing 31.2 **View Source for Figure 31.2.**

```
<h2>A complete brain-trust solution</h2>

<img src="images/bulb.gif" width="47" height="84" style="float: left;">

<p>When you consult with us, you'll be amazed at the results. You won't believe what
we'll come up with next.</p>

<p>We have won several international awards for our ideas alone, including the pres-
tigious Nobel Prize. You simply won't find better ideas anywhere.</p>
```

For instance, clearing the new paragraph to the left forces it to begin under-
neath the left-floating image instead of wrapping around it, as Figure 31.3 shows.

Figure 31.2

*Normally,
when you
break the text
into two blocks,
the second
block wraps
around the
floating image
nicely, just like
the first.*

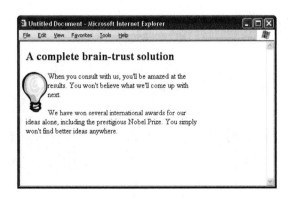

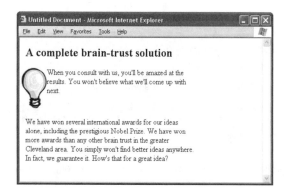

Figure 31.3

Clear the second paragraph to the left to make it begin directly under the left-floating image.

Listing 31.3 **View Source for Figure 31.3.**

```
<h2>A complete brain-trust solution</h2>

<img src="images/bulb.gif" width="47" height="84" style="float: left;">

<p>When you consult with us, you'll be amazed at the results. You won't believe what
we'll come up with next.</p>

<p style="clear: left;">We have won several international awards for our ideas
alone, including the prestigious Nobel Prize. You simply won't find better ideas
anywhere.</p>
```

To see what's happening here, add another inline image, and this time, float it to the right, as in Figure 31.4. The second paragraph clears the left-floating image but wraps around the right-floating image.

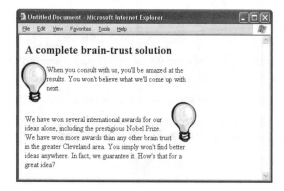

Figure 31.4

When you add a right-floating image, the second paragraph wraps around it, since you specified that it should only clear the left.

Listing 31.4 **View Source for Figure 31.4.**

```
<h2>A complete brain-trust solution</h2>

<img src="images/bulb.gif" width="47" height="84" style="float: left;">

<p>When you consult with us, you'll be amazed at the results. You won't believe what
we'll come up with next.</p>

<img src="images/bulb.gif" width="47" height="84" style="float: right;">

<p style="clear: left;">We have won several international awards for our ideas
alone, including the prestigious Nobel Prize. We have won more awards than any other
brain trust in the greater Cleveland area. You simply won't find better ideas any-
where. In fact, we guarantee it. How's that for a great idea?</p>
```

TIP

To clear a right-floating image, use the definition **clear: right;** instead.

If you want the second paragraph to clear the floating images on the left and the right, use the style definition **clear: both;**.

Table 31.1 summarizes CSS styles for floating and clearing.

Table 31.1 **Floating and Clearing with CSS**

STYLE	EFFECT
clear: both;	Prevents a block of text from wrapping around preceding left- and right-floating images
clear: left;	Prevents a block of text from wrapping around preceding left-floating images
clear: right;	Prevents a block of text from wrapping around preceding right-floating images
float: left;	Floats the image to the left of the blocks of text that follow
float: right;	Floats the image to the right of the blocks of text that follow

Designing Button States

Button states are the different appearances that a graphical button takes on depending on how the visitor interacts with it. DHTML-based Web sites generally define two button states: the default state, which determines how the button looks normally; and the onMouseOver state, which determines how the button looks when the visitor mouses over it. (A JavaScript rollover function switches between the two button states.) Sites built with Macromedia Flash usually include a third state: onClick, which determines how the button looks when the visitor clicks it.

Button states provide invaluable visual feedback on the average, link-infested Web page. With so much content crammed into a typical browser window, having things happen in response to mouse movements and clicks helps your visitors figure out how to use your site.

When it comes to designing states for your buttons, you want to capitalize on the psychology of what's going on. In other words, you want your visual effects to correspond to

What's with the strange nomenclature for button states?

Blame JavaScript. The names for the onMouseOver and onClick button states come from the corresponding JavaScript events.

the way your visitor's mind works. You don't want to contradict the psychology—doing the opposite of what your visitor's mind expects—or your site sends mixed messages, and your visual feedback creates confusion instead of improving usability.

Here's the theory: Design button states with increasing energy. To borrow the catchphrase of a famous TV chef, each successive button state needs to "kick it up a notch," following the logical order of how the visitor interacts with the button. Therefore, the default button state needs to be the one with the least amount of energy, since the visitor isn't interacting with it at all. The onMouseOver state needs to kick it up a notch, almost like the button absorbs the kinetic energy that the visitor generates by rolling the mouse. And the onClick state (if you have one) has to kick it up another notch to correspond to the additional kinetic energy of clicking the mouse.

What you're doing here is graphically duplicating the way a real-world object like a machine operates: Energy goes in, and something happens. Your computer's LED doesn't switch off when you power up and then stay on all night after you power down. That doesn't make intuitive sense. Yet how many graphical buttons have you seen on the Web that seem to switch off when you mouse over them? If you design your buttons so that they go down a notch when your visitor interacts with them, it seems like they're devouring energy and contradicting the laws of physics like a bad *Star Trek* plot.

When energy goes in, something happens. What happens exactly is up to you, but Table 32.1 offers some suggestions, and Figure 32.1 shows a few sequences of button states.

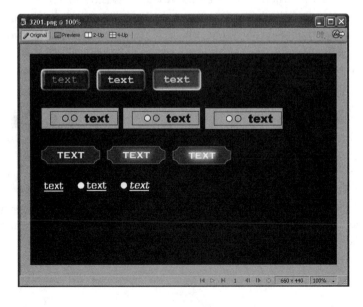

Figure 32.1

These button-state sequences go from lower energy to higher energy, just as the visitor intuitively expects.

Table 32.1 Design Suggestions for Button States

onMouseOver State (Highlighting)	onClick State (Activating)
■ Make the color of the text label brighter	■ Make the button look pressed in
■ Make the color of the button face brighter	■ Make the button look fully turned on (if the onMouseOver state looks partially turned on)
■ Add a border or glow around the button	
■ Nudge the entire button, or nudge the text label inside the button	■ Animate a quick flash of color in the element you changed or added in the onMouseOver state
■ Underline the text label	
■ Add a bullet to the left of the text label	■ Add a bullet to the text label (if you didn't already add one in the onMouseOver state)
■ Change the shape or size of the text label's bullet (if one already exists in the default state)	
■ Increase the point size of the type in the label	■ Add an underline to the text label (if you didn't already add one in the onMouseOver state)

TIP

Get creative with designs for the onMouseOver state, since what you want to do is highlight the button. Buckle down for the onClick state and go with the typical button metaphor of pressing—that is, make your button look pressed in, no matter what ingenious idea you came up with for the onMouseOver state. Making the button look pressed in is the most intuitive way to communicate to your visitors that they just activated your button.

TIP

Don't use a pressed-in design for the onMouseOver state, since it suggests to the visitor that the button has been activated (that is, clicked) when in fact it has only been highlighted. Save pressed-in designs for the onClick state in Flash sites.

33

Making Rollover Graphics

Rollover graphics are images that seem to change when the visitor rolls over them with the mouse pointer. This effect is actually something of a magic trick, because the graphic doesn't really change. Instead, there are two separate graphics files, and a JavaScript function pulls the old switcheroo, swapping between the two images depending on the position of the mouse pointer.

To create a rollover graphic, then, you need three things:

1. The default image file, or the normal state of the rollover
2. The onMouseOver image file, or the image that appears when the visitor mouses over the rollover
3. A JavaScript function that swaps between the images

You can use any two image files for the rollover. They don't have to look similar. They don't even need the same physical dimensions. That said, rollovers work best when the graphic files are different versions of the same image with the same dimensions. The rollover effect creates a kind of animation this way, and you get better consistency,

193

194

because the default image doesn't seem to disappear or change drastically on the visitor.

The JavaScript function is the secret ingredient that makes the rollover work. It relies on the extremely useful getElementById method, which recent versions of the most popular browsers support. Quite simply, the function locates the image you want to swap according to its ID code, and then it changes the source of that image from the default version to the onMouseOver version or from the onMouseOver version back to the default.

Two different JavaScript events on the image call the rollover function. The onMouseOver event triggers the switch from the default to the rolled-over state, and the onMouseOut event triggers the switch back. Without the onMouseOut event to return things to normal, the rollover image gets stuck in its rolled-over state, no matter where the visitor moves the mouse pointer.

TIP

For best results, always specify width and height attributes in the img tag of a rollover graphic. This way, if the onMouseOver image has different dimensions than the default image, the browser resizes the onMouseOver image to match the default image. Otherwise, the browser inserts the onMouseOver image at its native size and redraws the entire screen. Even more annoyingly, if the change in size causes the mouse pointer to fall outside the area of the onMouseOver image, the rollover function automatically swaps the default image back in, and you get a strobe effect.

TOOL KIT

Rollover Graphics

This DHTML document demonstrates how to create a rollover effect.

```
<html>
<head>
<title>Rollover Graphics</title>

<script language="JavaScript">

function doRollover(imageID, imageSource) {

/* This function takes two variables: imageID (the ID of the image you
want to change) and imageSource (the path to the image file you want to
swap in). A single JavaScript statement utilizing both variables does
the trick. */

  document.getElementById(imageID).src = imageSource;

}

</script>

</head>

<body>

<!-- For the purposes of this demo, a single rollover image appears
here, but you can fill the body of the document with whatever content
you want. -->
```

```
<img id="imageid"
    src="imagepath"
    width="imagewidth"
    height="imageheight"
    onMouseOver="doRollover('rolloverid', 'mouseoverimagepath');"
    onMouseOut="doRollover('rolloverid', 'defaultimagepath');">

<!-- Notes:

imageid is a unique string that identifies the image, such as img01 or
happyface. Give every image on your page a different ID.

imagepath is the path to the image, such as images/icecream.jpg. This
path can be document-relative, root-relative, or absolute.

imagewidth and imageheight are the width and height of the image in
pixels.

rolloverid is the ID of the target image, which is the image you want
to change with the rollover function. For a normal rollover, rolloverid
is the same as imageid. For a disjointed rollover, rolloverid is the ID
of whatever image you want to change. Make sure you enclose this value
in single quotes.

mouseoverimagepath is the path to the rolled-over version of the image,
such as images/icecream_ro.jpg. The path can be document-relative,
root-relative, or absolute. Put the entire path between single quotes.

defaultimagepath is the path to the default version of the image.
Again, the path can be document-relative, root-relative, or absolute,
and be sure to put the entire path between single quotes. For a normal
rollover, defaultimagepath is the same as imagepath. For a disjointed
rollover, defaultimagepath is the same as the src attribute of the tar-
get image.

-->

</body>
</html>
```

TIP

You can use the same function to create a disjointed rollover, or an image that triggers a rollover effect not for itself but for a different image entirely. To do this, define the onMouseOver and onMouseOut events in the trigger image, but point the function to the ID of the image that you want to change instead of the trigger image's own ID.

TIP

A few words on nomenclature: Do yourself a favor and name the onMouseOver image the same as the default image with the addition of a suffix like _ro or _over. For example, if your default image is button.gif, make the onMouseOver image **button_ro.gif** or **button_over.gif**. This helps you to keep track of your images.

Of course, different designers have different preferences for naming their images. One of the editors of this book prefers a system like this: **NavHomeOff.gif** for the default image and **NavHomeOn.gif** for the rollover. Use whatever system makes sense to you. But all designers agree that you should use one system or another.

About IDs: If you're at a loss as to what IDs to use, just come up with a generic prefix such as **img** and number your images like this: img01, img02, img03, and so on. You can use the filenames for the images as their IDs, but only if the same image doesn't appear more than once on the same page. Remember, each image needs to have a unique ID.

Making Images More Accessible

onscientious Web designers make their Web sites as compatible as possible with accessibility tools such as screen readers, text-to-speech converters, and text-to-Braille converters for the benefit of the visually impaired.

Making HTML text accessible is easy—you do nothing whatsoever. Accessibility tools are smart enough to ferret out the text on the page and turn it into spoken words or Braille. However, the technology does not yet exist for these tools to examine the content of an image and render an accessible description. It falls to you, the Web builder, to write these descriptions yourself and embed them in the HTML for screen readers and the like to find.

You put the description in the alt attribute of the img tag, like this:

```
<img src="neptune.jpg" width="300" height="150" alt="An image of the planet Neptune
as seen by the Hubble Space Telescope. The face of Neptune appears cobalt blue with
faint bands of blue-gray cloud.">
```

Notice that the description doesn't skimp on the details. The idea is to give the visually impaired a comparable experience of the image. That is, you want to convey the same information in your description that the picture provides visually. Therefore, when you add alt-text descriptions to your images,

TIP

As a value-added bonus, as the marketing department might say, some search engines specifically look for the text in the alt attribute to catalog your site more accurately. Therefore, supplying intelligent alt text may help your site to rank higher in search results.

pretend you're writing a novel. Make your description conjure the image in the mind's eye.

In the preceding example, you find that the text does a pretty good job of conveying the visual information. You wouldn't want to give a description like this:

```
<img src="neptune.jpg" width="300" height="150" alt="The planet Neptune">
```

Few would dispute the accuracy of this description, yet it doesn't have enough detail to conjure the image of Neptune in the mind's eye. Visually impaired people who hear this description already have to know what Neptune looks like to have a comparable experience of the image, which puts them at a disadvantage, since the image itself makes no prior assumptions. Someone who has never seen Neptune before can look at the image and learn what the planet looks like, so your text description needs to do the same thing.

TIP

Be sure to give text descriptions for all the images on a page. Purely functional images, like logos or buttons, don't need detailed descriptions: "About Us button" or "Home Page button" do the trick nicely. But definitely give very detailed descriptions for illustrations, charts, graphs, and other content images, or images that add to or expand upon the text on the page.

35

Creating Image Maps

Image maps are images that have one or more clickable regions called **hotspots**. Each hotspot acts as a separate link. The links can go to different pages or execute different scripts, which makes image maps more useful than regular old clickable graphics, where the entire image acts as a single link.

In an image map, there's nothing special about the image file itself. You can start with any Web graphic. What turns the image into an image map is a block of HTML code that defines the shape, location, and function of the hotspots. So, an image map consists of two parts:

1. The image file itself
2. The block of code that defines the hotspots

Put them together, and you have something like Figure 35.1. Notice that the img tag gets the usemap attribute, which tells the browser which map definition to apply. You can have as many image maps per page as you like, and you can even use the same definition for completely different images.

Figure 35.1

*An image map
consists of an
image file and
a block of
HTML code
that defines the
hotspots.*

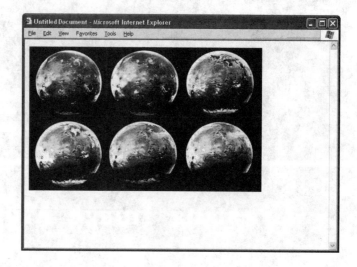

Listing 35.1 **View Source for Figure 35.1.**

```
<img src="images/mars.jpg" width="500" height="300" usemap="#mars">

<!-- Begin hotspot definitions -->

<map name="mars">
  <area shape="rect" coords="9,3,164,148" href="mars01.htm">
  <area shape="rect" coords="172,2,328,149" href="mars02.htm">
  <area shape="rect" coords="334,5,487,149" href="mars03.htm">
  <area shape="rect" coords="9,151,163,294" href="mars04.htm">
  <area shape="rect" coords="171,153,327,296" href="mars05.htm">
  <area shape="rect" coords="334,152,488,295" href="mars06.htm">
</map>

<!-- End hotspot definitions -->
```

TIP

You can put your map tags anywhere in the HTML, but the most convenient place for
them is at the bottom of the HTML document. This way, you always know where to find
your image-map definitions if you need to modify them or move them to another page.

The definition itself appears between the map tags. The name attribute of the map tag corresponds to the usemap attribute of the img tag, with the notable exception that the usemap attribute prefixes the name of the definition with a number sign (#), while the name attribute has no prefix.

Each hotspot in the image map gets its own area tag, so if you have six hotspots like the image map in Figure 35.1, you need six area tags. These area tags can appear in any order. As you might expect, the attributes of the area tag determine where and how the hotspot appears:

- The shape attribute determines which of the three possible hotspot shapes you're using: rectangular (rect), circular (circle), or polygonal (poly).

- The coords attribute determines the position and size of the hotspot. Depending on the value of the shape attribute, the values in the coords attribute have different meanings (see Table 35.1). The upper-left corner of any image is coordinate (0,0). The bottom-right corner of a 500-by-300 image is coordinate (500,300).

- The href attribute contains the hotspot's link. Its value can be a path to a new page, or it can open a blank email window (href="mailto:mars@email.eml"), or launch a script (href="javascript:doMars();").

So, if you want to make circular hotspots instead of rectangular ones for the image mars.jpg, you simply change the shape and update the coordinates:

```
<img src="images/mars.jpg" width="500" height="300" usemap="#mars">

<!-- Begin hotspot definitions -->
```

FAQ

What about server-side image maps?

This topic describes client-side image maps, where the HTML code contains the hotspot definitions. There are also server-side image maps, where the hotspot definitions reside in a separate file on the Web server. Images with server-side definitions are less dependent on the browser and easier to move from page to page, since you don't have to worry about moving the block of HTML that defines the hotspots. But server-side image maps are more cumbersome to code. They don't perform as quickly as their client-side cousins, and you can't make them accessible.

While server-side image maps used to be the standard in the early days, they have all but disappeared, now that all the major browsers support client-side mapping.

TIP

The name of the image map doesn't have to correspond to the name of the image file, but using the same name for both is a convenient way for you to keep track of which image map goes with which image.

TIP

Be careful that your hotspot areas don't overlap. When this happens, browsers get confused, and your image map probably won't work correctly.

```
<map name="mars">
    <area shape="circle" coords="85,76,70" href="mars01.htm">
    <area shape="circle" coords="245,76,70" href="mars02.htm">
    <area shape="circle" coords="410,76,70" href="mars03.htm">
    <area shape="circle" coords="85,225,70" href="mars04.htm">
    <area shape="circle" coords="245,225,70" href="mars05.htm">
    <area shape="circle" coords="410,225,70" href="mars06.htm">
</map>

<!-- End hotspot definitions -->
```

TIP

You can mix and match shapes in the same image map. Your hotspots don't all have to be the same shape.

Table 35.1 **Meaning of Coords Attribute Values**

SHAPE	NUMBER OF COORDS	MEANING	EXAMPLE
circle	Always 3	x position of center point, y position of center point, radius of circle in pixels	coords="10,12,20"
poly	At least 6, and always in multiples of 2	x position of shape point, y position of shape point (repeat for as many shape points as you need to describe the polygon)	coords="100,150,200,100,50,150" coords="275,50,300,150,350,100,400,150,450,50"
rect	Always 4	x position of top-left corner, y position of top corner, x position of bottom-right corner, y position of bottom-right corner	coords="0,0,100,150"

36

Making Image Maps More Accessible

Everybody knows that, to make an image more accessible, you write a detailed text description. Accessibility tools such as screen readers go specifically for the text, and the visually impaired visitor hears a verbal description of what the image shows.

But an image map is a special case, because it isn't just an image. An image map combines an image with clickable areas that work like links. Therefore, it only stands to reason that a more accessible image map requires both an overall text description and a text description for each clickable area.

Use the alt attribute of the img tag to give a text description for the overall image, just as you would for any other image on your site:

```
<img src="images/mars.jpg" width="500" height="300" usemap="#mars" alt="An image map
showing the decline of surface water on the planet Mars.">
```

The alt attribute of the area tag serves nicely for a clickable area's text description:

```
<map name="mars">
   <area shape="rect" coords="9,3,164,148" href="mars01.htm" alt="Phase 1">
   <area shape="rect" coords="172,2,328,149" href="mars02.htm" alt="Phase 2">
   <area shape="rect" coords="334,5,487,149" href="mars03.htm" alt="Phase 3">
   <area shape="rect" coords="9,151,163,294" href="mars04.htm" alt="Phase 4">
   <area shape="rect" coords="171,153,327,296" href="mars05.htm" alt="Phase 5">
```

```
<area shape="rect" coords="334,152,488,295" href="mars06.htm" alt="Phase 6">
</map>
```

Your favorite standards body, the World Wide Web Consortium (W3C), advises you to include redundant text links for the clickable areas of the image map so that text-only browsers and other devices that do not display images can still readily access the image map's content, as in Figure 36.1. Adding a short bit of instruction text doesn't hurt, either.

> **TIP**
>
> Always separate the links in a horizontal list with some type of typographical character such as parentheses, brackets, or pipes (vertical bars). Doing this helps your sighted visitors distinguish the links, and it helps screen readers figure out where one link ends and another begins.
>
> In other words, don't do this:
>
> Phase 1 Phase 2 Phase 3 Phase 4
>
> Try this:
>
> [Phase 1] [Phase 2] [Phase 3] [Phase 4]
>
> Or this:
>
> (Phase 1) (Phase 2) (Phase 3) (Phase 4)
>
> Of course, brackets and parentheses give you a blocky, tech-terminal, math-geeks-only look. For something a bit more aesthetic, try pipes instead:
>
> Phase 1 | Phase 2 | Phase 3 | Phase 4

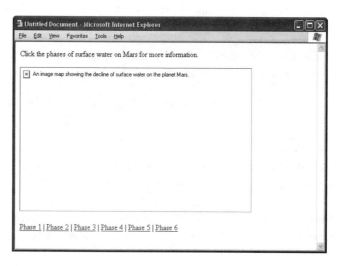

Figure 36.1

This page may never win a beauty prize with a broken image, but its image map is completely useable.

Listing 36.1 **View Source for Figure 36.1.**

```
<p>Click the phases of surface water on Mars for more information.</p>

<img src="images/mars.jpg" width="500" height="300" border="0" usemap="#mars"
alt="An image map showing the decline of surface water on the planet Mars.">

<p><a href="mars01.htm">Phase 1</a> | <a href="mars02.htm">Phase 2</a> | <a
href="mars03.htm">Phase 3</a> | <a href="mars04.htm">Phase 4</a> | <a
href="mars05.htm">Phase 5</a> | <a href="mars06.htm">Phase 6</a></p>

<map name="mars">
  <area shape="rect" coords="9,3,164,148" href="mars01.htm" alt="Phase 1">
  <area shape="rect" coords="172,2,328,149" href="mars02.htm" alt="Phase 2">
  <area shape="rect" coords="334,5,487,149" href="mars03.htm" alt="Phase 3">
  <area shape="rect" coords="9,151,163,294" href="mars04.htm" alt="Phase 4">
  <area shape="rect" coords="171,153,327,296" href="mars05.htm" alt="Phase 5">
  <area shape="rect" coords="334,152,488,295" href="mars06.htm" alt="Phase 6">
</map>
```

37

Using Background Images in Table Cells

ou probably know that you can place an image inside a table cell, like this:

```
<td><img src="mercury.jpg" width="200" height="200"></td>
```

You probably also know that you can set the background color of a table cell, like this:

```
<td bgcolor="#FF0000">Behold, the planet Mercury</td>
```

But did you also know that you can use an image as the background of a table cell? It works like this:

```
<td background="mercury.jpg" width="200" height="200">Behold, the planet Mercury</td>
```

Doing it like this allows you to superimpose HTML content, as Figure 37.1 shows.

> **TIP**
> The width and height attributes of the td tag describe the size of the table cell, not the size of the image. Older browsers may clip the size of the cell to match the amount of content it contains, even when you specify precise width and height values, which can crop your background image.

Figure 37.1

When you use
an image as
the back-
ground of a
table cell, you
can superim-
pose HTML
content.

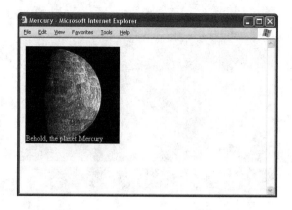

Listing 37.1 **View Source for Figure 37.1.**

```
<table>
  <tr>

<!-- Set the valign attribute to bottom to push the text to the bottom of the table
cell. -->

    <td valign="bottom" width="200" height="200"
        background="images/mercury.jpg">
      Behold, the planet Mercury
    </td>
  </tr>
</table>
```

GEEKSPEAK

Tiling is repeating an image to fill a given area.

This technique works best when the amount of
content you want to superimpose is not likely to
cause the table cell to expand beyond the width
and height values of the image. Otherwise, the
browser **tiles** or repeats the image to fill the extra
area, as in Figure 37.2, which may not be the effect
you want to achieve.

TIP

Make sure that your text is legible against the background image, unlike the examples in
this topic. One of the most common design problems on the Web is poor contrast
between foreground and background. If you can't find a color or style of text that stands
out enough from the background image, don't use a background image.

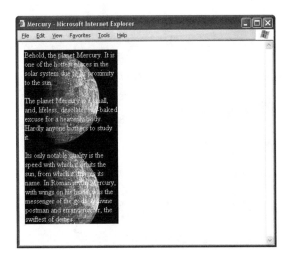

Figure 37.2

If the size of the cell expands beyond the size of the background image, the browser tiles the image to fill the extra area.

Listing 37.2 **View Source for Figure 37.2.**

```
<table>
  <tr>

<!-- You don't need to specify the valign attribute here, since the text fills the
200-by-200 cell. -->

    <td width="200" height="200" background="images/mercury.jpg">
      <p>Behold, the planet Mercury. It is one of the hottest places in the solar
system due to its proximity to the sun.</p>
      <p>The planet Mercury is a small, arid, lifeless, desolate, sun-baked excuse
for a heavenly body. Hardly anyone bothers to study it.</p>
      <p>Its only notable quality is the speed with which it orbits the sun, from
which it derives its name. In Roman myth, Mercury, with wings on his heels, was the
messenger of the gods, a divine postman and errand runner, the swiftest of
deities.</p>
    </td>
  </tr>
</table>
```

Unfortunately, HTML doesn't give you additional attributes for fine-tuning the behavior of background images, but CSS does (see Topic 38).

38

Using Background Images in CSS Divs

ackground images in table cells are either there or not, as you saw in Topic 37. You either define them in the HTML, or you don't, and the browser takes care of the rest. If the amount of content in the table cell exceeds the physical size of the image, the browser tiles the image. If this is the effect you want, then good for you. If you don't want this effect, then too bad.

Not so with background images in CSS divs. CSS provides a number of design options. You may tile the image if you like in a variety of ways, or you may display it one time and one time only. You may also specify where in the div your background image should appear.

Start with a typical div, like this:

```
<div id="mercury" style="width: 200px;">
  <p>Behold, the planet Mercury. It is one of the hottest places in the solar system
due to its proximity to the sun.</p>
  <p>The planet Mercury is a small, arid, lifeless, desolate, sun-baked excuse for a
heavenly body. Hardly anyone bothers to study it.</p>
  <p>Its only notable quality is the speed with which it orbits the sun, from which
it derives its name. In Roman myth, Mercury, with wings on his heels, was the mes-
senger of the gods, a divine postman and errand runner, the swiftest of deities.</p>
</div>
```

To add a background image to the div, use the background-image attribute, like so:

```
<div id="mercury" style="width: 200px;
     background-image: url(images/mecury.jpg);">
```

Notice that you enclose the path to the image within the url(...) construction.

Adding the background-image CSS attribute alone gives you a div that behaves very much like a table cell in that the background image tiles, as Figure 38.1 shows. Other CSS style definitions allow you to fine-tune the behavior of the background image.

If you do not want the background image to tile, say so in the background-repeat attribute, as in Figure 38.2.

Listing 38.1 View Source for Figure 38.2.

```
<div id="mercury" style="width: 200px;
     background-image: url(images/mecury.jpg);
     background-repeat: no-repeat;">
```

To position the background image in the div, specify a value for the background-position attribute, as in Figure 38.3.

> **TIP**
>
> If you want the background image to tile only in the horizontal direction, set background repeat to **repeat-x**. Use **repeat-y** to make the background image tile only in the vertical direction.

Figure 38.1

When you specify the background-image CSS attribute and nothing else, the background image tiles.

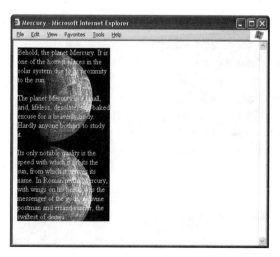

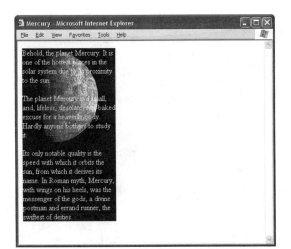

Listing 38.2 **View Source for Figure 38.3.**

```
<div id="mercury" style="width: 200px;
    background-image: url(images/mecury.jpg);
    background-repeat: no-repeat;
    background-position: center;">
```

Table 38.1 shows common values for CSS attributes related to background images. Remember, you should test your pages thoroughly before posting them on the Web, since browsers do strange things when you give them style definitions.

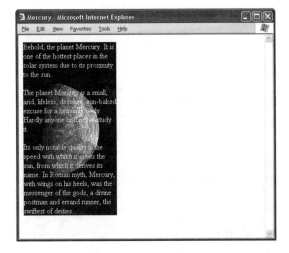

Table 38.1 Common CSS Attributes for Background Images in Divs

STYLE	CONTROLS	POSSIBLE VALUES	EXAMPLE
background-repeat	How or if the background image tiles	repeat-x, repeat-y, no-repeat, repeat	background-repeat: repeat-y; background-repeat: repeat;
background-position	The position of the background image inside the div	Any combination of the following: left, right, center, top, bottom	background-position: left; background-position: right bottom; background-position: center left; background-position: center;

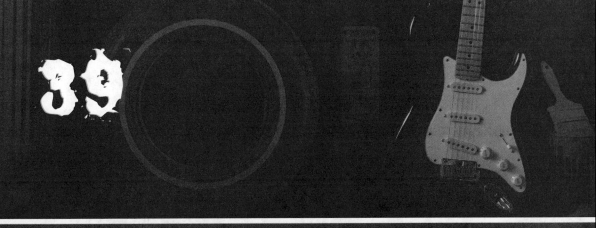

Using Background Images on Web Pages

here are two ways to add a background image to a Web page. One is to use HTML attributes. The other is to use CSS style definitions. With HTML, you get limited design options but solid reliability across browsers. With CSS, you get more design options but less reliability.

In HTML, you add the background attribute to the body tag, like this:

```
<body background="images/ufo.gif">
```

The browser tiles or repeats the image across all available real estate in the browser window, as in Figure 39.1.

Cascading Style Sheets produce the same effect:

```
<body style="background-image: url(images/ufo.gif);">
```

The preceding example creates a tiling background image, exactly as in Figure 39.1. However, CSS gives you additional options to control exactly how the background image behaves, including background-repeat, background-position, and background-attachment.

Use background-repeat to control how (or if) the background image tiles, as in Figure 39.2.

TIP

Beware of background images that overwhelm the content of the page. Stick to washed-out images that don't interfere with the legibility and clarity of your text.

Figure 39.1

When you add a background image to the page with HTML, the browser automatically tiles the image to fill the page.

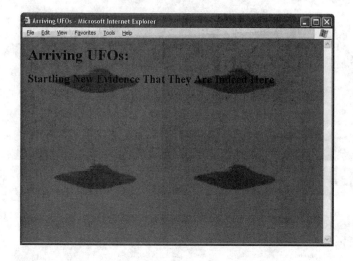

Listing 39.1 **View Source for Figure 39.2.**

```
<body style="background-image: url(images/ufo.gif);
             background-repeat: repeat-y;">
```

Determine where on the page the background image appears with the background-position attribute, as in Figure 39.3.

The background-attachment attribute determines how the background image responds to scrolling. Set background-attachment to **fixed** to make the

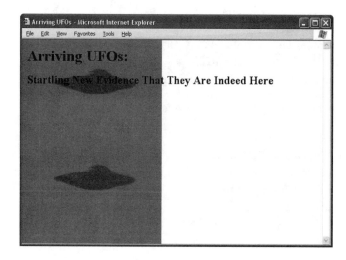

Figure 39.2

You can specify vertical-only tiling when you use CSS for background images.

Figure 39.3

Move the background image around the screen by including background-position in your style definition.

background image resist scrolling; that is, the background image remains rooted to its position in the browser window. The page content may scroll, but the background image does not, as in Figure 39.4.

Listing 39.2 View Source for Figure 39.3.

```
<body style="background-image: url(images/ufo.gif);
             background-repeat: repeat-y;
             background-position: right;">
```

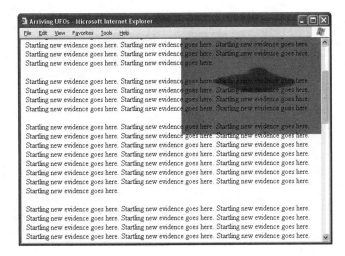

Figure 39.4

With CSS, you can even make the background image impervious to scrolling.

Listing 39.3 **View Source for Figure 39.4.**

```
<body style="background-image: url(images/ufo.gif);
             background-repeat: no-repeat;
             background-position: right;
             background-attachment: fixed;">
```

TIP·

The background-attachment style definition works best with images that don't tile.

To make the background image scroll with the
rest of the page content, set background-attachment
to **scroll**.

For your coding pleasure, Table 39.1 lists CSS
options for background images.

Table 39.1 **Common CSS Options for Background Images**

STYLE	CONTROLS	POSSIBLE VALUES	EXAMPLE
background-repeat	How or if the background image tiles	repeat-x, repeat-y, no-repeat, repeat	background-repeat: repeat-y; background-repeat: repeat;
background-position	The position of the background image inside the div	Any combination of the following: left, right, center, top, bottom	background-position: left; background-position: right bottom; background-position: center left; background-position: center;
background-attachment	How the background image reacts to scrolling	fixed, scroll	background-attachment: fixed; background-attachment: scroll;

PART IV:
Text Topics

Using Text Elements Properly

Using Phrase Elements Properly

Adding Cascading Style Sheets

Replacing Formatting Tags
with CSS

Creating Custom Formatting Styles

Changing the Look of a Text
Element

Defining Class Styles

Controlling the Typeface

Controlling Type Size

BLOG: Sizing up Type Sizing

Controlling Spacing

Controlling Justified and
Ragged Type

Controlling Indents

Building Lists

Highlighting Text with Color

Rehabilitating Horizontal Rules

Adding a Dateline and
Timestamp

Designing Data Tables

Using Pseudo-Elements

Defining ID Styles

40

Using Text Elements Properly

Just about every Web designer has done it at one time or another: using an HTML tag to mark up some text based on how the result looks in a browser instead of what the tag is supposed to mark up. Need a quick line of bold text? Who among us hasn't been at least tempted to reach for a header tag, even if the text in question doesn't really function as a header? Need to add some whitespace? The blockquote tag does the trick, even when you aren't trying to format an offset quote.

Now that Cascading Style Sheets (CSS) have become somewhat reasonably reliable in most browsers, the old arguments for doing whatever works don't hold as much water. CSS allows any HTML element to look however you, the designer, want it to look, so you don't have to borrow a tag on the basis of its appearance—which means that HTML tags can go back to their original purpose of defining the structure of the page. When you mark something up as a header, in other words, it really ought to function as a header on your page. When you mark something up as a blockquote, it should be an offset block of text, not an image that needs a little extra whitespace.

If you have been designing Web sites for any length of time, you may have gotten into some bad HTML habits, and you might forget exactly what HTML text tags are supposed to mark up. Enter Table 40.1.

Table 40.1 Common HTML Text Tags

TAG	IDENTIFIES	EXAMPLE
address	Your street address, phone number, email address, or other form of contact information	<address>Your address goes here</address>
blockquote	An offset quote	<blockquote>An offset quote goes here.</blockquote>
h1	First-level heading	<h1>A heading goes here</h1>
h2	Second-level heading	<h2>A heading goes here</h2>
h3	Third-level heading	<h3>A heading goes here</h3>
h4	Fourth-level heading	<h4>A heading goes here</h4>
h5	Fifth-level heading	<h5>A heading goes here</h5>
h6	Sixth-level heading	<h6>A heading goes here</h6>
p	Paragraph	<p>A paragraph goes here.</p>
q	Inline quote	<q>An inline quote goes here.</q>

Working with Header Tags

HTML provides six levels of headers—h1 through h6—in descending order of structural and visual importance, as Figure 40.1 shows. First-level headings are bold and large, like the main headline on the front page of a newspaper. Second-level headings are not quite as large, like the supplemental or section headlines in the paper. On it goes, until you get to sixth-level headings, which are like the bold text at the beginning of a classified ad: not much of a headline, but a headline nonetheless.

Your well-coded HTML document should use the header tags to denote the logical structure of your page. That is, the main headline of your page should use the h1 tag. A subsection under this heading gets the h2 tag; a sub-subsection gets the h3 tag, and so on. Ideally, if you remove all the running text from your

---

TIP

If the content on your page does not fall into a logical hierarchy, then all the headers on your page should be the same.

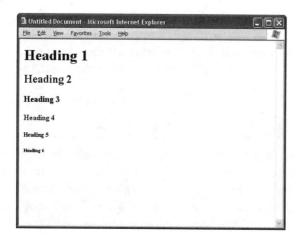

Figure 40.1

*HTML defines
six levels of
headings.*

page, a properly structured set of header tags gives you a complete and accurate outline of the information on your page, like this:

Welcome to my home site (h1)
    What you will find on my site (h2)
        About the games page (h3)
        About the news page (h3)
        About my online gift store (h3)
    Information about me (h2)
        My résumé (h3)
            Current employment (h4)
            Previous employment (h4)
            Education (h4)
                Graduate studies (h5)
                College (h5)
    My hobbies (h3)
        Shoelace art (h4)
            Favorite techniques (h5)
            Links to shoelace sites (h5)
        Basket-weaving (h4)
            Favorite techniques (h5)
            Links to basket-weaving sites (h5)
    My contact information (h3)
        Street address (h4)
        Telephone/fax (h4)
        Email (h4)

Remember, it doesn't matter so much what effect these tags have on the appearance of your text, since you can use CSS to make the tags generate whatever typography you want. The important thing is to make sure you use the tags consistently and as HTML designed them to be used.

Marking up Paragraphs

The lowly paragraph tag is probably the most neglected tag in all of HTML. Who wants to slow the production process to include those annoying <p> and </p> symbols before and after every single block of running text? Yet the benefits for making the extra effort can be extraordinary. CSS provides a wide range of typographic possibilities for running text, even the least of which is a significant improvement over the cramped, unattractive blocks of poorly set lines of type that HTML spits out (see Figure 40.2). The key to harnessing CSS is to mark up your document properly, and that means marking everything that is supposed to be a paragraph as a paragraph.

Using Quote Elements

HTML gives you two tags for marking up quotations: quote and blockquote. The quote tag works with inline quotations, like the dialog in a novel, while the blockquote tag marks up offset quotes, as Figure 40.3 shows.

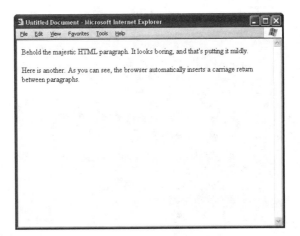

Figure 40.2

HTML paragraphs are so unattractive that it's hard to blame you for ignoring proper markup. But get into the habit of marking up paragraphs anyway so that you can use CSS to improve your site's typography.

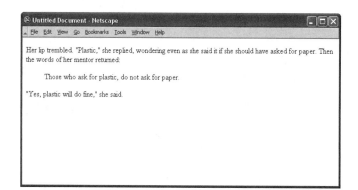

Figure 40.3

The quote tag is for inline quotations, while the blockquote tag is for offset quotes.

The World Wide Web Consortium (W3C) recommends that you specify the language of the quote in the lang attribute of the quote tag, like this:

```
<p>Her lip trembled. <q lang="en-us">Plastic,</q> she
replied, wondering even as she said it if she should have
asked for paper.</p>
```

Why? Because browsers are supposed to add the quotation marks automatically, depending on the conventions of the language. (Different languages have different symbols and conventions for rendering quotation marks.) The Netscape browser adds quotes when it encounters quote tags, but Internet Explorer does not.

TIP

The blockquote element doesn't automatically add quotation marks in any browser, nor does the HTML specification require it, so you don't have to give the language in the opening blockquote tag.

Displaying Addresses

Insert contact information about you or your organization in address tags, like so:

```
<address>
  The Old Software Company<br>
  100 Main St, Ste. 500<br>
  Youngstown, OH 92123
</address>
```

Notice the br tags at the end of each line to force a carriage return. The results look something like Figure 40.4 in a browser.

You shouldn't use the address tags to format any old address on your page. Try to reserve these tags specifically for contact information relating to your site, since search engines and the like might look to the address tags to mine

Figure 40.4

Use address tags to mark up contact infor- mation about you or your organization.

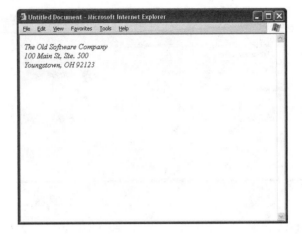

information about the site's owner. If you need to format several addresses, like the contact information for your site's membership or something to that effect, you should avoid the address tag and define a custom style in CSS.

41

Using Phrase Elements Properly

hrase elements are a series of HTML tags for identifying the particular structure of a segment of text within a larger element such as a paragraph.

The phrase elements typically create special typographic effects like boldface and italics, so designers tend to use them for their results rather than for what they are supposed to represent. You read in Topic 40 an impassioned plea to return to more responsible coding practices, now that CSS is at least somewhat reliable much of the time in many browsers, and the same argument applies here. Mark up your HTML properly, with the right tags for the job. If you want extra typographical effects, or if you need different ones than the tags provide by default, create these effects yourself with CSS styles.

With that in mind, see Table 41.1 for a comprehensive list of phrase elements.

Most of the phrase elements are self-explanatory, but the abbreviation and acronym tags need further clarification.

First, a quick refresher. An **abbreviation** is a group of letters that stands for a word or a series of words. You pronounce each letter in some abbreviations separately, even if the abbreviation is pronounceable. A good example is the abbreviation **UN**, which stands for **United Nations**. When you see this abbreviation, you don't say "unn," but "you, enn."

Table 41.1 HTML Phrase Elements

Tag	Identifies	Typically Displays As	Example
em	Emphasized text	Italic	What did you say?
strong	Really emphasized text	Boldface	You can't be serious!
cite	A citation; a reference or source	Italic	What's up, doc? <cite>-- Bugs Bunny</cite>
dfn	A term that is defined in the following text	Italic	A <dfn>tag</dfn> is an HTML markup element.
code	Computer code	Monospaced text	The <code>em</code> tag identifies emphasized text.
samp	Sample output from a computer program, function, etc.	Monospaced text	When this happens, the computer displays <samp>Error: Please Reboot.</samp>
kbd	Keys or text that the user presses or enters	Monospaced text	Press <kbd>Enter</kbd> to continue.
var	A variable in a computer program, equation, etc.	Italic	Check the value of <var>x</var> before you continue.
abbr	An abbreviation	Normal text*	Your site looks fantastic, but the <abbr title="World Wide Web Consortium">W3C</abbr> would not approve, as usual.
acronym	An acronym	Normal text	Send your complaints to <acronym title="National Aeronautics and Space Administration">NASA</acronym>.

* In Netscape, an abbreviation displays with a dotted underline. When the visitor mouses over the term, a tip appears, giving the full-text equivalent from the title attribute. IE does not offer anything like this feature.

You don't pronounce certain abbreviations at all, instead replacing them with the actual words that they represent. Consider the abbreviation for the state of California, CA. Typically, when you see this abbreviation, you just say "California" instead of "see, ay."

An **acronym**, by contrast, is an abbreviation that you pronounce as if it were a word. When you see the acronym NASA (National Aeronautics and Space Administration), you don't say "enn, ay, ess, ay," but "nassuh," and rarely do you substitute the agency's real name. You just pronounce the acronym and get on with your life.

What difference does marking up acronyms and abbreviations make to most of your visitors? None whatsoever. As Table 41.1 shows, the abbr and acronym tags don't add special typographical formatting to the marked-up text (at least not in Internet Explorer, the most popular browser by far). Most people who come to your site will never know that you went to the trouble of typing **National Aeronautics and Space Administration** every time you used the acronym **NASA**. But those visitors who use screen readers and other accessibility aids will thank you profusely for your consideration.

Screen readers and the like are too dumb to realize when they are looking at an abbreviation or an acronym, so you must tell them by way of your markup. When a screen reader comes to a phrase marked up as an acronym, it knows that it should try to pronounce the text as a word. When the screen reader comes to an abbreviation, it knows to pronounce each letter separately or to substitute the full text, which appears in the title attribute of the tag.

You also improve the performance of your site in search engines when you mark up abbreviations and acronyms correctly and include the full text in the title attribute. Some search engines catalog your page according to the words in the title attribute and the abbreviation or acronym itself, so your site appears to people who search for HTML as well as Hypertext Markup Language.

GEEKSPEAK

An **abbreviation** is a group of letters that stands for a word or a series of words. An **acronym** is an abbreviation that you pronounce as if it were a word.

How can I contribute a new word to my native language?
Come up with a really successful acronym. Some acronyms work so well as words that they become actual words, especially acronyms that describe technical concepts that most people don't care to understand. **Laser, radar,** and **scuba** were all once acronyms.

42

Adding Cascading Style Sheets

ascading **Style Sheets** (**CSS**) describe the style or appearance of elements on a Web page. You can use CSS to redefine the way the browser displays an HTML tag or sequence of tags, or you can build entirely new styles and apply them to whatever pieces of content you like. In this regard, CSS is extremely useful in separating the **structure** of a document—the purely technical description of a Web page that identifies individual pieces of content as particular **elements**, or types of things: paragraphs, images, headers, quotes, and so on— from the presentation of the document—what each element looks like in a browser.

When HTML first came out, it was supposed to be a structural language, with the browser software determining what each element looked like. The role of a Web builder was simply to identify what pieces of content

were which types of things—that is, to describe the structure of the page—and the browser handled the presentation. Graphically savvy Web builders found this way of working unacceptable. They demanded more and more control over the look of a Web page, until HTML itself became a mishmash of structural elements and presentation elements that had nothing to do with structure at all. To coding-minded Web builders like the fine folks at the W3C, this way of working was equally unacceptable.

Enter CSS, which, at least in theory, satisfies both types of Web people. The graphic heads get more and better design choices for pixel-perfect control over how a Web page looks, and the coding heads have a way to reclaim HTML as a purely structural language. The downside is that, although CSS has been around for years, it is still an emerging technology. Graphic heads were slow to embrace it, because it is very code-oriented, and it is harder and less intuitive to use than HTML markup. It assumes a level of technical understanding that many visually oriented people never possessed and never bothered to learn in the frenzied days of dot-com start-ups and IPOs. Further, browser makers like Microsoft and Netscape didn't feel compelled to support CSS with anything like consistency or completeness.

These days are slowly drawing to a close. CSS now enjoys a passably acceptable level of support in the major browsers, so using it effectively has become at least feasible. However, since CSS is nowhere near as stable as the much-maligned HTML presentation tags, he who dabbles in CSS must test and test and test his pages in a variety of browsers to troubleshoot the inevitable glitches, bugs, and inconsistencies that crop up.

GEEKSPEAK

A **style sheet** is a block of CSS code that appears between **style tags** in an HTML document or in a separate CSS file. It consists of style rules, or presentation instructions for the browser. A **style rule** has a style selector, which is the elements that you are formatting, and a **style definition**, which tells the browser exactly how to display the selector.

TIP

When your style sheet appears in its own file, you don't need the style tags before and after the CSS code. Only use style tags when you embed your style sheet in an HTML document.

Writing CSS

There are two ways to add CSS to your Web page: write up a style sheet or put CSS code into the style attribute of the tag that you want to format.

Writing a Style Sheet

A **style sheet** is a block of CSS code. It appears between style tags in an HTML document, or it exists as a separate file that you import into the HTML document. A style sheet consists of one or more **style rules**, or presentation instructions for the browser. A style rule, in turn, consists of a **style selector**, which is the element that you are formatting; and a **style definition**, which gives attribute/value pairs that tell the browser how to display the selector.

A style sheet looks something like this:

```
<style type="text/css">

  h1 {
    font-family: Arial;
    font-weight: bold;
    font-size: 24px;
  }

  p {
    font-family: "Times New Roman";
    font-size: 16px;
  }

</style>
```

This style sheet contains two style rules: one for the h1 selector and one for the p selector. Remember, the selectors are the elements that you are styling. In this case, you're styling the h1 and p tags for first-level headers and paragraphs, respectively. The code between the angle brackets ({, }) following each selector is the definition for that selector.

A style definition consists of attribute/value pairs. In HTML, attribute/value pairs take this form:

```
attributename="value"
```

where the attribute name is all one word, you separate the attribute from the value with an equals sign (=), and the value appears inside quotes. But in CSS, the coding convention is different:

```
attribute-name: value;
```

> **TIP**
>
> When the name of a font consists of multiple words, like **Times New Roman**, put the font name in quotes in your style definition. When the name of the font is a single word, like **Arial**, you don't need quotes.

where you separate the parts of the attribute name with the hyphen character (-) instead of mashing the whole thing together; you use the colon character (:) to separate the attribute from the value, not the equals sign; and you put the semicolon character (;) at the end of the line. Typically, you don't need to enclose the value between quotes, although there are some good exceptions to this rule, such as when the name of a font contains more than one word, like **Times New Roman** in the previous example.

Don't let this coding style stop you. Just by bluffing through the definition, you can guess that first-level headers display in Arial bold at a size of 24 pixels, while paragraphs use Times New Roman 16 pixels. The result of these styles looks something like Figure 42.1 in a browser.

When you change the style sheet, like this:

```
<style type="text/css">

    h1 {
        font-family: "Times New Roman";
        font-weight: bold;
        font-size: 96px;
    }

    p {
        font-family: Verdana;
        font-size: 8px;
    }

</style>
```

the presentation of your Web page changes, as in Figure 42.2.

Style definitions can be as complex or as simple as you need them to be. In other words, you don't have to supply values for every conceivable attribute in your definition. In the previous examples, the definitions say nothing about the spacing or the color of the text, which are certainly definable in CSS. When you omit information from your definition, the browser fills in its default preferences. Therefore, unless you specifically mention that a paragraph should appear in red type, the browser just assumes you want black type, the default

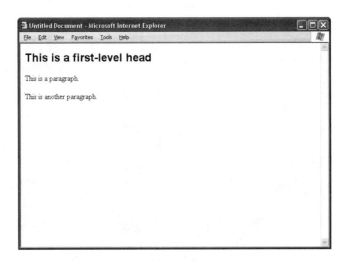

Figure 42.1

This HTML document contains a style sheet that defines styles for the h1 and p tags.

Figure 42.2

Change the style definition, and the appearance of the Web page changes.

color. Likewise, if you hadn't specifically told the browser to use Verdana or Arial in the previous examples, the browser would have just substituted its default font.

Now, what makes CSS cascading is that child elements inherit the styles of their parents, kind of like human kids wind up with the genes of their parents. A **parent element** is an HTML tag that contains another HTML tag. The **child element** is the HTML tag that the parent element contains. Take this block of HTML code:

```
<p>
  Welcome back, my friends, to the <em>Show That Never Ends</em>!
</p>
```

The paragraph tag is the parent, and the emphasis tag is the child, since the emphasis tag sits inside the opening and closing paragraph tags. But in this case:

```
<body>
  <p>
    Welcome back, my friends, to the <em>Show That Never Ends</em>!
  </p>
</body>
```

the emphasis tag is still the child of the paragraph tag, but both the paragraph tag and the emphasis tag are the children of the body tag.

Cascading works like this: The child inherits the style of the parent. So any style that you give to the body tag:

```
<style type="text/css">

body {
  font-family: Arial;
}

</style>
```

automatically applies to all its children, which, in this example, are the paragraph tag and the emphasis tag, as Figure 42.3 shows. Even though the browser's default font is Times New Roman, you don't have to tell the browser to use Arial for paragraphs or emphasis tags, since these tags automatically inherit the Arial font from their body-tag parent.

The cascading nature of CSS means that the style definitions of child elements refine or clarify the styles of the parents. In this style sheet:

```
<style type="text/css">

body {
  font-family: Arial;
}

p {
  font-style: italic;
}

</style>
```

TIP

A few CSS attributes don't propagate from parent to child, but that's OK, because you wouldn't want the children to inherit these properties anyway. Take the margin-top attribute, which defines the size of the top margin of the page. This attribute typically goes in the body tag. You don't want all the paragraphs, headers, images, and other children of the body tag to have the exact same top margin, or all the content of your page would crowd together at the top of the browser window.

Figure 42.3

In Cascading Style Sheets, the child element inherits the style of its parents. You don't have to tell the browser to display paragraphs in Arial if the body tag already has Arial in its style definition.

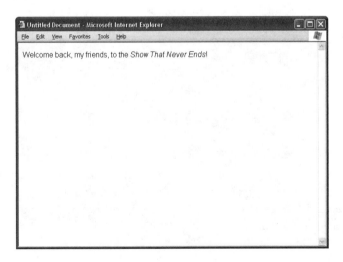

paragraphs appear in Arial italic, while other body ele-ments—such as h1 tags—display in normal Arial. First-level headers are children of the body tag, just like paragraphs, and all children of the body tag display in Arial. But in this style sheet, only the paragraph children have the extra clarification of displaying in italic, so the browser applies this extra bit of styling to p tags and leaves all the other child tags alone. Figure 42.4 shows the results.

Embedding Style Sheets

To embed a style sheet in your HTML page, put the CSS code between style tags, and put the entire style block inside the head section of the page, like this:

```
<html>
  <head>
    <title>My HTML Page</title>
    <style type="text/css">

      body {
        font-family: Arial;
      }

      p {
        font-style: italic;
      }
```

TIP

When a child style definition contra-dicts the style definition of a parent, the browser goes with the child style. For example, if a parent definition calls for Verdana but a child definition calls for Arial, the browser uses Arial in the child's presentation. At least the browser is supposed to do this. Browsers don't always handle inheritance correctly, so be sure to check the effects of your style sheets in a variety of browsers.

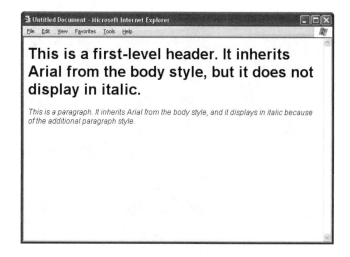

Figure 42.4

Use additional style definitions to clarify and expand upon the styles that children ele-ments inherit from their parents.

```
    </style>
  </head>
  <body>

    <!-- The body of the page goes here. -->

  </body>
</html>
```

TIP

To hide your CSS code from older browsers that do not support Cascading Style Sheets, you can put comment tags (<!--, -->) around the block of CSS. Put the opening comment tag immediately after the opening style tag, and put the closing comment tag immediately before the closing style tag.

All the elements on your page reference an embedded style sheet, but elements of other pages do not, unless you paste the style sheet onto the other pages of your site.

Importing Style Sheets

As a way to work around the problem of including the exact same style sheet on every page of your site, you may decide to put the style sheet in a separate file, save this file with the .css extension, and then import this style sheet into every page that needs it. This way, you only have to write the style sheet once, and you don't have to go through the copying and pasting rigmarole. Better still, if you decide you need to change a style, you only have to change it once, in the CSS file. If you embed your style sheet instead, you have to update the style on every single page of your site.

To import an external CSS file, use the @import rule in place of your embedded style sheet:

```
<html>
  <head>
    <title>My HTML Page</title>
    <style type="text/css">

      @import url("styles/mystyles.css");

    </style>
  </head>
  <body>

    <!-- The body of the page goes here. -->

  </body>
</html>
```

Following the @import rule, supply the Web address of your CSS style sheet using the **url("path")** construction. The path can be document-relative, root-relative, or absolute, just like the path of a link.

You may import more than one style sheet:

```
<style type="text/css">

  @import url("styles/styles01.css");
  @import url("styles/styles02.css");
  @import url("styles/styles03.css");

</style>
```

And, for good measure, if you want to supplement your imported style sheets with additional, page-only styles, by all means, please do so:

```
<style type="text/css">

  @import url("styles/styles01.css");
  @import url("styles/styles02.css");
  @import url("styles/styles03.css");

  p {
    color: #FF0000;
  }

</style>
```

If one of the imported style sheets also contains a paragraph style and you want the browser to use your page-specific paragraph style instead, mark up the page-specific style like so:

```
<style type="text/css">

  @import url("styles/styles01.css");
  @import url("styles/styles02.css");
  @import url("styles/styles03.css");

  p {
    color: #FF0000;
    !important;
  }

</style>
```

The **!important** declaration tells the browser to use this style in the event of a conflict. It ignores any paragraph styles in the imported style sheets on this page only.

> **TIP**
> Older browsers don't understand the @import style rule, but you can use this to your advantage. Embed basic style definitions in the HTML of the page, and then use @import to bring in more advanced styles, like the kind that don't work as well in older browsers. Just don't mark the basic, embedded styles with !important—otherwise, the bland styles will override the souped-up @import versions.

Using the HTML Style Attribute

Writing a style sheet makes sense when you have a global style that applies to all the elements of a particular type. But when you have a one-off style that applies to a particular instance of an element on your page and never again, it makes more sense to put the definition in the style attribute of the element's tag.

Say you want a particular paragraph to display in bold, red type when all the other paragraphs use the browser's default appearance. You don't want to write up a style sheet for the paragraph tag, since that will change all paragraphs to bold and red. You solve the problem like this:

```
<p>This is a normal paragraph, neither bold nor red.</p>

<p>This is another normal paragraph, neither bold nor red.</p>

<p style="font-weight: bold; color: #FF0000;">This is a special paragraph, both bold and red.</p>

<p>Back to normal paragraph style here, neither bold nor red.</p>
```

The style attribute of the paragraph tag applies an instant CSS definition to that particular paragraph, as well as any children of the paragraph, but the presentation reverts to normal as soon as the browser encounters the closing paragraph tag, as Figure 42.5 shows.

> **TIP**
> Notice that the definition inside the style attribute follows CSS conventions, even though the surrounding code uses HTML conventions.

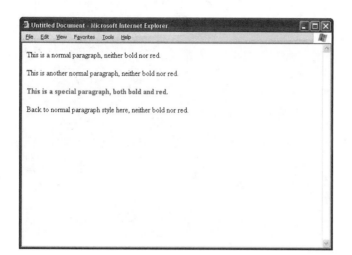

Replacing Formatting Tags with CSS

Formatting tags are HTML tags that explicitly turn on typographic effects such as boldface, underlining, and italics. Unlike phrase elements, formatting tags do not identify the structure of the text they mark up. They simply indicate that a particular string of text should display as bold, italic, or underlined.

The formatting tags are b (for boldface), i (for italic), u (for underline), and s or strike (for strikethrough). Figure 43.1 shows them in action.

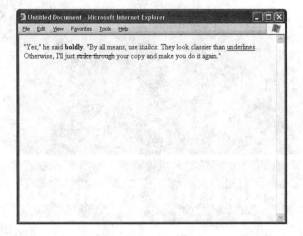

Since formatting tags have nothing to do with structure, and since HTML is supposed to be a structure-only markup language, formatting by way of these tags nowadays is a design faux pas. You should use CSS style definitions instead, like the kind in this topic's Toolkit.

Copy these definitions into your site's style sheet, or put them between style tags in the head section of your HTML file. Then, to format a piece of text with them, use the span tag, as Figure 41.2 demonstrates. Put the name of the style that you want to use in the class attribute.

TOOL KIT.

CSS Style Definitions to Replace Formatting Tags

This Toolkit gives you four CSS style definitions to replace the HTML formatting tags of bold, italic, underline, and strikethrough.

```css
.b {
    font-weight: bold;
}

.i {
    font-style: italic;
}

.u {
        text-decoration: underline;
}

.s {
        text-decoration: line-through;
}
```

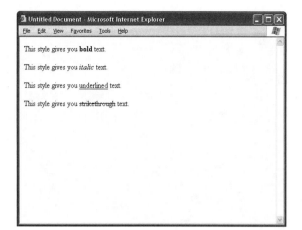

Figure 43.2

Instead of formatting tags, use CSS style definitions. They work just as well, and free up HTML to be a purely structural language once again.

Listing 43.1 **View Source for Figure 43.2.**

```
<p>This style gives you <span class="b">bold</span> text.</p>

<p>This style gives you <span class="i">italic</span> text.</p>

<p>This style gives you <span class="u">underlined</span> text.</p>

<p>This style gives you <span class="s">strikethrough</span> text.</p>
```

TIP

The abbreviated names of the style classes—b, i, u, and s—come from the names of the corresponding formatting tags as a way to trick old-school Web designers into using CSS. If you'd prefer more descriptive names, say like **bold** or **ital**, feel free to give these in the style definitions. Make sure the class attributes of your span tags reflect your revised class names.

44

Creating Custom Formatting Styles

For as beloved as HTML's formatting tags are in certain circles of Web design, these tags are pretty limited. They give you only the most basic formatting options: boldface, italic, underline, and strikethrough.

You saw in Topic 43 how to mimic the effects of HTML's formatting tags with a simple style sheet. CSS opens the door to many other possibilities for formatting, as Table 44.1 shows.

TIP
The formatting tags in HTML include b (boldface), i (italic), u (underline), and s or strike (strikethrough).

Table 44.1 **Common CSS Formatting Attributes**

CSS ATTRIBUTE	POSSIBLE VALUES	EXAMPLE
font-weight	bold, bolder, lighter, normal	font-weight: bolder;
font-style	italic, oblique, normal	font-style: oblique;
font-variant	normal, small-caps	font-variant: small-caps;
text-decoration	underline, overline, line-through, none	text-decoration: overline;
text-transform	capitalize, uppercase, lowercase, none	text-transform: capitalize;

248

The bolder and lighter font weights don't have a noticeable effect on screen, but you may be able to see a difference in hard copy. Additionally, in current browsers, the oblique font style looks identical to the italic font style, although future versions of browsers may display oblique text differently.

Want an overline instead of an underline? No problem. See Figure 44.1.

Listing 44.1 **View Source for Figure 44.1.**

```
<style type="text/css">

  .o {
    text-decoration: overline;
  }

</style>

<p>
  <q>I thought we went <span class="o">over</span> this,</q> said Captain Steward.
</p>
```

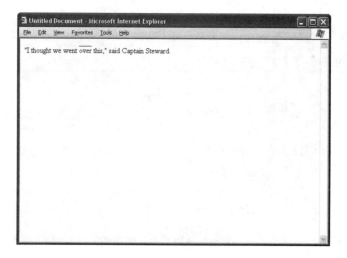

Figure 44.1

Use CSS to create overlines instead of underlines.

You can also render a string of text in small-caps style, which converts lowercase letters in the source code to smaller versions of capital letters in the browser, as in Figure 44.2.

Listing 44.2 **View Source for Figure 44.2.**

```
<style type="text/css">

  .sc {
    font-variant: small-caps;
  }

</style>

<p>
  <span class="sc">The Buck Stops Here.</span> That's what the placard on his desk
said.
</p>
```

Similarly, use the values **capitalize**, **uppercase**, and **lowercase** with the text-transform attribute to alter the sentence casing of the source code. In capitalized text, the first letter of each word displays with a capital letter. Uppercase text becomes all capitals in the browser, and lowercase text becomes all lowercase letters, no matter how the text appears in the source code, as you can see in Figure 44.3.

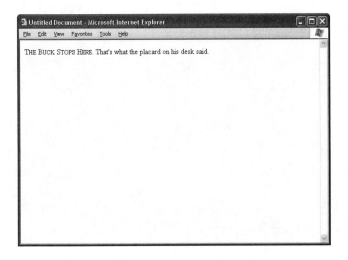

Figure 44.2

Convert lowercase letters in the source code to small caps in the browser.

Change sentence casing with the values of the text-transform attribute.

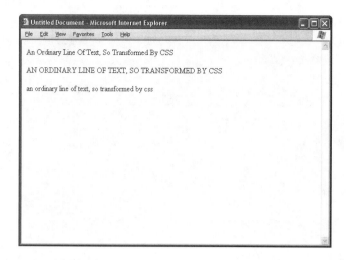

Listing 44.3 View Source for Figure 44.3.

```
<p style="text-transform: capitalize;">an ordinary line of text, so transformed by
CSS</p>

<p style="text-transform: uppercase;">an ordinary line of text, so transformed by
CSS</p>

<p style="text-transform: lowercase;">an ordinary line of text, so transformed by
CSS</p>
```

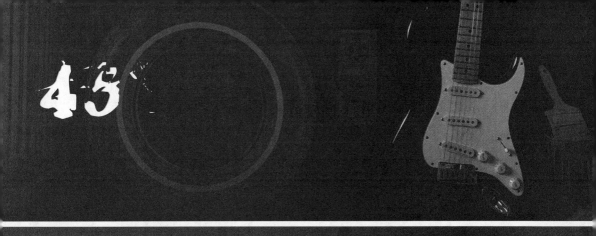

45

Changing the Look of a Text Element

n CSS, the simplest style selector is just the name of an HTML tag. The style definition for this simple selector determines how the browser displays the element wherever it appears on the page:

```
h1 {
  font-family: Arial;
  font-weight: bold;
}

p {
  font-family: Verdana;
}
```

So it goes for redefining the generic appearance of HTML text tags. But CSS allows you to choose much more specific selectors for entire sequences of tags to get precisely the typographical effect you have in mind, as Table 45.1 shows.

Defining Contextual Selectors

A **contextual selector** is a style selector that identifies all HTML tags of a particular type that appear somewhere within the tag of another type. You use this kind of selector to style all emphasis tags that appear inside a table, for instance,

Table 45.1 CSS Selectors for HTML Tags

SELECTOR	DESCRIPTION	EXAMPLE SYNTAX	EXAMPLE DESCRIPTION
Simple	All HTML tags of a type	p	All paragraphs
Contextual	All HTML tags of a type that are somewhere within a tag of another type	table em	All emphasis tags that appear somewhere inside a table
Child*	All HTML tags of a type that have as their immediate parent a tag of another type	td > p	All paragraphs that have table cells as their immediate parents
Sibling*	All HTML tags of a type that follow a tag of another type but aren't the children of this other tag	h1 + p	All paragraphs that immediately follow first-level heads

* These selectors don't always work very well in IE.

GEEKSPEAK

A contextual selector is a style selector that identifies all HTML tags of a particular type that appear somewhere within the tag of another type, such as all strong tags that appear inside an ordered list.

or all strong tags that appear inside an ordered list. In these examples, the browser ignores emphasis tags that don't appear in a table or strong tags that don't appear in an ordered list, unless of course you provide additional style rules for these instances.

The syntax for this type of selector looks something like this:

```
container-tag target-tag
```

As you can see, you separate the tag names with a singe space. So, to define a style for all strong tags that appear somewhere inside an ordered list, the style rule looks something like this:

```
ol strong {
    font-style: italic;
}
```

The browser displays only those strong tags that appear inside an ordered list in type that is both bold *and* italic. Why bold, you might wonder, when the style doesn't mention anything about boldface? Because, by default, browsers

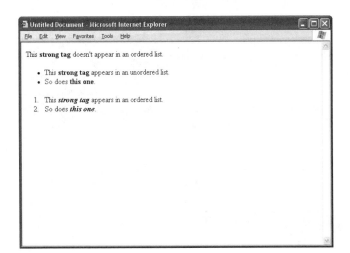

Figure 45.1

With a contextual selector, only those strong tags that appear inside an ordered list get the additional styling.

give strong tags the bold treatment. The rest of the strong tags on the page simply display as bold, without the extra enhancement of italics, as in Figure 45.1.

You can get really picky with contextual selectors. Say you want to style only those emphasis tags that appear inside paragraph tags that appear inside table cells that appear inside div elements:

```
div td p em {
    font-weight: bold;
}
```

The browser follows your instructions to the letter, as Figure 45.2 shows.

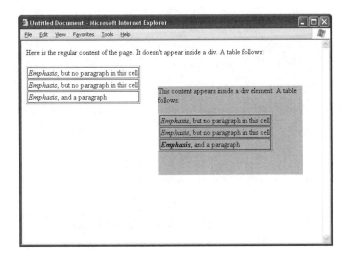

Figure 45.2

String a number of tags together for a very specific contextual selector. This style only affects emphasis tags inside paragraph tags inside table cells inside div elements.

Defining Child Selectors

A **child selector** is a style selector that identifies all HTML tags of a particular type that have as their immediate parent a tag of another type, like all paragraphs that are the immediate children of table cells. If the tag in question is not the immediate child of the parent tag, your style rule doesn't apply.

The syntax for this type of selector looks like this:

```
parent-tag > child-tag
```

Separate the tag names with the greater-than sign (>). The following style rule affects only those paragraphs that appear inside table cells:

```
td > p {
    font-weight: bold;
}
```

The browser leaves all other paragraphs alone, as in Figure 45.3.

The exact genealogy of a tag is important here. For a child selector to work, the tag in question must be the **immediate** child of the parent. So, a style rule that looks like this:

```
td > em {
    font-weight: bold;
}
```

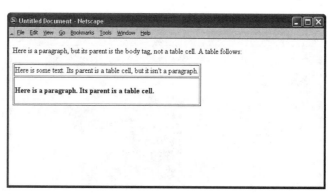

Figure 45.3

With a child selector, the browser selects only those tags of a particular type that have as their immediate parents the tags of another type. In this case, only paragraphs that are the children of table cells turn bold.

has no effect on the following block of HTML:

```
<td>
  <p>This is a paragraph with <em>emphasis</em>.</p>
</td>
```

but works correctly here:

```
<td>
  This is unformatted text with <em>emphasis</em>.
</td>
```

Why? In the first case, the immediate child of the table cell is the paragraph tag, not the emphasis tag. Sure, the table cell is the grandparent of the emphasis tag, but that's not the way a child selector works. The emphasis tag has to be the immediate child of the parent tag, as in the second case.

To affect all emphasis tags inside table cells regardless of the exact genealogy, use a contextual selector instead:

```
td em {
  font-weight: bold;
}
```

This style rule applies to both previous cases, since, in both cases, the emphasis tag is somewhere inside a table cell.

Back to child selectors: You can give an entire tag genealogy as the selector to get really specific results. This style rule only selects emphasis tags that are the children of h1 tags that are the children of table cells:

```
td > h1 > em {
  font-weight: bold;
}
```

Defining Sibling Selectors

A **sibling selector** is a style selector that identifies all HTML tags of a particular type that follow a tag of another type but aren't the children of this tag. Consider a paragraph tag that follows a first-level head inside a table cell. The paragraph isn't the child of the header, since the paragraph tag doesn't appear inside the header tag. These tags are siblings instead, like brother and sister. Their common parent is the table cell that encloses them both:

```
<td>
  <!-- This table cell is the proud parent of these two children. -->
  <h1>I am the older sibling. I am way too serious for my own good.</h1>
  <p>I am the younger sibling. I always get my own way.</p>
</td>
```

GEEKSPEAK

A **sibling selector** is a style selector that identifies all HTML tags of a particular type that follow a tag of another type but aren't the children of this tag, like all paragraphs that follow first-level heads.

So to select all paragraphs that follow first-level headers, use this syntax:

```
older-sibling + younger-sibling
```

for a style rule that looks like this:

```
h1 + p {
  font-weight: bold;
}
```

Paragraphs that follow first-level heads display in boldface, while other kinds of paragraphs don't, as Figure 45.4 shows.

Notice that the second paragraph under the first-level head doesn't acquire the boldface style. Why? Because, technically, this paragraph follows a paragraph, not a first-level head. A sibling selector only selects the tag immediately after it, and then only when the second tag isn't the child of the first tag. So the following style rule:

```
td + em {
  font-weight: bold;
}
```

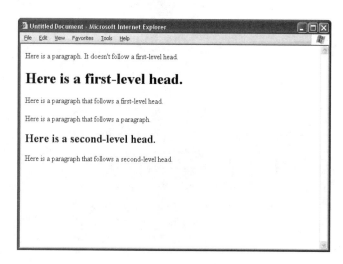

Figure 45.4

Use a sibling selector to affect tags that follow other tags but aren't the children of these tags.

has no effect on the following block of HTML:

```
<td>
  This is unformatted text with <em>emphasis</em>.
</td>
```

As with the other selectors, you can get super-anal about your level of precision. This style rule affects only those paragraphs that follow fourth-level heads that follow third-level heads that follow second-level heads that follow first-level heads:

```
h1 + h2 + h3 + h4 + p {
  font-weight: bold;
}
```

Mixing It Up

CSS is flexible enough to apply the same style definition to multiple selectors of different types. Simply separate the selectors with commas. Take this example:

```
p, h1, h2 + h3, td > strong {
  color: #FF0000;
}
```

This style rule applies to all paragraphs, all first-level heads, all third-level-head siblings of second-level heads, and all strong-tag children of table cells. It turns all these elements red.

The following style sheet has the same effect, but it isn't nearly as concise:

```
p {
  color: #FF0000;
}

h1 {
  color: #FF0000;
}

h2 + h3 {
  color: #FF0000;
}
```

```
td > strong {
  color: #FF0000;
}
```

By all means, use the long form if it helps you to keep the styles straight in your head. But once you get accustomed to the ways of CSS, remember that you can write very efficient style rules without sacrificing precision.

46

Defining Class Styles

You saw in Topic 45 about how to redefine the appearance of HTML tags with great precision. But what happens if you need a style that doesn't necessarily apply to any particular HTML tag or logical sequence of tags? Never fear. CSS, like the Buddha, provides. Simply define your own style selector, called a **class**.

A typical class style rule looks something like this:

```
.bolditalic {
  font-weight: bold;
  font-style: italic;
}
```

Come up with a name for your class, and put a period in front of it, as in **.bolditalic** in the preceding code. Then, just write the style definition. It's as easy as that.

A CSS class is kind of like a club that any HTML tag can join, but membership is by invitation only. To invite an HTML tag into the club, fill out the tag's class attribute, as in the Listing 46.1.

GEEKSPEAK

A **class** is a custom-made style selector that doesn't necessarily apply to any particular HTML tag or sequence of tags.

TIP

When you fill in the class attribute of an HTML tag, don't include the period at the beginning of the class name. Just give the name.

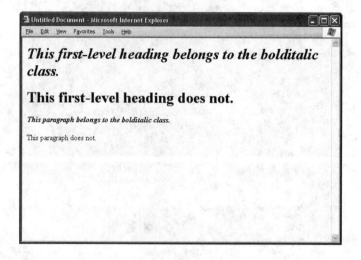

Listing 46.1 **View Source for Figure 46.1.**

```
<style type="text/css">

.bolditalic {
  font-weight: bold;
  font-style: italic;
}

</style>

<h1 class="bolditalic">This first-level heading belongs to the bolditalic
class.</h1>

<h1>This first-level heading does not.</h1>

<p class="bolditalic">This paragraph belongs to the bolditalic class.</p>

<p>This paragraph does not.</p>
```

The Listing 46.1 reveals a couple of interesting things. First, you can use your class style on any type of tag. Remember, a class is like a club that any tag can join. Second, the class style doesn't override the default appearance of the tags in your browser, unless the style directly contradicts the browser's default. First-level heads are bold by default, so your h1 tag that belongs to the club simply turns italic; it's already bold. If the class style had specified the font weight as normal, then the h1 tag would appear in normal type, not bold, since the style definition contradicts the browser's default choice of boldface.

GEEKSPEAK
A span is a segment of content identified by span tags in an HTML document.

Now consider this paragraph:

`<p>This paragraph contains text that belongs to the bolditalic class.</p>`

How can you make just the word **text** join the bolditalic club? You can't define the class attribute of the paragraph tag, since all the text in the paragraph would turn bold and italic, not just the word **text**. What you need for the job is a cunningly placed span tag:

`<p>This paragraph contains <span>text</span> that belongs to the bolditalic class.</p>`

The span tag has no visible effect in the browser window. Its sole purpose is to mark off a segment or **span** of content. Now that you have a tag in exactly the right place, you can ask the span to join the club:

`<p>This paragraph contains <span class="bolditalic">text</span> that belongs to the bolditalic class.</p>`

See the results in Figure 46.2.

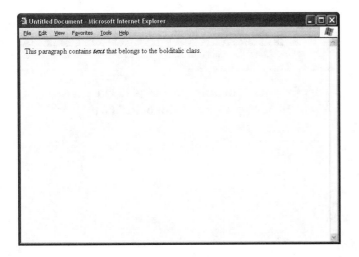

Figure 46.2
If you don't have a tag in the right place, put the span tag exactly where you need it, and then bring the span into your class style.

Forming an Exclusive Club

If regular class styles are like clubs that any tag can join, then you can also define exclusive clubs that only tags of a particular type can join. For instance, you can create a class style that doesn't affect all paragraphs in a document but only those paragraphs that belong to the class. First-level headers, second-level headers, and all the rest can't belong to the class unless you add them to the style selector.

Such a style rule looks like this:

```
p.bolditalic {
  font-weight: bold;
  font-style: italic;
}
```

See Figure 46.3 for an example of this style in action.

Listing 46.2 View Source for Figure 46.3.

```
<p class="bolditalic">Only paragraphs can join the p.bolditalic class.</p>

<p>This paragraph opts not to join, so it doesn't enjoy the benefits of member-
ship.</p>

<h1 class="bolditalic">This first-level heading belongs to the class, but it doesn't
get any of the benefits, because it isn't a paragraph.</h1>
```

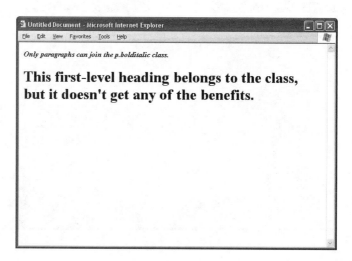

Figure 46.3

By combining a tag selector with a class name, you create a class style to which only tags of that particular type can belong.

As you can see, nothing is stopping the h1 tag from trying to join the class, but the browser flat-out ignores it, since it isn't a paragraph. Of course, the browser still displays the first-level header in bold, but that's just because these elements appear in bold by default. The boldface here has nothing to do with the style sheet.

TIP
When you fill out the class attribute, don't include the tag selector in the name of a tag-specific class. Just type the name of the class.

TIP
Any type of tag selector—simple, contextual, child, or sibling—can have a special class designation. Just append a period and the name of the class after the selector. See Topic 45 for more information on the types of selectors.

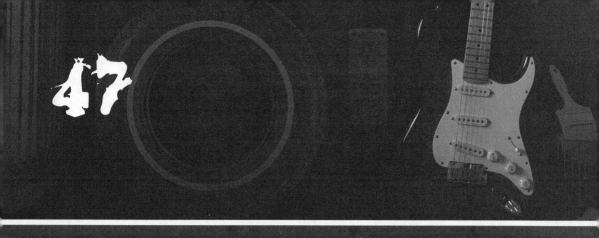

47

Controlling the Typeface

Normally, a browser displays text in its default typeface or font, which is almost always Times New Roman on Windows computers. HTML offers the creaky font tag to let you change the typeface for a particular section of text. The font tag works like this:

```
<p>
  <font face="Arial">This paragraph displays in Arial.</font>
</p>
```

The value of the face attribute is the name of the font that you want to use.

You may play with the position of the font tags to apply the font to several text elements in a row:

```
<font face="Arial">
  <h1>This header displays in Arial.</h1>
  <p>So does this paragraph.</p>
  <p>So does this paragraph.</p>
</font>
```

But now that CSS is here, you don't need the font tag. The font-family attribute performs the same function. You can add it to the style definition of an HTML tag:

```
p {
  font-family: Arial;
}
```

or a class style:

```
.arialtext {
  font-family: Arial;
}
```

CSS makes typeface management easier, too. If you define a style rule so that all paragraphs display in Arial, as in the first CSS example, you can forget about those annoying font tags. Whenever you add a paragraph to your page, it automatically displays in Arial.

It gets better. Let's say you want all the text on a page to display in Arial. Simply put the font-family attribute in the style rule for the body tag:

```
body {
  font-family: Arial;
}
```

TIP

If the name of a font contains multiple words, like **Times New Roman** or **Courier New**, make sure you put the name in quotes in the CSS style definition.

Troubleshooting Fonts

For both the font tag and the font-family attribute to work properly, the visitor's computer must have the font that you specify. It doesn't matter if your computer has the font. The visitor's computer is the one that matters.

So, how do you know which fonts are on your visitor's computer? The short answer is, you don't. But don't let that stop you from making some educated guesses. All typical personal computers come with standard fonts. The typefaces in Table 47.1 are almost always safe choices. See also Figure 47.1.

To minimize your risk further, you may specify a range of typeface preferences in the font tag or font-family CSS attribute. Simply give your preferences in order, and separate font names with commas:

```
<font face="Arial, Helvetica, sans-serif">
```

or:

```
body {
  font-family: Arial, Helvetica, sans-serif;
}
```

GEEKSPEAK

A **sans serif** typeface such as Arial doesn't have little decorations on the ends of the letters. A **serif** typeface such as Times New Roman does. A **monospace** typeface such as Courier New displays typewriter-style text, where all the characters and symbols have the same amount of spacing between them.

	Table 47.1 **Safe Typefaces for Web Pages**	
WINDOWS FONT	MACINTOSH EQUIVALENT	CATEGORY
Times New Roman	Times	Serif
Arial	Helvetica	Sans serif
Georgia	Times	Serif
Verdana	Geneva	Sans serif
Courier New	Courier	Monospaced

In these cases, the browser first tries to render the text in Arial. If the visitor's computer doesn't have Arial, it goes to Helvetica. If the browser strikes out there, too, it renders the text in its default sans serif font, whatever that font happens to be.

TIP

A smart list of font preferences goes like this: Begin with the Windows font, follow with the Mac equivalent, and end with the generic font category: **serif**, **sans-serif**, or **monospace**.

If you want to use a more exotic typeface on your page, list that font as your first preference, but follow it with one of the safe fonts from Table 47.1, just in case.

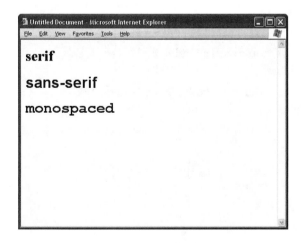

Figure 47.1

A serif font has decorations on the ends of the letters, while a sans serif font doesn't. In a monospaced font, all the letters use the same spacing, typewriter-style.

TIP

At the end of a list of font preferences, always include **serif**, **sans-serif**, or **mono**, depending on what kind of font you'd like to display. These three generic fonts don't stand for any one specific typeface. Rather, they correspond to the visitor's default serif, sans serif, and monospaced fonts, whatever these fonts happen to be.

Invoking the generic fonts is a failsafe choice. If all else goes wrong with your selections, at least you can guarantee that the broad category of the typeface is the same.

Choosing the Best Typeface

Any book designer will tell you that typeface has a great deal to do with conveying the character of the book. If the book is supposed be a serious, authoritative examination of a weighty topic or a carefree, lighthearted pleasure-read, the designer tries to choose a typeface that visually suggests a similar mood or feeling. Not too many books about the Hegelian philosophy have been done up in comic book lettering. Also, the size of the text helps the designer choose the right typeface. Some kinds of type work well at small sizes because they're more legible, while others work better in larger sizes for the same reason.

Having said that, Web typography isn't nearly as complex as the print equivalent. There are far fewer typefaces from which to choose, and there aren't as many variables, even in a robust language like CSS, which narrows your design options but, at the same time, makes choosing the best typeface fairly straightforward.

Here are a few rules of thumb:

- Serif fonts such as Times New Roman work best for Web sites with serious, sober content.

- Sans serif fonts such as Arial work best for Web sites with lighter, more playful content.

- Serif fonts at regular sizes tend to be easier to read when you have long passages of text.

- A wide typeface such as Verdana or Georgia works best at small type sizes. At larger type sizes, these fonts tend to be too big.

- Sans serif fonts generally work better than serif fonts for headings.

Controlling Type Size

n Topic 47, you saw how the font tag in HTML and the font-family attribute in CSS allow you to set the typeface of a Web page. Along similar lines, you can set the size of the type in the size attribute of the font tag or the font-size attribute of CSS.

Using the Font Tag

The font tag's size attribute looks something like this:

```
<font face="Arial, Helvetica, sans-serif" size="4">
```

The value in the size attribute isn't pixels, points, picas, inches, feet, millimeters, or miles. Instead, it corresponds to one of seven predefined text sizes in HTML. Normal text on a Web page displays at size 3. So this text, at size 4, is one size larger. The smallest text is size 1, and the largest is size 7, as Figure 48.1 demonstrates.

Another possible value for the size attribute is a relative size, where you express the size of the font as some number plus or minus the current size. A relative size looks like this in the HTML:

```
<font face="Arial, Helvetica, sans-serif" size="+1">
```

or

Figure 48.1

When you use the font tag, you have only seven type sizes from which to choose, numbered 1 through 7.

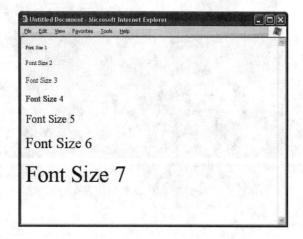

```
<font face="Arial, Helvetica, sans-serif" size="-3">
```

In the first example, the type jumps up one size from whatever size the previous text happens to be, while the type in the second example goes down three sizes. The smallest relative size is –6, and the largest is +6.

Using the Font-Size Attribute

Can I get more than seven HTML type sizes?

Clever Web designers have tried to squeeze additional type sizes out of HTML by setting a font tag to size 7 for starters and then increasing the size with a relative font tag immediately afterward. If this is you, then give yourself a pat on the back for your craftiness, but unfortunately the browser is on to you. The maximum size you can get out of HTML is size 7. The browser ignores relative values that add up to more than 7 (or less than 1).

If seven type sizes seems ridiculous to you, you're not alone. CSS saves the day with virtually unlimited type sizes. Simply add the font-size attribute to your style definition, and supply the value and the units you want to use:

```
p {
    font-family: Arial, Helvetica, sans-serif;
    font-size: 18px;
}
```

Paragraph tags using this style rule appear in the browser as in Figure 48.2.

Table 48.1 summarizes the variety of units for type size that CSS provides. However, be aware that sizing type in the browser is a risky proposition. Since browsers offer somewhat shaky support for CSS, and since no two browsers choke on the same kinds of issues, you're better off using a relative unit for type size. As Table 48.1 shows, the relative units include em, ex, and px; but browsers are

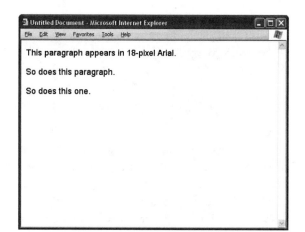

Figure 48.2

With CSS, you may specify any type size in a variety of units.

notorious for butchering the em and ex units, which leaves you with good old pixels as the only real alternative.

A relative unit isn't relative in the sense that the value changes. Instead, the actual size of the unit changes depending on a number of factors. For instance, screen resolution determines the size of a pixel. If your machine displays at 800 pixels by 600 pixels, then your pixels are larger than someone's whose machine displays at 1600 by 1200 pixels, assuming you both have the same size monitor screen.

Relative units allow the browser to accommodate the visitor's particular screen setting. If you use absolute units instead, like points, picas, or inches,

Table 48.1 **CSS Length Units**		
UNIT	SIGNIFIES	CATEGORY
cm	Centimeters	Absolute
em	Ems; 1 em is roughly the width of the capital letter M	Relative
ex	X-heights; 1 ex is roughly the height of the lowercase letter x	Relative
in	Inches	Absolute
mm	Millimeters	Absolute
pc	Picas	Absolute
pt	Points	Absolute
px	Pixels	Relative

your page is at the mercy of the browser to determine exactly how big an inch is on screen. Not surprisingly, in older browsers especially, the computer's reasoning is not so good, and your visitor may end up with illegibly small text and no way to resize it.

Using Length Constants in CSS

If type sizing with relative or absolute units leaves you cold because of the potential problems, you may substitute one of seven CSS length constants. You guessed it: These constants are roughly equivalent to the seven type sizes of HTML, as in Figure 48.3, so you're back to the sizing game, but at least this way you don't give the browser as much of a chance to render your page illegibly.

The seven length constants are **xx-small**, **x-small**, **small**, **medium**, **large**, **x-large**, and **xx-large**. You put one of these keywords in place of the number and units in a style definition, like so:

```
p {
   font-size: x-large;
}
```

You may also specify a relative length constant to adjust the size of type according to the current type size, whatever that happens to be. Use **larger** to make the type one size larger, or use **smaller** to make the type one size smaller:

```
<p style="font-size: x-large;">
   This type size is x-large, but <span style="font-size: smaller;">this type size is
one size smaller.</span>
</p>
```

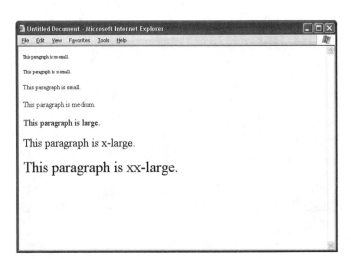

Figure 48.3

When in doubt, CSS gives you seven length constants that correspond roughly to the seven type sizes of HTML.

BLOG: Sizing up Type Sizing

ifferent people come at the problem of CSS type sizes differently. Some tell you never to size type, period. Others tell you to stick to the length constants. Still others suggest that sizing is all right as long as you use relative units.

Based on the overwhelming number of people surfing the Web with more or less recent browsers, it seems that type sizing with relative units is safe enough for general-purpose Web sites. This conclusion assumes that most Web surfing happens by way of Microsoft Internet Explorer on Windows desktop or laptop computers. This isn't a product endorsement. It's simply a fact of life. The last couple of versions of IE for Windows handle CSS pixel units pretty well, so the problem is, for all practical purposes, solved. However, if you expect a larger-than-usual proportion of visitors coming to your site with wireless phones, PDAs, Macintoshes, Netscapes, or older Windows browsers, you would be wise to heed the warnings of the more conservative type-sizers among us.

The first goal of a Web site is to present content. This content must be accessible and usable, and therefore it must be legible. Any aesthetic or design concerns must always defer to usability, no matter how it pains your inner arteest.

Of course, the correlation between effective design and usability is not trivial. You'll find no argument here about that. But it's one thing to strive for an effective and intuitive graphical layout, and it's another to split hairs over online typography. So if type sizing has to go to make your site more usable to more of your audience, then go it must.

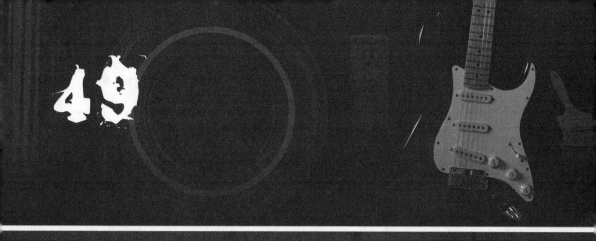

Controlling Spacing

n HTML, the browser pretty much determines the amount of space between elements. It's all built into the browser's understanding of what each tag looks like. Sure, you can force a line break with the br tag, but this method is crude and imprecise. Graphic designers understand that empty or negative space is just as important as occupied or positive space. Space a crucial element of design, and it demands pixel-perfect control. You don't have to build too many Web pages before you start wanting better options for managing space than HTML is willing to provide.

Thank the gods for CSS. It delivers all kinds of space control: space around elements, space inside elements, space between lines of text, space between words, and space between letters. Topic 26 discusses the issue of setting page margins with CSS. This topic looks at other kinds of CSS spacing, particularly as it relates to text.

Controlling Space around Elements

CSS' margin attributes apply to more than just the borders of the page. You can apply margins to any element, thereby adjusting the space around it, as in Figure 49.1.

Figure 49.1

This paragraph has a bottom margin of 200 pixels, which creates a nice chunk of whitespace to separate the paragraph from what comes after.

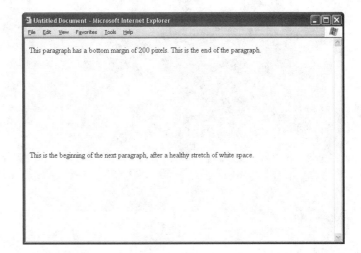

Listing 49.1 **View Source for Figure 49.1.**

```
<p style="margin-bottom: 200px;">This paragraph has a
bottom margin of 200 pixels. This is the end of the
paragraph.</p>

<p>This is the beginning of the next paragraph, after a
healthy stretch of white space.</p>
```

TIP

When you space multiple elements with margins, it's usually a good idea to choose either the top or bottom margin and the left or right margin and stick with your choice consistently for each element's style rule. In other words, don't specify the top margin in one element and the bottom margin in another. This way, you don't run into problems if, say, a 200-pixel bottom margin butts up against a 200-pixel top margin, creating an effective gap of 400 pixels.

There are four margin attributes: margin-top, margin-bottom, margin-left, and margin-right. Each can have a different value and unit (see Topic 48 for a table of valid CSS units). As the View Source for Figure 49.1 shows, you don't have to set all four margin attributes. Just specify the margins you need for proper spacing.

TIP

As a shortcut, feel free to use the generic margin attribute. Supplying a single value for this attribute creates equal margins on all four sides of the element, like this:

```
margin: 200px;
```

You can also give four different values, representing the top, right, bottom, and left margins, respectively, like so:

```
margin: 100 50 200 25px;
```

Controlling Space inside Elements

The padding attributes affect the amount of whitespace between an element's borders and the beginning of the element's content. To get a better idea of how padding works, imagine that every element on screen has its own invisible rectangular box, as in Figure 49.2. Padding adds whitespace between the edge of the box and the content inside.

As with margins, there are four padding attributes: padding-top, padding-bottom, padding-left, and padding-right. You can set each separately, and you can omit the ones that you don't need in your style definition:

```
p {
    padding-top: 20px;
    padding-left: 10px;
}
```

> **TIP**
>
> As with margins, CSS gives you a generic padding attribute. It works the same way: Supply a single value to add equal padding to all four sides, or give four different values for top, right, bottom, and left:
>
> ```
> padding: 20px;
> padding: 10 12 18 8px;
> ```

Controlling Space between Lines of Type

Use the line-height attribute to control the amount of space between lines of type. This trick is handy for improving the legibility of long passages of text, as you can see in Figure 49.3.

The line-height attribute takes a number and a unit for its value, like so:

```
p {
    font-size: 18px;
    line-height: 27px;
}
```

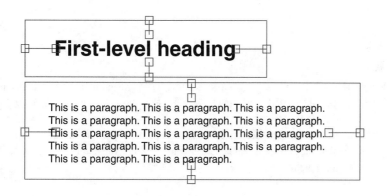

Figure 49.2

Padding determines the amount of whitespace between an element's outer border and the content inside.

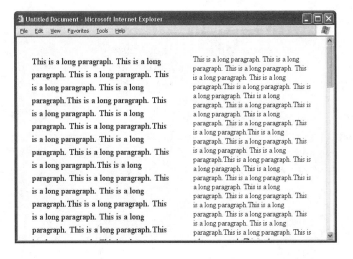

FAQ

Is line-height in CSS the same as leading?

Yes. In the print-publishing game, **leading** is the name for the amount of space between lines of type. In the olden days, when print-shop apprentices needed extra space between lines of type, they physically inserted thin lead plugs. The lead plugs are long gone in modern, electronic typesetting, but the name remains.

Controlling Space between Words

Another way to improve legibility, particularly when you work with small type sizes, is to increase the amount of space between words, as in Figure 49.4.

The attribute for the job is word-spacing. This attribute is different from the others so far in that the browser adds whatever value you give to its default amount of word space. So, the following style definition:

```
word-spacing: 3px;
```

doesn't set the word spacing to 3 pixels, but puts three additional pixels of space between words. Similarly, the style definition:

```
word-spacing: -3px;
```

TIP

When it comes to long passages of on-screen text, a good rule of thumb is to set the line height to one and one-half times the type size. For example, if the type size is 10 pixels, set the line height to 15 pixels.

If you want even more space, try double-spacing, just as you did when you typed your high school book reviews. For double-spacing, multiply the font size by 2, and set this as the line height.

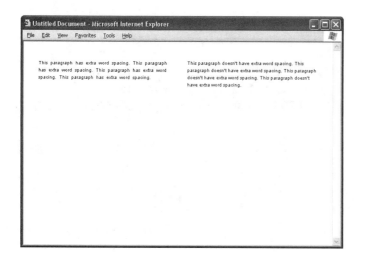

Figure 49.4

Just three pix-els of extra word spacing make the para-graph on the left easier to read.

takes away three pixels of space, making your lines of type tighter. To set word spacing to the browser's default, type this in your style definition:

```
word-spacing: normal;
```

Controlling Space between Letters

Finally, CSS allows you to adjust the amount of space between the letters in an HTML element with the letter-spacing attribute, as Figure 49.5 shows. Like the word-spacing attribute, letter-spacing adds its value to the browser's default, and it accepts negative values to decrease the default amount of space between letters.

In a style definition, letter-spacing looks something like this:

```
letter-spacing: 1px;
```

or, for a net loss in letter space:

```
letter-spacing: -1px;
```

or, for the browser's default amount of letter space:

```
letter-spacing: normal;
```

TIP

In general, large type sizes require less word space, while small type sizes require more. In addition, wide fonts such Verdana often benefit from a little extra word space, while condensed fonts look better with slightly less.

Figure 49.5

Use the letter-spacing attribute to increase (or decrease) the default amount of space between letters in an element.

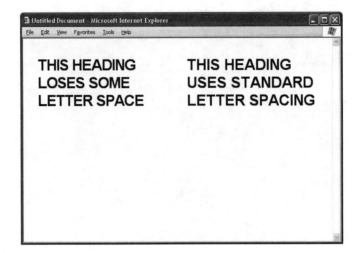

TIP

Increased letter spacing tends to improve the legibility of small type, while decreased letter spacing tends to look better in large type. In addition, typefaces with wide characters tend to like more letter space, while typefaces with narrow characters like less.

Controlling Justified and Ragged Type

Justified lines of type have the same length. To create this effect, the browser pads shorter lines with extra space, as in Figure 50.1.

One way to create justified text in HTML is to set the align attribute of the tag in question to the value **justify**:

```
<p align="justify">This paragraph has justified text.</p>
```

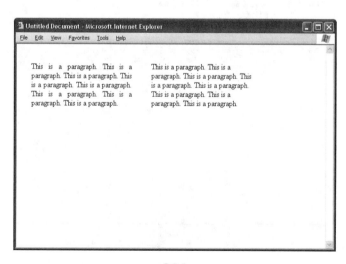

Figure 50.1

The paragraph on the left is justified. In justified type, the browser pads shorter lines with extra space so that they're all the same length.

But CSS makes this method obsolete. Include the text-align CSS attribute in your style definition instead:

```
<p style="text-align: justify;">This paragraph has justified text.</p>
```

A word to the wise: The browser's built-in calculations for justifying text aren't very sophisticated, which often makes justified blocks of type on the Web look pompous in the worst way, worse than the most low-budget local newspaper you've ever seen. When done right, with skill and precision, justification often brings a classy touch to books and other printed material. But ragged type tends to be easier to read on a monitor, and legibility trumps all in onscreen typography.

Speaking of ragged type, there are three kinds: ragged right, ragged left, and ragged center. **Ragged right** type lines up on the left margin, leaving the right side ragged; while **ragged left** lines up on the right margin, leaving the left side ragged. In **ragged center** type, both sides are ragged, and the lines of type appear centered in their block, as Figure 50.2 demonstrates. By default, browsers display ragged right type.

Specifying ragged type is actually counterintuitive, in that the proper value for HTML's align attribute or CSS' text-align attribute is the opposite of

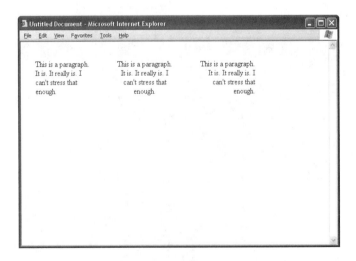

Figure 50.2

The paragraph on the left has ragged right type, while the paragraph in the middle has ragged center type, and the paragraph on the right has ragged left type.

what it should be. For ragged right type, the correct value is **left**, and for ragged left type, the correct value is **right**:

```
<p align="left">This paragraph has ragged right type.</p>
```

```
<p style="text-align: right;">This paragraph has ragged left type. </p>
```

If your mind is twisting, try to think of it in terms of where the text lines up, which is probably how the people who designed HTML and CSS were thinking back in the day. In ragged right type, the text aligns on the left, so, in this sense, **text-align: left;** seems pretty reasonable.

This leaves ragged center type, which takes the value **center**:

```
<p align="center">This paragraph has ragged center type.</p>
```

```
<p style="text-align: center;">This paragraph has ragged center type. </p>
```

51

Controlling Indents

The standard solution to creating an indent with HTML is the blockquote tag, which doesn't make the standards police very happy. Strictly speaking, the purpose of the blockquote tag is to offset a chunk of display text like the quote at the beginning of a scholarly essay, as in Figure 51.1. But you'd be hard pressed to find a more practical, results-oriented bunch than Web designers under deadline constraints. In the fog of rapid production, they drafted the blockquote tag early on to jury-rig page indents, as in Figure 51.2.

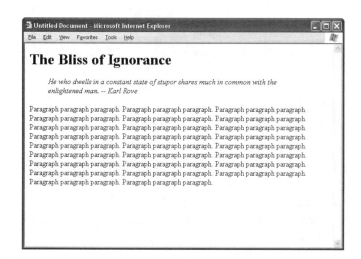

Figure 51.1

The blockquote tag is supposed to offset chunks of display text, like this.

286

Figure 51.2

In the hands of crafty designers, the block-quote tag became the de-facto method for creating page indents, much to the dismay of standards-conscious Web heads.

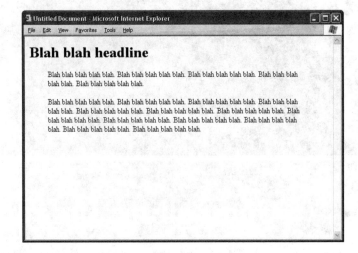

In both cases, the HTML coding is the same. Simply place blockquote tags around the content that you want to indent, like so:

```
<blockquote>
  <p>This paragraph is indented.</p>
  <p>This paragraph is indented.</p>
  <p>This paragraph is indented.</p>
</blockquote>
```

You can also nest blockquote tags to increase the amount of indentation:

```
<blockquote>
  <blockquote>
    <blockquote>
      <p>This paragraph is very indented.</p>
      <p>This paragraph is very indented.</p>
      <p>This paragraph is very indented.</p>
    </blockquote>
  </blockquote>
</blockquote>
```

Notice, though, that you can't control the precise amount of indentation. For each blockquote tag, the browser just pushes the text some distance to the right according to a default setting.

A better solution overall is to use CSS. The margin-left attribute does the job handily, and it gives you the added flexibility of adjusting the precise amount of indentation, as Figure 51.3 shows.

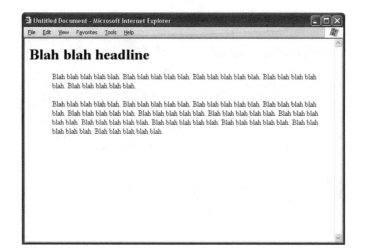

Figure 51.3

You're better off creating indents with CSS. This way, you can specify the precise amount of indentation.

Listing 51.1 **View Source for Figure 51.3.**

```
<head>
  <style type="text/css">

    p {
      margin-left: 50px;
    }

  </style>
</head>

<body>
  <h1>Blah blah headline</h1>

  <p>Blah blah blah....</p>

  <p>Blah blah blah....</p>
</body>
```

CSS does you one better, too. It allows you to specify additional indentation for the first line of any text element, be it a paragraph, a heading, or what have you. The attribute responsible is text-indent, and it works as in Figure 51.4.

Figure 51.4

*Use the text-
indent attribute
to indent the
first line of any
text element.*

Figure 51.4

*Use the text-
indent attribute
to indent the
first line of any
text element.*

Listing 51.2 **View Source for Figure 51.4.**

```
<head>
  <style type="text/css">

    p {
      text-indent: 30px;
    }

  </style>
</head>

<body>
  <h1>Blah blah headline</h1>

  <p>Blah blah blah....</p>
</body>
```

Notice that the second and subsequent lines of text fall along the left margin of the element. The text-indent attribute only affects the first line of text. In the View Source for Figure 51.4, the value of 30 pixels is 30 pixels of **additional** indentation. So, if the style rule for a paragraph had been:

```
p {
  margin-left: 50px;
```

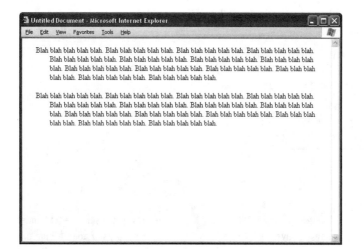

Figure 51.5

To create a hanging indent, establish a standard left margin for the block of text, and then set the text-indent attribute to a negative value.

```
    text-indent: 30px;
}
```

the total actual indentation in the first line of type is 80 pixels, or 50 + 30. In the second and subsequent lines of type, the indentation jumps back to 50 pixels.

Which segues nicely into an interesting CSS trick: creating a hanging indent. A **hanging indent** is like a paragraph indent in reverse: The first line of type pushes out to the left from a block of text, not in to the right. The first line seems to hang in midair beyond the left border of the block of type, hence the name.

To create a hanging indent, first set the left margin of the text element to some value, say 50 pixels. Then set the text indent to a negative value, like –30 pixels. See Figure 51.5 for the results. The first line of type shoots 30 pixels further left than the standard left margin of 50 pixels.

GEEKSPEAK

A hanging indent is a paragraph indent in reverse. The first line of type pushes out to the left, not in to the right.

Listing 51.3 **View Source for Figure 51.5.**

```
<head>
  <style type="text/css">

    p {
      margin-left: 50px;
      text-indent: -30px;
    }
```

```
    </style>
  </head>

  <body>
    <p>Blah blah blah...</p>

    <p>Blah blah blah....</p>
  </body>
```

TIP

In a hanging indent, if your left margin has a value of x, make sure the text-indent attribute doesn't have a value smaller than –x. In other words, if your left margin is 50 pixels, don't give –80 pixels as the length for the first-line indent, or you'll push your hanging indent off the left side of the page.

52

Building Lists

In HTML, there are two kinds of lists: ordered (or numbered) lists and unordered (or bulleted) lists. The markup for a list begins with either the ol or ul tag for ordered and unordered lists, respectively, followed by a series of li tags for each item in the list. See Figure 52.1 for examples of both types of lists.

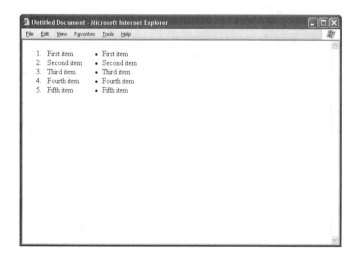

Figure 52.1

In HTML, you get ordered (numbered) and unordered (bulleted) lists. The markup is the same, except for the list tag.

Listing 52.1 **View Source for Figure 52.1.**

```
<table>
  <tr>
    <td>

<!-- Ordered list begins here -->

      <ol>
        <li>First item</li>
        <li>Second item</li>
        <li>Third item</li>
        <li>Fourth item</li>
        <li>Fifth item</li>
      </ol>

<!-- Ordered list ends here -->

    </td>
    <td>

<!-- Unordered list begins here -->

      <ul>
        <li>First item</li>
        <li>Second item</li>
        <li>Third item</li>
        <li>Fourth item</li>
        <li>Fifth item</li>
      </ul>

<!-- Unordered list ends here -->

    </td>
  </tr>
</table>
```

As you can see, the HTML code for the lists is exactly the same, with the exception of the list tag. Therefore, changing an ordered list to an unordered list is a simple matter of changing the ul tag to an ol tag.

Notice also that you don't have to type the numbers in an ordered list. The browser keeps track of them for you and displays them automatically.

Table 52.1 **HTML List Attributes**

ATTRIBUTE	APPLIES TO	CONTROLS	POSSIBLE VALUES	EXAMPLES
type	ol	The leading character	A (capitalized alphabetical), a (lowercase alphabetical), I (capitalized Roman numeral), i (lowercase Roman numeral), 1 (decimal)	`<ol type="A">` `<ol type="i">`
type	ul	The shape of the bullet	circle (hollow), disc (solid), square	`<ul type="circle">` `<ul type="square">`
start	ol	The starting number or letter in the list	Any numeric*	`<ol start="4">`

* In ordered lists other than standard decimal numbered lists, the start attribute indicates the **n**th value in the sequence. So an alphabetical list with a start value of 4 begins with the letter D, since D is the fourth letter of the alphabet. Likewise, a list with Roman numerals begins with X (ten) when the start value equals 10.

In a surprise turn of events for the topics in this section, HTML gives you a number of handy attributes for controlling list appearance. Table 52.1 summarizes them.

Nesting Lists in HTML

Nested lists are lists that appear inside other lists. In HTML markup, a nested list takes the place of a list item, like so:

```
<ol>
  <li>First item of the main list</li>
  <li>Second item of the main list</li>
  <li>Third item of the main list</li>

<!-- Here comes the nested list -->

  <ol>
    <li>First item of the nested list</li>
    <li>Second item of the nested list</li>
    <li>Third item of the nested list</li>
  </ol>
```

```
<!-- There went the nested list -->

  <li>Fourth item of the main list</li>
  <li>Fifth item of the main list</li>
</ol>
```

You may nest list within lists within lists if you so choose:

```
<ul>
  <li>First item of the main list</li>
  <li>Second item of the main list</li>
  <li>Third item of the main list</li>

<!-- Here comes the nested list -->

  <ul>
    <li>First item of the nested list</li>
    <li>Second item of the nested list</li>

<!-- Here comes a nested list within the nested list -->

    <ul>
      <li>First item of the very nested list</li>
      <li>Second item of the very nested list</li>
    </ul>

<!-- There went the nested list within the nested list -->

    <li>Third item of the nested list</li>
  </ul>

<!-- There went the nested list -->

  <li>Fourth item of the main list</li>
  <li>Fifth item of the main list</li>
</ul>
```

GEEKSPEAK

Nested lists are lists that appear inside other lists.

When you nest unordered lists, the browser typically cycles through the bullet types for each successive nested list. So, if you start the list with a disc (filled) bullet, a nested list gets the circle (hollow) bullet, a nested list within the nested list gets the square

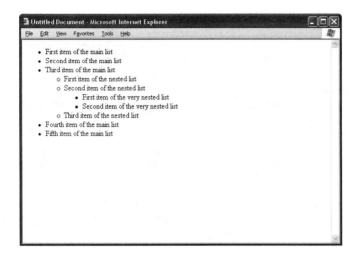

bullet, and a nested list within the nested list within the nested list gets the disc again, and so on, as Figure 52.2 shows.

TIP

You don't get the same treatment with ordered lists. To create an outline effect with an ordered list, you must explicitly set the type attribute for each nested list—or whip up a style sheet. See the Toolkit at the end of this topic for details.

Adjusting List Properties with CSS

Cascading Style Sheets introduce a few extra list-formatting possibilities, as Table 52.2 shows.

Replacing Bullets with an Image

Probably the most fun of these attributes is list-style-image, which allows you to specify an image file instead of a standard disc, circle, or square bullet, as in Figure 52.3.

Changing the Position of the Leading Character

The list-style-position attribute determines where the bullet or leading character appears in relation to the list items. Setting this attribute to **outside** hangs the leading character outside the main block of the list, while setting list-style-position to **inside** brings the character inside the main block, as in Figure 52.4.

Table 52.2 CSS List Attributes

ATTRIBUTE	CONTROLS	POSSIBLE VALUES	EXAMPLE

list-style-image	The image to display in place of a bullet or leading character	url(*imagepath*), none	ul {
			   list-style-image: url(../images/bullet.gif);
			}

list-style-position	The position of the bullet or leading character in relation to the list items	inside, outside	ol {
			   list-style-position: inside;
			}

list-style-type	The type of bullet or leading character to display	disc, circle, square, decimal, lower-roman, uppper-roman, lower-alpha, upper-alpha, none	ol {
			   list-style-type: lower-roman;
			}

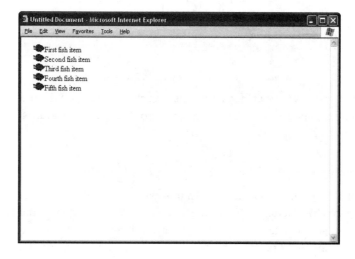

Figure 52.3

Use the list-style-image attribute to replace standard bullets with your own image file.

Listing 52.2 **View Source for Figure 52.3.**

```
<head>
  <style type="text/css">

    ul {
      list-style-image: url(images/fish.gif);
    }

  </style>
</head>

<body>
  <ul>
    <li>First fish item</li>
    <li>Second fish item</li>
    <li>Third fish item</li>
    <li>Fourth fish item</li>
    <li>Fifth fish item</li>
  </ul>
</body>
```

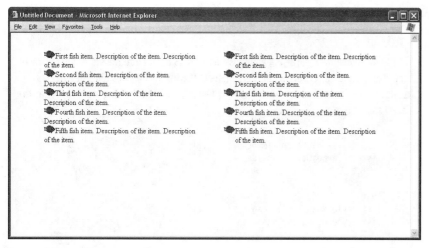

Figure 52.4

Use the list-style-position attribute to determine where the bullet or leading character appears in relation to the list items. The list on the left has a value of **inside** *for this attribute, while the list on the right has a value of* **outside**.

```
<style type="text/css">

/* First, change the bullet of all ul tags, regardless of class. */

  ul {
    list-style-image: url(images/fish.gif);
  }

/* Now, define classes for the values of list-style-position. */

  ul.in {
    list-style-position: inside;
  }

  ul.out {
    list-style-position: outside;
  }

</style>
```

TIP

The View Source for Figure 52.4 employs a handy CSS trick. First, the style rule for the ul tag changes the bullets of all unordered lists to the fish image. Two tag-specific class styles follow, one for each value of list-style-position. The following style sheet has the exact same effect:

```
  ul.in {
    list-style-image: url(images/fish.gif);
    list-style-position: inside;
  }

  ul.out {
    list-style-image: url(images/fish.gif);
    list-style-position: inside;
  }
```

The advantage to writing the style sheet as in Figure 52.4 is that you don't have to repeat yourself with the list-style-image attribute. Instead, you give it once, in the global redefinition of the tag. The two classes simply fine-tune this general style.

Redefining the Browser's Default List Type

The list-style-type attribute is handy for redefining the ol and ul HTML tags so that you don't have to keep setting the individual type attributes for every list on your page:

```
ul {
  list-style-type: square;
}
```

A page with this style rule automatically formats all unordered lists with the square bullet.

TIP

To create a "nude" list without bullets or leading characters of any kind, set the list-style-type attribute to none in the style definition for that list.

TOOL KIT.

Creating an Automatic Outline Style for Ordered Lists

When you nest ordered lists, HTML doesn't cycle through list types to give you an outline effect like it typically does for unordered lists.

A simple style sheet remedies this oversight (see Figure 52.5). Place this style sheet between style tags in the head section of your HTML page, or copy it exactly as it is and save it in an external CSS file.

Figure 52.5

This outline style sheet automatically displays nested ordered lists in outline format.

How many levels can I add to my outline?

This style sheet works with outlines up to five levels deep. If your outline extends beyond five levels, the browser reverts to normal list numbering. You can counter this effect by adding style rules for as many outline levels as you want, following the pattern that the existing style rules establish.

```
/* Order the first level of the outline with capital Roman numerals (I,
II, III, etc.). */

ol {
  list-style-type: upper-roman;
}

/* The second level of the outline is a nested list, or an ol tag
somewhere inside another ol tag. A contextual selector does the job. */

ol ol {

/* Order the second level of the outline with capital letters (A, B, C,
etc.). */

  list-style-type: upper-alpha;
}

/* The third level of the outline is a nested list within a nested list,
or an ol tag somewhere inside another ol tag somewhere inside another ol
tag. You need another contextual selector. */

ol ol ol {

/* Order the third level of the outline with decimal numbers (1, 2, 3,
etc.). */

  list-style-type: decimal;
}
```

```
/* The fourth level of the outline is a nested list within a nested list
within a nested list, or four ol tags deep. */

ol ol ol ol {

/* Order the fourth level of the outline with lowercase letters (a, b, c,
etc.). */

  list-style-type: lower-alpha;
}

/* The fifth level of the outline is a nested list within a nested list
within a nested list within a nested list, or five ol tags deep. */

ol ol ol ol ol {

/* Order the fifth level of the outline with lowercase Roman numerals (i,
ii, iii, etc.). */

  list-style-type: lower-roman;
}
```

TIP

If you feel like tinkering, use CSS to adjust the spacing of the li elements and the margins of the ol tag to create a more attractive presentation.

53

Highlighting Text with Color

n Topic 5, you saw how to set the default text color of a Web page along with the default background color and link colors. This topic looks at how to change the color of specific text elements or pieces of text within an element without affecting the default text color.

If you're one of those diehard Web designers who insist on using the font tag, you'll be happy to know that the color property of this tag does the job:

```
<font face="Arial, Helvetica, sans-serif" color="#FF0000">
  <h3>Note</h3>
  <p>You <strong>must</strong> supply your current email address.</p>
</font>
```

Just as the typeface of the font tag applies to all the text elements nested inside it, the font color also applies. In the preceding example, both the h3 tag and the paragraph tag acquire the color red (#FF0000), no matter what the default text color of the page happens to be.

You can achieve the same effect with the color attribute of CSS:

```
<h3 style="color: #FF0000;">Note</h3>
<p style="color: #FF0000;">You <strong>must</strong> supply your current email
address.</p>
```

FAQ

What, exactly, am I coloring when I add a background color to a text element?

When you set the background-color attribute of a text element, you are actually coloring its **block**, or the rectangular area in which the text element sits. Normally, this block is transparent.

If you need to change the color of a string of text within an element, either nest font tags inside the element:

```
<p>Roses are <font color="#FF0000">red</font>, and violets
are <font color="#0000FF">blue</font>.</p>
```

or, for CSS, drop span tags around the text that you want to color:

```
<p>Roses are <span style="color: #FF0000;">red</span>, and
violets are <span style="color: #0000FF;">blue</span>.</p>
```

CSS also gives you the ability to color the background area of a text element, creating an effect like a highlighter pen, as you can see in Figure 53.1.

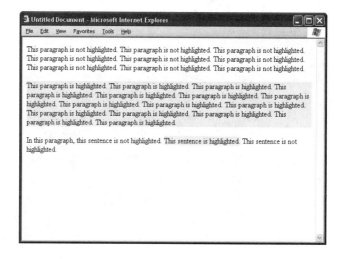

Figure 53.1

CSS is as good as any high-lighter pen.

Listing 53.1 **View Source for Figure 53.1.**

```
<p>This paragraph is not highlighted....</p>

<p style="background-color: #FFFF00;">This paragraph is highlighted....</p>

<p>In this paragraph, this sentence is not highlighted. <span style="background-
color: #FFFF00;">This sentence is highlighted.</span> This sentence is not high-
lighted.</p>
```

Changing the background color in this fashion usually makes more sense than changing the color of the type itself. You aren't as likely to trick your visitors into thinking that the text is a hyperlink. Why? Because you leverage the power of a metaphor.

Most people know what a printed page looks like when someone has gone over it with a highlighter pen. When you change the background color of a text element, the effect on screen looks very similar. Therefore, people tend to assume that your background color has the same function—to call attention to an important passage.

When the text itself changes color, people tend to associate it with a different metaphor: the hyperlink. This spells nothing but trouble, because it confuses your audience. They click and click on the colored text, and nothing happens, because it isn't a hyperlink. It just looks like one.

TIP

Who says your highlighter has to be yellow? Try aqua (#00FFFF), hot pink (#FF0099), gray (#CCCCCC), or chartreuse (#99FF00).

To call even more attention to the highlighted text, add the following line to the style definition:

```
font-weight: bold;
```

With this modification, the text inside the highlighted region becomes bold.

TOOL KIT

Yellow Highlighter Style Rule

The short style rule in this Toolkit gives you a virtual yellow highlighter to apply to any text on your page. It creates a class called **highlight**. To highlight an entire text element, set the class attribute of its tag to **highlight**:

```
<p class="highlight">Text goes here.</p>
```

To highlight a string of text within an element, mark off the string with span tags, and set the span's class to **highlight**:

```
<p>Text goes here. <span class="highlight">Highlighted text goes
here.</span> Text goes here.</p>
```

Place this rule between style tags in the head section of your page, or copy it as is and save it in an external CSS file.

```
.highlight {
  background-color: #FFFF00;
}
```

Rehabilitating Horizontal Rules

ne of the most useful but least used elements in all HTML is the humble horizontal rule. Its goal is a simple but noble one: to create a visual dividing line between the sections of a page.

The best thing about this element is that it's a free graphic. The browser generates it internally. Your visitors don't have to download it, which reduces the overall graphics load and improves the performance of your site.

Part of the problem with the horizontal rule is that, out of the box, it's too long, too blocky, and too obtrusive, as Figure 54.1 shows. Most designers would rather separate the sections of their page with elegant whitespace, not this ugly thing. But if you take the time to adjust its attributes, you can create some truly classy effects, as in Figure 54.2.

Table 54.1 presents the HTML attributes for the hr tag, which generates horizontal rules. You'll modify most of these attributes to make horizontal rules more respectable.

The first order of business is getting rid of the default shading effect, which accounts for most of the clumsiness of the horizontal rule:

```
<hr noshade>
```

The noshade attribute doesn't take a value. It either appears in the hr tag, or it doesn't.

Next, to make the horizontal rule subtler, reduce its height. By default, the rule is 2 pixels tall in Internet Explorer and 3 pixels tall in Netscape. Setting

Figure 54.1

*Unmodified,
HTML's hori-
zontal rule is
an aesthetic
train wreck.*

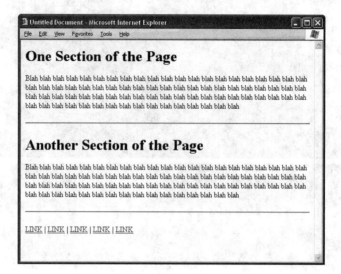

the size attribute to 1 not only standardizes the appearance of the element across browsers, it improves its effectiveness. Slimmer is better; you don't want the horizontal rule calling too much attention to itself. So:

```
<hr noshade size="1">
```

The standard horizontal rule is also too long. By default, it fills the entire width of the page or whatever container element it happens to be in, such as a table cell or a CSS div. Truncated horizontal rules work better. They introduce extra whitespace into your design, which helps your layout to breathe.

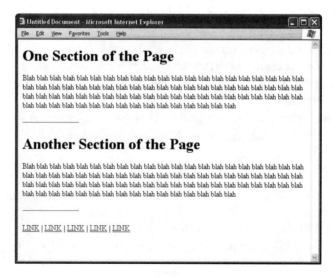

Figure 54.2

*With a little
attribute modi-
fication, the
horizontal rule
shows promise.*

Table 54.1 HTML Attributes for Horizontal Rules

ATTRIBUTE	CONTROLS	POSSIBLE VALUES	EXAMPLES
align	The horizontal position of the element	left, right, center	<hr align="left"> <hr align="center">
noshade	That the horizontal rule doesn't appear with a 3D shading effect	No value	<hr noshade>
size	The height of the element in pixels	Any numeric	<hr size="10">
width	The horizontal size of the element in pixels	Any numeric, including percentages	<hr width="50"> <hr width="33%">

Some designers prefer to give precise pixel measurements for the width of the horizontal rule, like this:

```
<hr noshade size="1" width="200">
```

The precise amount depends on the width of the area that the horizontal rule occupies. If you're working with a fixed-width design, then this option is probably your best bet. However, if you have a liquid design that changes size depending on the size of the browser window, a fixed-width horizontal rule might give you trouble. It may look just right in a maximized browser window, but it might be too big in a smaller browser window.

To solve this problem, just make the horizontal rule liquid, too, by specifying its width as a percentage:

```
<hr noshade size="1" width="20%">
```

A value of 20% scales the width of the horizontal rule to 20% of the width of the

TIP

You may alter the color of horizontal rules with CSS, but browsers don't agree on which CSS attribute is the right one for the job. Internet Explorer prefers the color attribute, while Netscape insists on background-color. Setting the color attribute in Netscape does nothing in IE. Similarly, setting the background color in IE does nothing in Netscape.

One possible workaround is to specify both attributes in your style definition:

```
hr {
   color: #FF0000;  /* For IE */
   background-color: #FF0000;  /* For Netscape */
}
```

TIP

Another classy effect is to set the height of a horizontal rule to some modest amount, like 4 or 5 pixels, and remove the noshade attribute. Doing this creates a hollow, rectangular box.

area it occupies. So if the horizontal rule is in a table cell that happens to be 600 pixels wide, the width of the horizontal rule becomes 120 pixels, or 20% of 600.

The browser centers horizontal rules by default—not that you can tell, because the element expands to its full width automatically. Centering becomes more apparent when you shorten the width. Leave the rule centered if you like, but many designs work better when you position the rule to the left or right:

```
<hr noshade size="1" width="20%" align="left">
```

The horizontal rules in Figure 54.2 use these precise attributes.

Creating End Signs

Here's another trick involving horizontal rules: By manipulating the width and size attributes, you can create boxes to position at the end of a section of text, much like a magazine signs off with an **end sign**, or a special character or bullet at the end of an article. See Figure 54.3 for an example.

To create a box, set the width and size of the horizontal rule to the same amount:

```
<hr size="10" width="10">
```

Specify the noshade attribute to make the box solid, or leave the noshade attribute out to make the box hollow. Notice in Figure 54.3 that the hollow box looks clickable because of the shading's 3D effect, so watch out. You're probably better off using solid boxes for end signs.

Figure 54.3

Create solid or hollow boxes with horizontal rules. (The indents on the paragraphs come courtesy of the margin-left CSS attribute.)

Adding a Dateline and Timestamp

 dateline is a piece of text that gives the current date, and it usually appears at the top of a page. Similarly, a **timestamp** is a piece of text that gives the current time, and it often appears at the bottom of a page. Both are handy for creating a sense of freshness. Nothing pleases your audience more than visiting an utterly current, up-to-the-second-fresh site.

GEEKSPEAK

A dateline is a piece of text that gives the current date. A timestamp is a piece of text that gives the current time.

Even if you update your content on a sporadic basis, the appearance of the current date or the current time helps to make your site feel fresher.

Datelines and timestamps can be yours with some straightforward JavaScript functions. See the Toolkits for complete information.

TOOL KIT

Generating a Dateline

This JavaScript function comes in two parts. The main script goes between script tags in the head section of your HTML file or in a separate JS file. You need an additional script tag inside the body of your Web page wherever you want the dateline to display.

TIP

The browser renders the dateline in the visitor's local time or whatever time the internal clock of the visitor's computer shows.

311

You'll get to that momentarily. First, here is the main script:

```
function doDateline() {

/* First, get the current date. JavaScript's Date object does just
that. This line of code gets the current date and puts it in a variable
called now. */

   var now = new Date();

/* The following lines extract the day of the week, the month, the cal-
endar date, and the year from the now variable. These values are all
numerical. */

   var day = now.getDay();
   var month = now.getMonth();
   var date = now.getDate();
   var year = now.getYear();

/* Internet Explorer returns the correct year, while Netscape and Opera
are off by exactly 1900 years. The following if/then block makes sure
everyone's in the right century. */

   if (year < 2000) {
     year += 1900;
   }

/* Initialize the dateline variable. This variable will eventually con-
tain the text of the dateline. */

   var dateline = "";

/* Now build the text of the dateline. The day of the week currently
exists in numerical form, from 0 to 6 representing Sunday through
Saturday. The following if/then blocks add the correct name of the day
to the dateline variable depending on the numerical value in the day
variable.

Notice the comma and the trailing space after the name of the day. You
need the space so that the next item, the month, doesn't appear
squished up against the comma.

If you want a simple dateline, such as 12/22/2005, omit this block of
code. */

   if (day == 0) {
     dateline = "Sunday, ";
   }
   if (day == 1) {
     dateline = "Monday, ";
   }
   if (day == 2) {
     dateline = "Tuesday, ";
   }
   if (day == 3) {
     dateline = "Wednesday, ";
   }
```

```
  if (day == 4) {
    dateline = "Thursday, ";
  }
  if (day == 5) {
    dateline = "Friday, ";
  }
  if (day == 6) {
    dateline = "Saturday, ";
  }
```

/* The month also exists in numerical form, with 0 for January, 1 for
February, 2 for March, and so on, until you get to 11 for December.
These if/then blocks append the correct month name to the dateline
variable. Notice again the trailing space for proper formatting.

If you want to use European style for your dateline, switch the order
of this block and the next block.

If you want a simple dateline, replace this block of code with the following line:

```
  dateline += (month + 1) + "/";
*/
```

```
  if (month == 0) {
    dateline += "January ";
  }
  if (month == 1) {
    dateline += "February ";
  }
  if (month == 2) {
    dateline += "March ";
  }
  if (month == 3) {
    dateline += "April ";
  }
  if (month == 4) {
    dateline += "May ";
  }
  if (month == 5) {
    dateline += "June ";
  }
  if (month == 6) {
    dateline += "July ";
  }
  if (month == 7) {
    dateline += "August ";
  }
  if (month == 8) {
    dateline += "September ";
  }
  if (month == 9) {
    dateline += "October ";
  }
  if (month == 10) {
    dateline += "November ";
  }
```

```
   if (month == 11) {
     dateline += "December ";
   }
```

/* The next line appends the numerical date to the dateline and adds a comma character followed by a space.

For European formatting, switch this block with the preceding one, delete the comma and space, and add the comma after the name of each month in the preceding block of code.

If you want a simple dateline, replace this line with the following:

```
   dateline += date + "/";
   */
```

```
   dateline += date + ", ";
```

/* The next line appends the numerical year to the dateline. */

```
   dateline += year;
```

/* Your dateline is ready for display. This line writes the dateline to the page. */

```
   document.write(dateline);
 }
```

So much for the main script. Now, in the place where you want the dateline to appear on your page, add the following code:

```
<script language="JavaScript">doDateline();</script>
```

If you prefer, you may mark up this script tag as a paragraph, header, or any other type of text element:

```
<p><script language="JavaScript">doDateline();</script></p>
```

Put the main script together with the doDateline callout, and you get something that looks like Figure 55.1. The simple version looks like Figure 55.2.

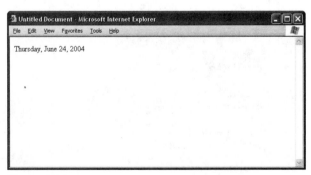

Figure 55.1

Add a dateline to any Web page.

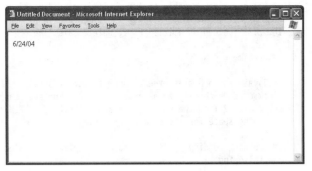

Figure 55.2

If you prefer, you can create a simple dateline.

Generating a Timestamp

This JavaScript function works much the same way. The main script goes between script tags in the head section of your HTML file or in an external JavaScript file. An additional script tag inside the body of your page displays the timestamp.

> **TIP**
>
> As with the dateline, this timestamp script generates times according to the internal clock of the visitor's computer.

Here's the main script:

```
function doTimestamp() {

/* Like before, begin by getting the current date and putting it in a
variable called now. */

  var now = new Date();

/* Mine the now variable for the hour, minutes, and seconds. */

  var hour = now.getHours();
  var minutes = now.getMinutes();
  var seconds = now.getSeconds();

/* Initialize the timestamp variable, which will hold the string of
text that the browser displays. */

  var timestamp = "";
```

```
/* Set the time variable to A.M., with a preceding space for formatting
reasons. If you wish to display the timestamp in 24-hour format, as
16:12:25 instead of 4:12:25 P.M., delete this line of code. */

  var time = " A.M.";

/* JavaScript hours use the 24-hour format by default. The following
block of code checks if the hour variable is greater than 12. If so, it
subtracts 12 from the value and changes the time to P.M., again with a
preceding space for the proper formatting.

If you want to display 24-hour format, replace this block of code with
the following:

  if (hour < 10) {
    hour = "0" + hour;
  }

This if/then block adds a zero to the left of the hour where needed, so
that the sixth hour displays as 06, not 6. */

  if (hour > 12) {
    hour -= 12;
    time = " P.M.";
  }

/* Similarly, these next if/then blocks format minutes and seconds so
that they display with zeroes to the left when needed. */

  if (minutes < 10) {
    minutes = "0" + minutes;
  }

  if (seconds < 10) {
    seconds = "0" + seconds;
  }

/* Now build up the timestamp string. */

  timestamp = hour + ":" + minutes + ":" + seconds + time;

/* Write the timestamp into the page. */

  document.write(timestamp);
}
```

Add the following code in the place where you want the timestamp to appear on your page:

```
<script language="JavaScript">doTimestamp();</script>
```

You probably want to juice it up with some extra formatting:

```
<p>
  <em>This page generated at
  <script language="JavaScript">doTimestamp();</script></em>
</p>
```

See the results for yourself in Figure 55.3.

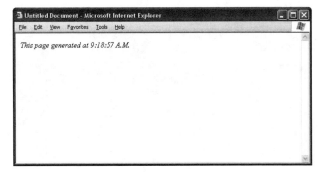

Figure 55.3

Add a timestamp.

56

Designing Data Tables

ata tables are table elements that hold—brace yourself—rows and columns of data. As far as the W3C is concerned, data tables are the only type of table worth talking about, since the HTML spec defines table tags for precisely this purpose. The W3C hates it when you borrow table tags for heretical purposes such as creating page layout.

Table 56.1 displays common HTML table tags. Many of these tags don't make sense in the context of layout tables, so you may not be familiar with

Table 56.1 **Common HTML Table Tags in Order of Appearance in the Code**

TAG	INDICATES
table	A table
caption	The caption of the table
col	A column in the table
colgroup	A group of related columns in the table
thead	The head section of a table

Table 56.1 *(Continued)*

TAG	INDICATES
tfoot	The foot section of a table
tbody	The body section of a table; may appear more than once in a table to denote different sections in the table body
tr	A row in the table
th	A table cell that holds the header of a row or column
td	A table cell that holds an ordinary piece of data

them. But when you build a data table, keep them in mind, because proper markup improves the accessibility of your work.

Figure 56.1 shows a data table that uses all ten of the tags from Table 56.1. Look over the View Source for this figure to see how the markup works.

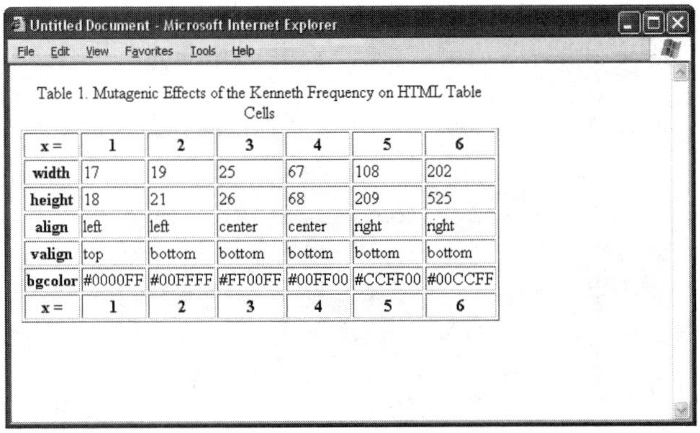

x =	1	2	3	4	5	6
width	17	19	25	67	108	202
height	18	21	26	68	209	525
align	left	left	center	center	right	right
valign	top	bottom	bottom	bottom	bottom	bottom
bgcolor	#0000FF	#00FFFF	#FF00FF	#00FF00	#CCFF00	#00CCFF
x =	1	2	3	4	5	6

Figure 56.1

This data table uses all ten of the tags from Table 56.1.

Listing 56.1 View Source for Figure 56.1.

```
<table border="1">

<!-- The first piece of content is the table caption. -->
```

```
<caption>
  Table 1. Mutagenic Effects of the Kenneth Frequency on HTML Table Cells
</caption>
```

```
<!-- Next comes a description of the column structure of the table. The col and col-
group tags in this particular table indicate a structure of one column on the left
followed by a group of six columns. Notice that the col tag does not have a closing
version, while colgroup does. -->
```

```
<col>
<colgroup span="6"></colgroup>
```

```
<!-- Next comes the table head, which describes the top row of the data table. The
table cells use th tags instead of td tags to indicate that they are header cells. -->
```

```
<thead>
  <tr>
    <th>x =</th>
    <th>1</th>
    <th>2</th>
    <th>3</th>
    <th>4</th>
    <th>5</th>
    <th>6</th>
  </tr>
</thead>
```

```
<!-- Next comes the table foot, which describes the last row of the data table. It
must appear before any of the table body sections. The foot section often matches
the head section exactly, like it does here, but the foot can have unique content,
such as a Totals row. -->
```

```
<tfoot>
  <tr>
    <th>x =</th>
    <th>1</th>
    <th>2</th>
    <th>3</th>
    <th>4</th>
    <th>5</th>
    <th>6</th>
  </tr>
</tfoot>
```

322

<!-- Next comes the table body. This particular table divides its content into three
different body sections. The first one begins here. -->

```
  <tbody>
    <tr>
      <th>width</th>
      <td>17</td>
      <td>19</td>
      <td>25</td>
      <td>67</td>
      <td>108</td>
      <td>202</td>
    </tr>
    <tr>
      <th>height</th>
      <td>18</td>
      <td>21</td>
      <td>26</td>
      <td>68</td>
      <td>209</td>
      <td>525</td>
    </tr>
  </tbody>
```

<!-- Here is the second body section. -->

```
  <tbody>
    <tr>
      <th>align</th>
      <td>left</td>
      <td>left</td>
      <td>center</td>
      <td>center</td>
      <td>right</td>
      <td>right</td>
    </tr>
    <tr>
      <th>valign</th>
      <td>top</td>
      <td>bottom</td>
      <td>bottom</td>
      <td>bottom</td>
      <td>bottom</td>
```

```
    <td>bottom</td>
  </tr>
  </tbody>

<!-- Here is the third body section. -->

  <tbody>
    <tr>
      <th>bgcolor</th>
      <td>#0000FF</td>
      <td>#00FFFF</td>
      <td>#FF00FF</td>
      <td>#00FF00</td>
      <td>#CCFF00</td>
      <td>#00CCFF</td>
    </tr>
  </tbody>

<!-- Add a closing table tag to finish the markup. -->

</table>
```

Making the Most of the Grouping Tags

You may be wondering what good are the HTML grouping tags: col, colgroup, thead, tfoot, and tbody. After all, these tags don't add any content to the table. The col and colgroup tags simply describe the structure of the columns in the table, and the thead, tfoot, and tbody tags mark off the table's sections. Why go to the trouble of coding this information into a table in the first place?

Not only do the grouping tags improve the accessibility of your table by describing its structure in detail, they give you some handy formatting shortcuts. Take the table in Figure 56.1 as an example. Let's say that you want to align the content to the right in every table cell of the first column. You don't have to fuss with:

```
<td align="right">
```

in each table cell. Simply specify the align attribute once, in the col tag:

TIP

When you use col and colgroup tags with thead, tfoot, and tbody tags in the same table, the Netscape browser gets fussy and doesn't always apply the col and colgroup attributes. One easy way to solve this problem is not to use col and colgroup with thead, tfoot, and tbody. Pick one group of tags or the other—whichever makes more sense for your particular data table.

```
<col align="right">
```

Better, give the alignment as a CSS style definition:

```
<col style="text-align: right;">
```

This shortcut works with the colgroup tag, too:

```
<colgroup span="6" style="text-align: center;"></colgroup>
```

Add width attributes to specify the horizontal size of the columns:

```
<col style="text-align: right; width: 75px;">
<colgroup span="6" style="text-align: center; width: 100px;"></colgroup>
```

You can also apply HTML attributes and CSS style definitions to the thead, tfoot, and tbody sections:

```
<thead style="font-family: Arial, Helvetica, sans-serif; font-size: 10px; font-style: italic;">
  <!-- Content goes here -->
</thead>
```

Working with Colspans and Rowspans

Colspans and rowspans are the bane of layout tables, because they cause all sorts of strange breakage problems. These attributes come in handy for data tables, though, because that's what the people who dreamed up HTML designed colspans and rowspans for.

Technically speaking, the **colspan** attribute determines how many columns a particular table cell spans or straddles, while the **rowspan** attribute determines the number of spanned rows. The best way to understand how colspans and rowspans work is to look at an example, which Figure 56.2 provides.

> **GEEKSPEAK**
> The colspan attribute determines how many columns a table cell straddles, while the rowspan attribute determines the number of straddled rows.

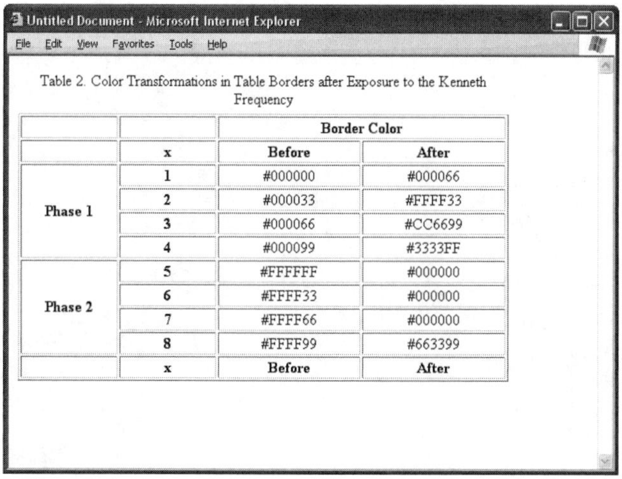

Figure 56.2

This data table uses the colspan and rowspan attributes.

Listing 56.2 **View Source for Figure 56.2.**

```html
<table border="1">

  <caption>Table 2. Color Transformations in Table Borders after Exposure to the
Kenneth Frequency</caption>

  <colgroup span="2" style="width: 100px;"></colgroup>
  <colgroup span="2" style="width: 150px; text-align: center;"></colgroup>

<!-- The head element contains two table rows here. A few of the cells contain non-
breaking spaces ( ). Use these to fill otherwise empty table cells.

The last cell in the first row contains the colspan. As you can see in Figure 56.2,
the Border Color cell straddles two columns: the Before column and the After column.
-->

  <thead>
    <tr>
      <th> </th>
      <th> </th>
      <th colspan="2">Border Color</th>
    </tr>
    <tr>
      <th> </th>
      <th>x</th>
```

```
      <th>Before</th>
      <th>After</th>
    </tr>
  </thead>

  <tfoot>
    <tr>
      <th> </th>
      <th>x</th>
      <th>Before</th>
      <th>After</th>
    </tr>
  </tfoot>


<!-- This table has two body elements. The first table cell in the first row con-
tains the rowspan. Looking at the figure, you see that the Phase 1 cell straddles
the 1, 2, 3, and 4 rows. -->

  <tbody>
    <tr>
      <th rowspan="4">Phase 1</th>
      <th>1</th>
      <td>#000000</td>
      <td>#000066</td>
    </tr>
    <tr>
      <th>2</th>
      <td>#000033</td>
      <td>#FFFF33</td>
    </tr>
    <tr>
      <th>3</th>
      <td>#000066</td>
      <td>#CC6699</td>
    </tr>
    <tr>
      <th>4</th>
      <td>#000099</td>
      <td>#3333FF</td>
    </tr>
  </tbody>
```

```
<!-- Here is the second body element. Again, the rowspan in the Phase 2 cell
causes this cell to straddle four rows. -->

  <tbody>
    <tr>
      <th rowspan="4">Phase 2</th>
      <th>5</th>
      <td>#FFFFFF</td>
      <td>#000000</td>
    </tr>
    <tr>
      <th>6</th>
      <td>#FFFF33</td>
      <td>#000000</td>
    </tr>
    <tr>
      <th>7</th>
      <td>#FFFF66</td>
      <td>#000000</td>
    </tr>
    <tr>
      <th>8</th>
      <td>#FFFF99</td>
      <td>#663399</td>
    </tr>
  </tbody>

</table>
```

As you can see from the Listing 56.2, the colspan and rowspan attributes appear in the tag for the table cell, either th or td, depending on whether you need a header cell or a regular cell to span. The values of these attributes determine the number of columns or rows to span.

You'll notice that a row that includes a colspanned or rowspanned cell seems to be missing some markup. For example, in the first row of the data table in Figure 56.2, you find three table cells:

```
<tr>
  <th> </th>
  <th> </th>
  <th colspan="2">Border Color</th>
</tr>
```

TIP
A single table cell can contain both colspan and rowspan attributes.

The very next row has four table cells:

```
<tr>
  <th> </th>
  <th>x</th>
  <th>Before</th>
  <th>After</th>
</tr>
```

The missing code in the first row is perfectly normal. In fact, this is the way it needs to be. The table cell with the colspan of 2 counts as two cells, not one, in which case both rows have four table cells after all.

Another point of note: The colgroup tags at the top of the table show the following structure:

```
<colgroup span="2"></colgroup>
<colgroup span="2"></colgroup>
```

The spans of the colgroup tags add up to four columns, not three, even though there seem to be three columns in the very first row of the table. Once again, you have to count the cell with the colspan of 2 as two columns, not one, so the math does add up. The colgroup tags describe four table columns, and there are indeed four columns in that section of the table.

Adjusting Cellpadding and Cellspacing

Normally, when you create a layout table, you set the table tag's cellpadding and cellspacing attributes to 0. But when you build a data table, cellpadding and cellspacing are useful formatting tools. **Cellpadding** determines the amount of interior whitespace between the edges of a table cell and its content, while **cellspacing** determines the amount of exterior whitespace between individual table cells.

When you set the cellpadding and cellspacing attributes in the table tag, their values apply to every cell in the table:

```
<table border="1" cellpadding="5" cellspacing="8">
```

Figure 56.3 shows a table with exactly these attributes. Compare it with the table in Figure 56.2 to see the difference in appearance that a little cellpadding and cellspacing make.

Use cellpadding and cellspacing to help dense data tables breathe a little. Tables are usually easier to read when they have a little extra whitespace.

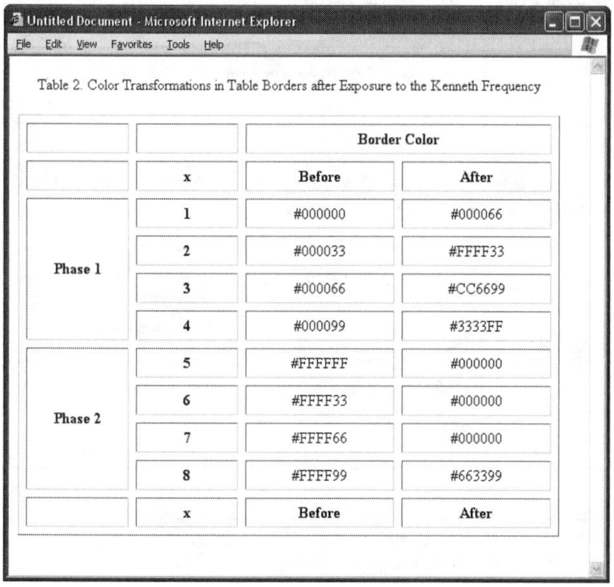
Untitled Document - Microsoft Internet Explorer
File Edit View Favorites Tools Help

Table 2. Color Transformations in Table Borders after Exposure to the Kenneth Frequency

		Border Color	
	x	**Before**	**After**
Phase 1	**1**	#000000	#000066
	2	#000033	#FFFF33
	3	#000066	#CC6699
	4	#000099	#3333FF
Phase 2	**5**	#FFFFFF	#000000
	6	#FFFF33	#000000
	7	#FFFF66	#000000
	8	#FFFF99	#663399
	x	**Before**	**After**

Figure 56.3

This data table adjusts the spacing inside and outside its cells with the cellpadding and cellspacing attributes.

Don't overdo it, though. Too much whitespace is just as bad as too little. Let your eye be the judge. If your table isn't legible enough, try nudging up the cellpadding and cellspacing.

GEEKSPEAK

Cellpadding determines the amount of interior whitespace between the edges of a table cell and its content. Cellspacing determines the amount of exterior whitespace between individual table cells.

If your data table uses background colors, the cellpadding attribute is probably the better choice for whitespace. Cellspacing often causes visible gaps between the cells, breaking the continuous field of background color, as in Figure 56.4. Cellpadding has no such effect, as Figure 56.5 shows, as long as you set the cellspacing attribute to 0.

TIP

Adjust the padding of an individual table cell with the padding-top, padding-bottom, padding-left, and padding-right CSS attributes, like this:

```
<td style="padding-top: 3px; padding-bottom: 4px; padding-left: 2px;
padding-right: 5px;">
```

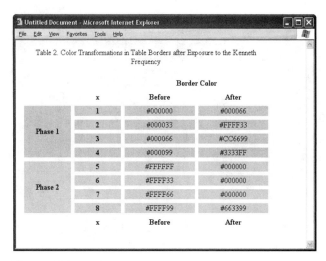

Figure 56.4

Watch out for cellspacing when your table cells have background colors. Cellspacing often breaks the continuous field of color.

Figure 56.5

Use cellpadding instead to keep the color field unbroken, and set cellspacing to 0.

Changing the Border

Hardly anyone uses table borders in layout tables, but just about everyone uses table borders in data tables. The table's border attribute controls the thickness of the border, and the bordercolor attribute determines the color:

```
<table border="5" bordercolor="#000000">
```

Figure 56.6 shows a table with these properties. The border around the outside of the table appears at a thickness of 5 pixels. The interior borders or **rules** retain their normal thickness but borrow the table border's color.

You can change the way the browser draws rules in the table by setting the table's rules attribute, like this:

```
<table border="5" bordercolor="#000000" rules="cols">
```

By setting the rules attribute to cols, the browser draws rules around the columns only, as you can see in Figure 56.7. Table 56.2 summarizes the possible values of the rules attribute.

> **GEEKSPEAK**
>
> **Rules** are the interior borders of a table. They retain their standard thickness, no matter the value in the border attribute, but they appear in the table border's color.

> **TIP**
>
> Table borders in Netscape appear with a 3D shading effect. In IE, table borders are solid.

Table 2. Color Transformations in Table Borders after Exposure to the Kenneth Frequency

		Border Color	
	x	Before	After
	1	#000000	#000066
Phase 1	2	#000033	#FFFF33
	3	#000066	#CC6699
	4	#000099	#3333FF
	5	#FFFFFF	#000000
Phase 2	6	#FFFF33	#000000
	7	#FFFF66	#000000
	8	#FFFF99	#663399
	x	Before	After

Figure 56.6

This table has a five-pixel, black (#000000) border.

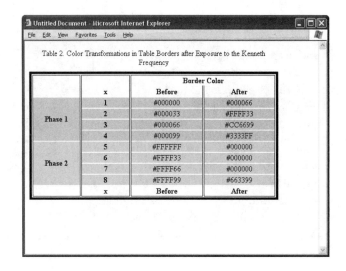

Table 56.2 **Values of the Rules Attribute**	
VALUE	DRAWS RULES AROUND
all	All table cells
cols	Columns only
rows	Rows only
groups	Groups only: col, colgroup, thead, tfoot, and tbody
none	Nothing; no rules drawn

With CSS, you can change the style of the border:

```
<table border="5" bordercolor="#000000" rules="groups" style="border-style: dotted;">
```

Figure 56.8 shows how the dotted border style looks in a browser. See Table 56.3 for more border styles.

You can set the borders of different sides of the table to different values, as in Figure 56.9:

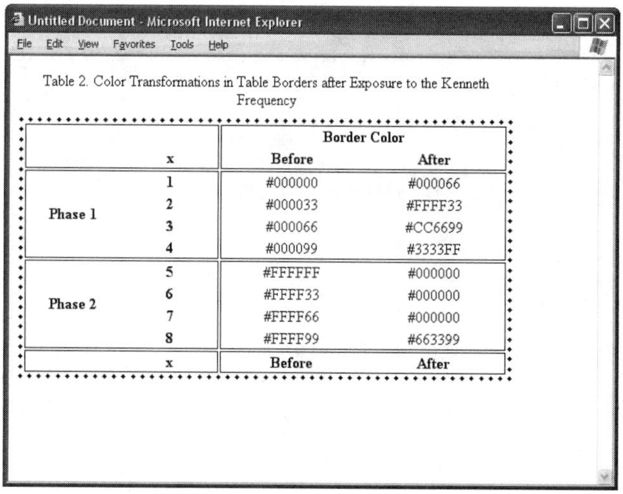

Table 2. Color Transformations in Table Borders after Exposure to the Kenneth Frequency

		Border Color	
	x	Before	After
Phase 1	1	#000000	#000066
	2	#000033	#FFFF33
	3	#000066	#CC6699
	4	#000099	#3333FF
Phase 2	5	#FFFFFF	#000000
	6	#FFFF33	#000000
	7	#FFFF66	#000000
	8	#FFFF99	#663399
	x	Before	After

Figure 56.8

Use CSS to change the style of the border.

Table 56.3 Common CSS Border Styles*

STYLE	APPEARANCE
solid	An unbroken, solid border
dashed	Dashed lines
dotted	Dotted lines
double	A pair of solid borders
none	No border

* CSS defines many other border styles, but not all browsers support them.

```
<table border="5" bordercolor="#000000" rules="groups"
style="border-top-style: dashed; border-bottom-style: dotted;
border-left-style: double; border-right-style: none;">
```

In fact, with CSS, you can set the border thickness and border color independently for all four sides. Table 56.4 runs down the list of common CSS border attributes at your disposal.

With CSS, the top, right, bottom, and left borders may all have different styles.

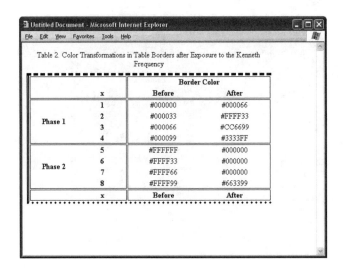

Table 56.4 **Common CSS Border Attributes***

ATTRIBUTE	CONTROLS	EXAMPLE
border-color	The color of all four sides of the border	border-color: #FF0000;
border-style	The style of all four sides of the border	border-style: dotted;
border-width	The weight or thickness of all four sides of the border	border-width: 10px;
border-bottom-color	The color of the bottom border	border-bottom-color: #00FF00;
border-bottom-style	The style of the bottom border	border-bottom-style: none;
border-bottom-width	The weight or thickness of the bottom border	border-bottom-width: 8px;
border-left-color	The color of the left border	border-left-color: #0000FF;
border-left-style	The style of the left border	border-left-style: solid;
border-left-width	The weight or thickness of the left border	border-left-width: 5px;
border-right-color	The color of the right border	border-right-color: #FFFF00;
border-right-style	The style of the right border	border-right-style: dashed;
border-right-width	The weight or thickness of the right border	border-right-width: 4px;

Table 56.4 *(Continued)**

ATTRIBUTE	CONTROLS	EXAMPLE
border-top-color	The color of the top border	border-top-color: #FFFFFF;
border-top-style	The style of the top border	border-top-style: double;
border-top-width	The weight or thickness of the top border	border-top-width: 6px;

*CSS defines other border attributes, but not all browsers support them.

Improving Accessibility

Using the right tags goes a long way toward making your data tables more accessible. You can go even further by adding some finishing touches to your markup.

FAQ

Do these accessibility tips work in today's browsers?

Not really. File these suggestions in the Forward Compatibility category. The most recent versions of the major browsers don't use this extra markup, and current accessibility tools don't, either. Use these techniques to make your data tables ready for the next generation of Web-browsing technologies.

If the text in your table headers is excessively wordy:

```
<th>Intensity of the Kenneth Frequency</th>
<th>Fluctuation in Beta Transmission</th>
<th>Margin of Error</th>
```

you can add your own abbreviations in the abbr attribute of the th tag. Screen readers substitute these abbreviations for the full phrase, which cuts down on the monotony of listening to the data table read aloud.

```
<th abbr="Intensity">Intensity of the Kenneth Frequency</th>
<th abbr="Fluctuation">Fluctuation in Beta Transmission</th>
<th abbr="Error">Margin of Error</th>
```

You can also specify exactly which table cells belong under which header cell. To do this, give each th tag in the table header group a unique ID. Then, for each table cell, specify this ID in the headers attribute, like this:

```
<table border="1" rules="groups">

  <caption>Table 3: Intensity of the Kenneth Frequency and Fluctuations in Beta
Transmission</caption>

  <col width="300" align="center">
  <col width="300" align="center">
  <col width="160" align="center">

  <thead>
    <tr>
      <th id="intensity" abbr="Intensity">Intensity of the Kenneth Frequency</th>
      <th id="fluctuation" abbr="Fluctuation">Fluctuations in Beta Transmission</th>
      <th  id="error" abbr="Error">Margin of Error</th>
    </tr>
  </thead>

<!-- This table doesn't have a foot section, which is completely fine. You don't
need to specify every possible group in every table. Just include the ones you need.
-->

  <tbody>
    <tr>
      <td headers="intensity">1</td>
      <td headers="fluctuation">90</td>
      <td headers="error">6%</td>
    </tr>
    <tr>
      <td headers="intensity">2</td>
      <td headers="fluctuation">128</td>
      <td headers="error">35%</td>
    </tr>
    <tr>
      <td headers="intensity">3</td>
      <td headers="fluctuation">2726</td>
      <td headers="error">32%</td>
    </tr>
    <tr>
```

```
      <td headers="intensity">4</td>
      <td headers="fluctuation">263443</td>
      <td headers="error">32%</td>
    </tr>
    <tr>
      <td headers="intensity">5</td>
      <td headers="fluctuation">2</td>
      <td headers="error">98%</td>
    </tr>
  </tbody>

</table>
```

> **TIP**
>
> The IDs of all tags on a page need to be unique. Don't use the same ID for another header tag or any other HTML element on the page.

For your viewing pleasure, this table appears in Figure 56.10.

Another way to improve the accessibility of your data table is to group cells into categories with the axis attribute. Your category names can be anything—just use the names consistently, as in the following example, where all intensity cells belong to the axis **intensities**, all fluctuation cells belong to the axis **fluctuations**, and all error cells belong to the axis **errormargins**.

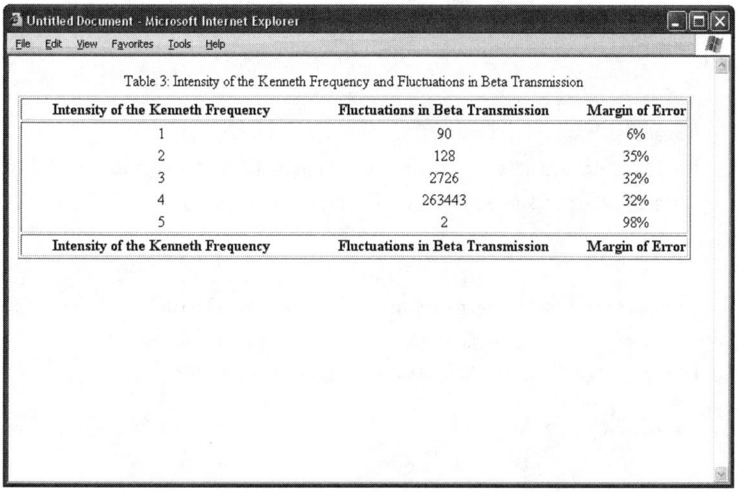

Figure 56.10

The browser doesn't display a data table any differently when you specify id and headers attributes, but this extra markup will make a difference with the screen readers of the future.

Table 3: Intensity of the Kenneth Frequency and Fluctuations in Beta Transmission

Intensity of the Kenneth Frequency	Fluctuations in Beta Transmission	Margin of Error
1	90	6%
2	128	35%
3	2726	32%
4	263443	32%
5	2	98%
Intensity of the Kenneth Frequency	Fluctuations in Beta Transmission	Margin of Error

> **TIP**
>
> If the table cell belongs to two or more headers, separate the header IDs with spaces, like this:
>
> ```
> <td headers="firstheader secondheader thirdheader fourthheader">
> ```

```
<table border="1" rules="rows">

  <caption>Table 4: Intensities of the Kenneth and Bradley Frequencies and
Fluctuations in Beta Transmission</caption>

  <col width="150">
  <colgroup span="3" width="150" align="center">

  <thead>
    <tr>
      <th> </th>
      <th id="intensity" abbr="Intensity" axis="intensities">Intensity</th>
      <th id="fluctuation" abbr="Fluctuation" axis="fluctuations">Fluctuations in
Beta Transmission</th>
      <th id="error" abbr="Error" axis="errormargins">Margin of Error</th>
    </tr>
  </thead>

  <tbody>
    <tr>
      <th id="kenneth" rowspan="5" abbr="Kenneth">Kenneth Frequency</th>
      <td headers="intensity kenneth" axis="intensities">1</td>
      <td headers="fluctuation kenneth" axis="fluctuations">90</td>
      <td headers="error kenneth" axis="errormargins">6%</td>
    </tr>
    <tr>
      <td headers="intensity kenneth" axis="intensities">2</td>
      <td headers="fluctuation kenneth" axis="fluctuations">128</td>
      <td headers="error kenneth" axis="errormargins">35%</td>
    </tr>
    <tr>
      <td headers="intensity kenneth" axis="intensities">3</td>
      <td headers="fluctuation kenneth" axis="fluctuations">2726</td>
      <td headers="error kenneth" axis="errormargins">32%</td>
    </tr>
    <tr>
```

```
      <td headers="intensity kenneth" axis="intensities">4</td>
      <td headers="fluctuation kenneth" axis="fluctuations">263443</td>
      <td headers="error kenneth" axis="errormargins">32%</td>
    </tr>
    <tr>
      <td headers="intensity kenneth" axis="intensities">5</td>
      <td headers="fluctuation kenneth" axis="fluctuations">2</td>
      <td headers="error kenneth" axis="errormargins">98%</td>
    </tr>
  </tbody>

  <tbody>
    <tr>
      <th id="bradley" rowspan="5" abbr="Bradley">Bradley Frequency</th>
      <td headers="intensity bradley" axis="intensities">1</td>
      <td headers="fluctuation bradley" axis="fluctuations">4</td>
      <td headers="error bradley" axis="errormargins">73%</td>
    </tr>
    <tr>
      <td headers="intensity bradley" axis="intensities">2</td>
      <td headers="fluctuation bradley" axis="fluctuations">45</td>
      <td headers="error bradley" axis="errormargins">35%</td>
    </tr>
    <tr>
      <td headers="intensity bradley" axis="intensities">3</td>
      <td headers="fluctuation bradley" axis="fluctuations">356</td>
      <td headers="error bradley" axis="errormargins">12%</td>
    </tr>
    <tr>
      <td headers="intensity bradley" axis="intensities">4</td>
      <td headers="fluctuation bradley" axis="fluctuations">32</td>
      <td headers="error bradley" axis="errormargins">11%</td>
    </tr>
    <tr>
      <td headers="intensity bradley" axis="intensities">5</td>
      <td headers="fluctuation bradley" axis="fluctuations">12</td>
      <td headers="error bradley" axis="errormargins">2%</td>
    </tr>
  </tbody>

</table>
```

This table appears in Figure 56.11.

Figure 56.11

Grouping cells into axis categories doesn't affect the appearance of the data table in the browser, but the screen readers of the future will use the axis names to better understand the layout of your table.

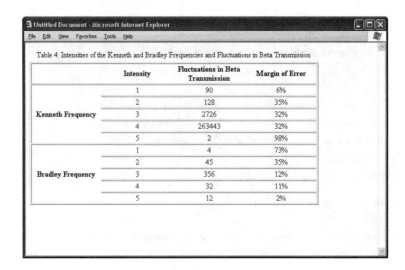

Table 4: Intensities of the Kenneth and Bradley Frequencies and Fluctuations in Beta Transmission

	Intensity	Fluctuations in Beta Transmission	Margin of Error
Kenneth Frequency	1	90	6%
	2	128	35%
	3	2726	32%
	4	263443	32%
	5	2	98%
Bradley Frequency	1	4	73%
	2	45	35%
	3	356	12%
	4	32	11%
	5	12	2%

Using Pseudo-Elements

In CSS, **pseudo-elements** are special add-ons to HTML tag selectors. They identify particular sections of the text inside the HTML element. Currently, there are two pseudo-elements: first-line and first-letter. You can apply them to any text tag or any tag that contains text, such as a table or a div.

Any old style sheet might identify a general paragraph style:

```
p {
  font-family: Arial, Helvetica, sans-serif;
  font-size: 14px;
}
```

Only an especially clever style sheet adds a pseudo-element that instructs the browser what to do with the first line in a paragraph:

```
p {
  font-family: Arial, Helvetica, sans-serif;
  font-size: 14px;
}

p:first-line {
  font-weight: bold;
  font-variant: small-caps;
}
```

GEEKSPEAK

A CSS pseudo-element is a special add-on to an HTML tag selector that identifies a particular section of the text inside the element.

See the effects for yourself in Figure 57.1.

342

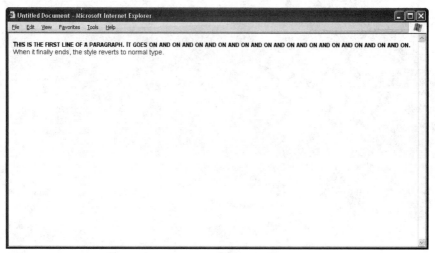

Figure 57.1

The first-line pseudo element identifies a special style for the first line of a text element, like this paragraph.

FAQ

How do I know where the first line ends?

The width of the browser window determines where the first line ends. Therefore, you, the designer, lose a degree of control over exactly which text gets the first-line treatment. If you like to remain in complete control of your text, you should forego the first-line pseudo-element and drop span tags around the exact string of text you want to change. Then, apply a special style definition to the span tag's style attribute.

The first-letter pseudo-element works much the same way, only it affects the first letter of the text, not the entire first line:

```
p {
    font-family: Arial, Helvetica, sans-serif;
    font-size: 14px;
}

p:first-letter {
    font-family: "Times New Roman", Times, serif;
    font-weight: bold;
    font-size: 48px;
}
```

Figure 57.2 shows these style rules in action.

TIP

Remember, even though the examples in this topic show paragraphs, you can use the first-line and first-letter pseudo-elements with any text tag or container tag, such as a table or div.

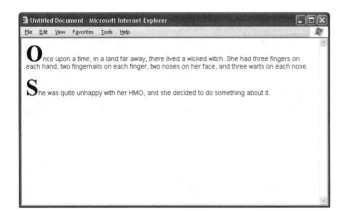

Figure 57.2

The first-letter pseudo element identifies a special style for the first letter of a text element.

Style Sheet for Drop Caps

In the publishing game, a drop cap is an oversized capital letter that usually appears at the beginning of a chapter. It's different from the example in Figure 57.2, though, in one notable way: It hangs below the baseline of the text, and the first three or so lines of type in the paragraph wrap around it, as in Figure 57.3.

GEEKSPEAK

A **drop cap** is an oversized capital letter that usually appears at the beginning of a chapter. It hangs below the baseline of the text, and the surrounding lines of type wrap around it.

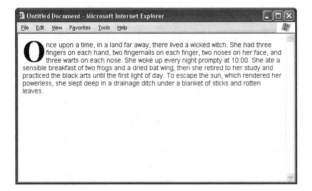

Figure 57.3

A drop cap is an oversized capital letter that hangs below the baseline of the text. The next couple of lines of type wrap around it.

344

Descenders are portions of letters that dip below the baseline of a line of type, like the stem of the lowercase letter **p**.

This Toolkit gives you a style rule for drop caps. Just copy and paste it into an existing style sheet. Don't be afraid to tinker with the font size. You'll probably need to fine-tune the style for your particular page, depending on the typeface and type size of the running text. The drop cap should clear three to four lines of type. Capital letters with **descenders**, or portions that dip below the baseline, like the capital letter Q in a serif typeface, clear four lines of type, while normal capital letters clear three.

Feel free also to add other CSS attributes to the style rule, such as a background color or some extra padding.

```
p.dropcap:first-letter {
  font-family: Georgia, "Times New Roman", Times, serif;
  font-weight: bold;
  font-size: 63px;

/* This font size assumes the running text is 14 pixels and that the
drop cap clears three to four lines of type. */

  float: left;

/* The float attribute is the secret weapon that makes the drop cap
work. When an element floats, the browser wraps surrounding elements
around it. An element can float to the left or right. */

  padding-right: 2px;

/* A little padding on the right side of the drop cap helps to avoid
collisions between the drop cap and the surrounding lines of type. */

}
```

To use this style rule, set any paragraph to the class **dropcap**:

```
<p class="dropcap">Once upon a time, in a land far away....</p>
```

Since the dropcap class in this Toolkit is exclusive to paragraphs, you can't add a drop cap to a header, table, or any other type of tag. If you want the dropcap class to work with any applicable element, including paragraphs, simply remove the paragraph tag from the selector, like so:

```
.dropcap:first-line {
```

FAQ

This drop cap looks ridiculous in Netscape. What gives?

Drop-cap styles, including the one in this Toolkit, tend to look better in Internet Explorer than in Netscape, because Netscape adds an inordinate amount of whitespace above the top of the drop cap. To improve the look of this style in Netscape, add a background color to the style definition. This puts the drop cap inside a colored box, which makes the whitespace above the letter less jarring.

For a better-looking yet patently silly workaround, you can add negative top and bottom margins to the style definition:

```
margin-top: -12px;
margin-bottom: -12px;
```

Doing this pushes the drop cap up, but it also gives you an extra 12 pixels of whitespace before the paragraph begins.

At least the negative margins don't affect the appearance of the drop cap in Internet Explorer, so this solution is cross-browser-friendly.

Defining ID Styles

An **ID selector** in CSS is much like a tag-specific class in that it is an exclusive club. It's so exclusive, in fact, that it applies to one and only one element per page. No two elements should belong to the same ID, even if the elements are of the exact same type: paragraphs, headings, images, links, or what have you.

To define an ID selector, you use special syntax—namely, the number sign (#), followed by the name of the ID:

```
#barney {
  font-weight: bold;
  color: #FF00FF;
}
```

Then, set the id attribute of the tag to which you want to apply the style:

```
<p id="barney">This paragraph has the ID of "barney."</p>
```

IDs come in handy as substitutes for style rules that appear in the style attribute of an HTML tag. You'll recall that putting CSS code in the style attribute works best for one-off styles. What is an ID if not a one-off style? So feel free to replace something like this:

```
<p style="font-weight: bold; color: #FF0000;">Alert!</p>
```

What happens if I apply the same ID to more than one element?

You won't go to prison, and your computer won't explode, and you won't crash the Internet. The browser treats IDs like classes, so, if you do happen to use the same ID for multiple elements, all the elements appear with the ID style.

However, you create all kinds of problems for yourself when it comes time to add JavaScript functions to your page that use the getElementByID method. If your IDs are not unique, your functions won't work properly.

So, if you want a class style, create a class style. Reserve IDs for special classes of one.

with something like this:

```
<style type="text/css">

 #alert {
   font-weight: bold;
   color: #FF0000;
 }

</style>

<body>

 <p id="alert">Warning!</p>

</body>
```

As you can see in Figure 58.1, both methods have the exact same effect. If you're a coding aesthete, the ID method may be a bit cleaner, a bit tastier to your palette, and a bit more authentic to the spirit of CSS. You'd probably rather use an ID than shove the style rule into the attribute of some clunky old HTML tag, although either method gets the job done.

Figure 58.1

An ID style (top) works just like the style attribute of an HTML tag (bottom) in that it defines a one-off style rule. The effects are identical.

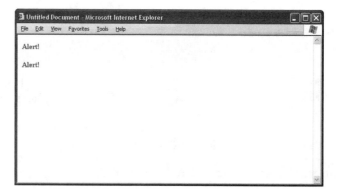

PART V:
Link Topics

59

Applying Styles to Hyperlinks

TML provides a basic set of attributes for controlling the appearance of hyperlinks on your page. These attributes appear in the body tag:

```
<body link="#0000FF" vlink="#FF00FF" alink="#FF0000">
```

Table 59.1 summarizes the link attributes. As you can see, HTML ties them to three link states: the unvisited state, the visited state, and the active state. You use color to tell the three states apart. An **unvisited link** is a link to a page that the browser doesn't remember visiting. The default color of unvisited links is blue. A **visited link** is a link to a page that the browser does remember visiting. The default color is purple or magenta. Finally, an

> ### GEEKSPEAK
> An **unvisited** link is a link to a page that the browser doesn't remember visiting. A **visited** link is a link to a page that the browser does remember visiting. An **active** link is a link that the visitor is currently clicking or highlighting.

Table 59.1 **HTML Link Attributes**

ATTRIBUTE	CONTROLS
link	The color of unvisited links
vlink	The color of visited links
alink	The color of links when clicked or highlighted

FAQ

How do I highlight a hyperlink?

Surely you know how to click a hyperlink, but not everyone knows how to highlight a hyperlink, mainly because most people don't realize that you can navigate Web sites in Internet Explorer and Netscape without a mouse.

Here's how it works: You cycle through the interactive elements on the page by pressing the Tab key, and then you press Enter to activate an element when you come to it. That's how you highlight a hyperlink: You tab onto it, giving it **focus**, in Web jargon. IE changes the link to its active color. If you tab past the hyperlink, it loses focus and reverts to its default color, either visited or unvisited.

While you can highlight links in Netscape, this browser doesn't change the color of the link to its active value.

active link is a link that the visitor is currently clicking. In Internet Explorer, the active-link color also appears when the visitor highlights a link.

To set custom colors for the link states on your page, specify them directly with the link, vlink, and alink attributes.

It's hard to believe that the Web got as popular as it did with so few design choices for the most essential element on any Web page. You have three link colors for three link states, and that's it. But the design doors open wide when you format links with Cascading Style Sheets (CSS) instead of HTML attributes.

At the most basic level, CSS mimics the roles of the link, vlink, and alink attributes with the link, visited, and active pseudo-classes. In CSS, a **pseudo-class** is a special addition to the anchor tag that tells the browser to which link state the style rule applies. In Topic 57, you looked at the pseudo-elements first-line and first-letter. Pseudo-classes are similar, but they apply only to the anchor tag at present.

GEEKSPEAK

A **pseudo-class** is a special addition to the anchor-tag selector that tells the browser to which link state the style rule applies.

The following block of CSS code has the same effect as the attributes in the body tag at the beginning of this topic:

```
a:link {
  color: #0000FF;
}
```

```
a:visited {
  color: #FF00FF;
}

a:active {
  color: #FF0000;
}
```

Those style rules are just begging to be elaborated. How about setting
unvisited links and active links in boldface but leaving visited links in normal
type?

```
a:link {
  color: #0000FF;
  font-weight: bold;
}

a:visited {
  color: #FF00FF;
  font-weight: normal;
}

a:active {
  color: #FF0000;
  font-weight: bold;
}
```

Figure 59.1 demonstrates these styles. Notice how the boldface helps
unvisited links to jump off the page, while visited links seem less important.

Some sites add a subtle background color around hyperlinks, creating a
box effect, as in Figure 59.2

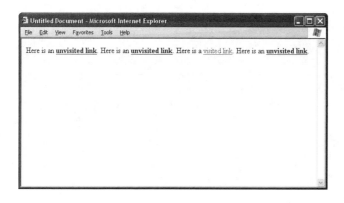

Figure 59.1

Use CSS to
change more
than just the
color of the
various link
states.

Figure 59.2

*Add a back-
ground-color
attribute to the
style rule for a
link or link state
to create a box
effect.*

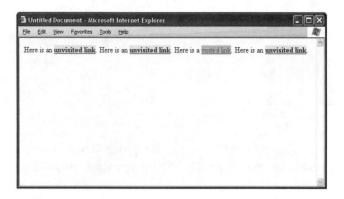

Listing 59.1 View Source for Figure 59.2.

```
a {
  font-weight: bold;
}

/* Each link state has a different background color in these style rules. */

a:link {
  color: #0000FF;
  background-color: #CCFFFF;
}

a:visited {
  color: #FF00FF;
  font-weight: normal;
  background-color: #CCCCFF;
}

a:active {
  color: #FF0000;
  background-color: #FFCCCC;
}
```

You can also turn off the default underline, as in Figure 59.3.

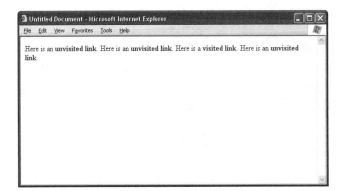

Figure 59.3

Turn off the hyperlink's underline.

Listing 59.2 **View Source for Figure 59.3.**

```
a {
  font-weight: bold;
  text-decoration: none;
}

/* You need some sort of visual cue other than just color to designate a hyperlink,
so these style rules allow boldface for all three states in absence of a hyperlink.
*/

a:link {
  color: #0000FF;
  background-color: #CCFFFF;
}

a:visited {
  color: #FF00FF;
  background-color: #CCCCFF;
}

a:active {
  color: #FF0000;
  background-color: #FFCCCC;
}
```

BLOG: In Defense of the Hyperlink Underline

CSS is great when it works. It lets you do all kinds of interesting things to HTML elements. You can even remove the most sacred of all things sacred, the underline of a hyperlink.

The very first Web site ever made had a hyperlink, and that hyperlink had an underline, so there's tradition to think about. But you want to keep the underline for more than just that.

For one thing, most hyperlinks are underlined. In fact, this is why removing the underline is so tempting. Designers like to lose the underline to make their sites unique, which is an important part of the designer's role. The Web would be much less interesting if every site used the same conventions.

There's just one problem. People who browse the Web are so used to the omnipresent underline that they click on anything that has one, even if it isn't a hyperlink. This is precisely why you should take great care not to underline elements that aren't hyperlinks. This is also why you should underline elements that are hyperlinks.

The Web is all about speed. People who like the Web like the ability to find information quickly. Moreover, Web surfers are skimmers. They don't actually read your text until they come to the information they want.

As a designer, you want to keep these facts in mind. You want your visitors to be able to move around your site with effortless speed, so you need something to attract their attention to the hyperlinks.

The underline works perfectly. Everyone knows that it indicates a hyperlink. It's easy to pick out, and your visitors don't have to think about it. Why ruin a good thing?

Besides, non-underlined hyperlinks compel your visitor to figure out what style convention you're using. Is it the boldface? The italic? The words in the colored boxes? Sure, it's obvious to you, but you're the designer. The learning experience is usually counterproductive to the browsing experience. In other words, your visitors can't leverage their knowledge about how the Web works to browse your site, which means that they can't tear through it at the blinding speeds to which they're accustomed.

By all means, design link states with CSS. Add boldface. Add italic. Change the typeface. Change the type size. Just think twice before you lose the underline.

60

Making Rollover Hyperlinks

In Topic 59, you looked at three CSS pseudo-classes—link, visited, and active—and you saw how they correspond to the three link states of HTML. CSS adds a fourth link state: the **hover state**, which describes a link when the visitor rolls over it with the mouse pointer. Another link state means another CSS pseudo-class, and another pseudo-class means another opportunity to create a custom style.

The following style sheet includes a rule for the hover state:

```
a {
  font-weight: bold;
  text-decoration: none;
}

a:hover {
  text-decoration: underline;
}
```

GEEKSPEAK

The **hover state** describes a link when the visitor rolls over it with the mouse pointer. Use the hover pseudo-class to create rollover styles for hyperlinks in CSS.

As you can see in Figure 60.1, links appear in boldface without an underline by default, thanks to the general style rule that governs all anchor tags. But when the visitor hovers over a link, the special style rule that applies only to rollovers kicks in, and the underline appears.

Notice that you don't have to include boldface in the style rule for the hover state. Everything in the general style for anchor tags automatically applies to

Figure 60.1

Figure 60.1

With the hover pseudo-class, you can create links that change appearance when the visitor mouses over them.

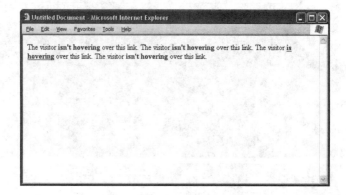

the pseudo-classes. So, when you write style rules for the link states, just include definitions for the extra formatting that you want to apply, including contradictions or changes to the general rules (like going from normal weight in regular links to boldface in rollovers). You don't have to repeat yourself for the style definitions that remain the same from state to state.

TIP

Some designers like to create link rollovers where the links have underlines by default, and rolling over the links causes the underlines to disappear. While this strategy makes sense in that the default underline helps the visitor to figure out which items on the page are hyperlinks, it doesn't make sense in that a rollover should go from a lower-energy state to a higher-energy state. Psychologically speaking, this is what the visitor expects. When the underline goes away, the link seems to be shutting off—it goes from a higher-energy state to a lower-energy state. Some visitors might conclude that the links aren't active after all.

If you don't want to remove the underline by default, then don't remove the underline in the rollover state. Find some other way to style the rollover, like going from normal weight to boldface or adding a background color. Whatever the style, the rollover link should look like it's powering up, not shutting down.

The hover style can include any CSS that applies to text. Therefore, a link rollover can increase in size or weight, change style, change color; change decoration, and so on. Just be careful about altering the default link too much. If the hover link doesn't fit in the same amount of space as the default link, the browser redraws the entire page on rollover, as in Figure 60.2, which may confuse your visitors or even make them motion-sick.

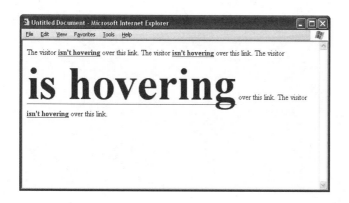

Figure 60.2

Compare this figure with Figure 60.1, and you see that the browser redraws the page to accommodate this extreme rollover style.

61

Choosing the Right Path

The **path** of a hyperlink is like a set of driving instructions for the browser. It tells the browser how to get to the page that loads when the visitor clicks the link.

There are three types of paths: absolute, document-relative, and root-relative. Which path you choose depends on which way you want to tell the browser how to get to the linked page. An **absolute path** tells the browser how to get to the desired page from anywhere on the Web. A **document-relative path** tells the browser how to get to the desired page from the current Web page, while a **root-relative path** tells the browser how to get to the desired page from the current Web site. Each type of path has its merits and drawbacks, as this topic shows.

Using Absolute Paths

An absolute path gives the full URL of the desired Web page, including the **http://www** part, like this:

```
<a href="http://www.pearson.com/">Absolute path</a>
```

GEEKSPEAK

An **absolute** path tells the browser how to get to the desired page from anywhere on the Web. A **document-relative** path tells the browser how to get to the desired page from the current Web page. A **root-relative** path tells the browser how to get to the desired page from the current Web site.

In other words, an absolute path is exactly the same as the URL that you type into a browser's Address field. To go to the page in question, you don't have to type a different URL when you use a different computer or if you're on a different Web site. That's what makes the path absolute—it's always the same, no matter where on the Web the browser happens to be looking.

Since absolute paths are always the same, you don't have to update them in the source code if you change the position of your page in your site's hierarchy. You can move a page with an absolute link anywhere on your site, and the link always connects to the desired page, as long as the URL in the href attribute is accurate.

But since you have to give the full URL whenever you write an absolute path, these paths can be cumbersome for **internal links,** or links that go to pages on your own Web site. Document-relative or root-relative links are generally better for internal links. Moreover, for absolute paths to work, your computer must be actively connected to the Web. If you open a browser window offline to test your site, clicking a link with an absolute path causes the browser to make an Internet connection.

Using Document-Relative Paths

In a document-relative path, you give the browser directions to the desired page from the current Web page. You do this by stepping the browser through your site's hierarchy.

It stands to reason, then, to write a good document-relative path, you need to know the hierarchy of your site. Take the following site structure:

- Home Page
  - Movies
    - Action
    - Comedy
    - Drama
    - Romance

- Mystery/Suspense
- Horror
- Sci-Fi
- Music
  - Popular
  - Jazz
  - Classical
- Games
  - PC
  - Console

Say that the current page is the home page. A document-relative path to the Movies page from the home page looks like this:

```
<a href="movies/movies.htm">Home Page to Movies</a>
```

while a document-relative path to the Action page within the Movies category looks like this:

```
<a href="movies/action/action.htm">Home Page to Action</a>
```

However, if the current page changes, so does the document-relative path. To go to the Action page from the Movies page instead of the home page, the path becomes:

```
<a href="action/action.htm">Movies to Action</a>
```

As you can see, you don't have to fuss with the **http://www** or the domain name of your site. A document-relative path assumes all that. All you have to do is direct the browser to the right directory and file, depending on the current page.

So it goes for drilling down into the site structure, but what if you want to climb back up? How do you write a document-relative path from the Sci-Fi page to the Movies page? You need a bit of technical nomenclature:

```
<a href="../movies.htm">Sci-Fi to Movies</a>
```

The two dots (..) is computer code for "Go up one level in the site structure." So, if the browser is sitting on the Sci-Fi page and sees two dots in the document-relative path, it understands that it must go back up one level in the hierarchy to find the file **movies.htm**. Similarly, if you need to go up more than one level, from Sci-Fi all the way to the home page, you need more than one set of double dots:

```
<a href="../../index.htm">Sci-Fi to Home Page</a>
```

This document-relative path instructs the browser to go up two levels in the site structure to find the file **index.htm**.

You can combine upward and downward movement in the same document-relative path. Say you want to go from the Horror page under Movies to the Classical page under Music. Your document-relative path looks like this:

```
<a href="../music/classical/classical.htm">Sci-Fi to Classical</a>
```

In plain English, the browser goes up one level in the hierarchy to find the music folder. It looks inside the music folder for the classical folder, and it looks inside the classical folder for the file **classical.htm**.

The great thing about document-relative paths is that they work offline just as well as they do online. In other words, you can test your site offline in a browser without logging on to the Web, and all the links with document-relative paths work perfectly. The main disadvantage of document-relative paths is that, if you move the page that contains the link to a different level of your site, the link no longer works. Remember, a document-relative path steps the browser up and down through your site hierarchy. If the page no longer holds the same position in the hierarchy, the steps won't match up. You don't have the same problem with absolute paths, since absolute paths don't depend on the browser's current location.

TIP

Site-management tools such as Macromedia Dreamweaver, Adobe GoLive, and Microsoft FrontPage automatically update document-relative paths when you move your pages around the site structure.

Using Root-Relative Paths

Root-relative paths are similar to document-relative paths in that you use them for internal links only, not external links, but they look more like absolute paths, although they don't have the **http://www** or the domain name of your site:

```
<a href="/index.htm">Root-Relative Path</a>
```

TIP

The root of a site is its uppermost level.

Root-relative paths begin with a forward slash (/), and they give the location of the target page from the **root**, or the uppermost level, of your site. Therefore, a root-relative path is always the same, like an absolute path. The path doesn't change depending on the browser's current location, since the site root itself doesn't change.

Taking the site hierarchy in the previous section as an example, a root-relative path to the Classical page looks like this:

```
<a href="/music/classical/classical.htm">From site root to Classical</a>
```

An absolute path to this page looks exactly the same, with the addition of the **http://www** and the domain name of the site.

On the face of it, root-relative paths seem to be more convenient than document-relative paths for internal links. You can move a page with a root-relative path to a different level of your site structure, and the link still works, since the path always begins at the root of the site. However, root-relative paths have one fatal flaw in that they only work on a Web server. You can't test links with root-relative paths offline, not even if you log on to the Web (unless you have a Web server on your personal computer). You must upload your pages to the Web server to test the links. Not only is this a pain, but also it's potentially embarrassing. Normally, you upload your pages to the server once you've thoroughly tested and debugged them. If you have to upload them to test them, your visitors might stumble across pages that aren't quite ready for prime time while you're in the process of testing and debugging.

So I can't test root-relative links offline?

Actually, you can, but you need special software or hardware. Professional Web builders work around the problem of root-relative links in one of two ways: installing a Web server on their personal computer, or uploading the pages to a staging server, which is a private Web server for debugging and testing.

62

Changing the Color of a Single Hyperlink

here's no way in straight HTML for you to change the color of a single hyperlink on your page. You have the link, vlink, and alink attributes in the body tag, which define the link colors for all links equally, but you don't have the option of making the default unvisited link color blue, for example, and one particular unvisited link red.

You don't have the option, that is, unless you use CSS, which gives you a couple of different ways to change the color of a particular link.

Changing the Default Color for All Link States

If you want to change a link's default color, and if you want to have the same color apply to the link regardless of state, simply add a style rule to the style attribute of the link's anchor tag:

```
<a href="../special.htm" style="color: #FF0000;">See Our Specials</a>
```

TIP

Watch out about changing individual link colors too frequently. Your visitors rely on the link colors to give them an idea about what pages of your site they've already seen. Any time you deviate from the pattern of your default link color scheme, you run the risk of confusing your audience.

However, a perfectly valid use of these techniques might be to change the color of script-launching links to separate them from normal hyperlinks. Doing this reinforces the idea that script-launching links are different kinds of things than page-loading links, which helps to make your site easier to use.

In this example, the hyperlink always appears in red, no matter the state of the link or the default link colors.

Alternately, if the same formatting applies to more than one link on the page, you can create a class style to control the special hyperlink color:

```
<style type="text/css">

  a.special {
    color: #FF0000;
  }

</style>

<body>

  <a class="special" href="../special1.htm">See Our Specials</a>
  <a class="special" href="../special2.htm">See More Specials</a>

</body>
```

Now, any anchor tag that belongs to the **special** class has the same color properties, no matter the state of the link or the default link colors.

Changing the Default Color for Individual Link States

If your special link color needs to change depending on the state of the link, the style attribute of the anchor tag doesn't really help you out, since you need access to the pseudo-classes of the anchor tag. Not a problem—just create a special class style, like this:

```
<style type="text/css">

  a.special:link {
    color: #FF0000;
  }

  a.special:visited {
    color: #CC0000;
  }
```

```
a.special:active {
  color: #990000;
}

a.special:hover {
  color: #660000;
}

</style>

<body>

 <a class="special" href="../special1.htm">See Our Specials</a>
 <a class="special" href="../special2.htm">See More Specials</a>

</body>
```

In this example, you have four style rules for the four CSS link states, each corresponding to a different color. But all the style rules belong to the same class—**special**—so when an anchor tag joins the class, all four style rules apply. The state of the link determines which color appears, regardless of the default color for this state.

TIP

You don't have to give style rules for all four link states. Just define the states that apply to your link. If your special link needs to have separate visited and unvisited colors but not active or hover colors, then just create styles for the link and visited states. The default links on your page may have active and hover states, but they won't apply to your special class.

63

Choosing the Right Text for a Hyperlink

reating a hyperlink is easy. You just drop a pair of anchor tags around the piece of text that you want the visitor to click.

Designing a hyperlink is another matter entirely. Exactly which text should you drop the anchor tags around?

The first rule of thumb for any text hyperlink is this: The link should tell the visitor what to expect with a click. That is, the text of the link should suggest where the hyperlink goes or what kind of information the visitor gets by following it.

Sometimes the choice is easy. If you have a list of links that functions as part of the site's navigation, you see right away that the links should be the full names of the nav categories, as in Figure 63.1. This wording satisfies the first rule of thumb of hyperlinks, because it tells the visitor exactly where the links go.

Listing 63.1 **View Source for Figure 63.1.**

```
<p>
  <a href="../index.htm">HOME</a> |
  <a href="../products/products.htm">PRODUCTS</a> |
  <a href="../services/services.htm">SERVICES</a> |
  <a href="../aboutus/aboutus.htm">ABOUT US</a>
</p>
```

Figure 63.1

When you have a list of links that functions as part of the site's navigation, drop your anchor tags around each nav choice.

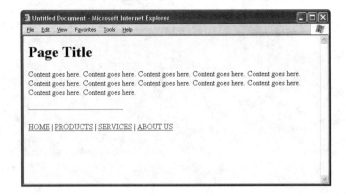

The same holds true if you have a list of links in a sidebar or a special section of the page, as in Figure 63.2. There's no question where the links go. The text of the links themselves give it away.

Listing 63.2 **View Source for Figure 63.2.**

```
<p><a href="http://external_site01">External Site 1</a></p>
<p><a href="http://external_site02">External Site 2</a></p>
<p><a href="http://external_site03">External Site 3</a></p>
<p><a href="http://external_site04">External Site 4</a></p>
<p><a href="http://external_site04">External Site 5</a></p>
```

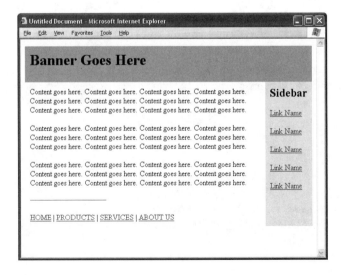

Figure 63.2

Likewise with links in sidebars.

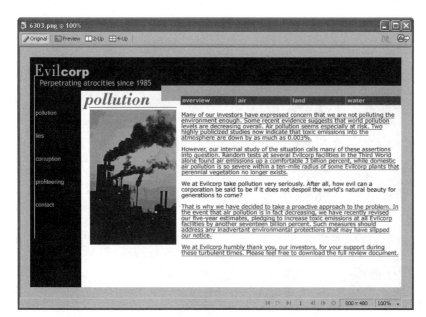

Figure 63.3

Here, entire paragraphs serve as hyperlinks. Does this make you want to click? Of course it doesn't. You don't have time for this.

But what happens if you have **inline links**, or links that appear within the running text of the page? You can't very well make the whole paragraph a link, although some designers like to try this, as in Figure 63.3. Technically, this strategy satisfies the first rule of thumb of hyperlinks, because it eventually tells the visitors where the links go, more or less. However, it breaks the second rule of thumb of hyperlinks, which is this: The link text should be as clear and concise as possible.

Why clear and concise? Because unclear and wordy go against the flow of the Web, which is to say that they slow your visitors down. Your visitors have to read the text carefully, usually more than once, to figure out where the links go. Remember, your visitors may be the biggest fans of the printed word since Stephen King, but they don't read text on the Web. They skim. They scan. They expect

> **GEEKSPEAK**
>
> Inline links are links that appear within the running text of the page.

the particular piece of information they're looking for to catch their eye, which simply doesn't happen when it blends in with everything else.

So how do you make a link clear and concise? The key is to make the link text work out of context. That is, if your visitors don't read any of the surrounding text (which is highly likely), they should still be able to figure out where the links go.

Take Figure 63.4. The link text is clearer, and it tells you what kind of information to expect at the other end without forcing you to read the entire paragraph. But the link text is still too wordy. Too much of it jumps off the page. You still need to read too much.

Figure 63.4

*Getting better.
More focused.
But the link text
is still too long.*

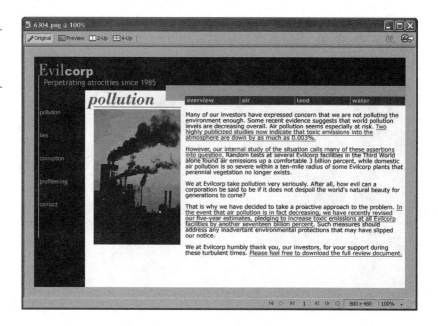

The design in Figure 63.5 is better still. The links are short enough, and they tell you where they go. Even if you don't read any of the surrounding text, you know that the first link goes to information about some studies. You know that the second link goes to information about an internal study. You know that the

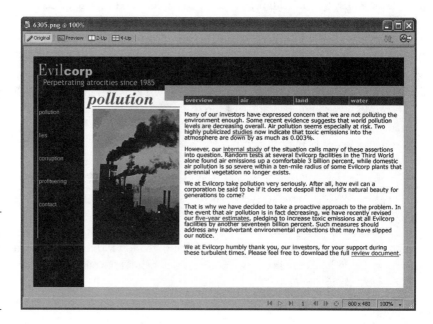

Figure 63.5

*Better still.
These links are
short, and they
tell the visitor
what kind of
information to
expect.*

third link goes to information about five-year estimates, and you know the last link goes to information about a review document.

Notice that the text of the first link doesn't have to spell out what kinds of studies appear on the linked page. Your visitors may be impatient, but they aren't stupid. They already know they're on the Pollution page. Put yourself in their shoes. If you had to guess what kinds of studies wait at the other end of the link, you'd probably guess pollution studies; and, as it turns out, you'd be absolutely right.

Notice also that the second link reads **internal study**, while the first link says **studies**. In the spirit of brevity, you might think that the second link should drop the **internal** and just say **study**. In some cases, you might be right. But in this case, the word **study** is too similar to the **studies** of the first link. The phrase **internal study** is brief enough, and it creates an instant contrast to the first link, helping to differentiate the two. In turn, your visitors expect that the links go to different pages, which they do. The words **studies** and **study** don't have the same contrast, so some visitors might expect them to go to the same page.

Finally, the last link doesn't use the word **download**, which some might expect. Why not? Because **download** doesn't make sense out of context. A hyperlink on the Pollution page that says **download** tells you nothing, except that clicking the link allows you to download something that probably relates to pollution. But a hyperlink on the Pollution page that says **review document** gives you a better idea about what to expect: a review document, presumably by Evilcorp, about pollution practices.

Which segues nicely into the closing point of this topic: What about the ever-popular **Click Here** link? The design in Figure 63.6 gives four variations of this all-time classic, and not one of them is a well-designed hyperlink. All but the first are concise, but are they clear? Do they make sense out of context?

There's only one way to find out: Skim the page. Do the links tell you where they go? Do they tell you what kind of information to expect? The closest one is the last one, which promises **information**, but that term is so general as to be virtually meaningless.

Click Here links read like instructions. They don't tell your visitors anything about what's on the linked page. Instead, they tell your visitors what to do. But your visitors already know how hyperlinks work. And if they don't, they'll figure it out. After all, who taught you how to click?

Your visitors already know where to click. They already know how to click. What they want from you is *why* to click, which **Click Here** doesn't provide.

FAQ

What about punctuation marks? Are they part of the link text?

The text of an inline link doesn't usually include beginning or ending punctuation marks such as parentheses, periods, or commas. This general style is exactly the opposite of print publishing, where highlighted words and phrases usually do include beginning and ending punctuation.

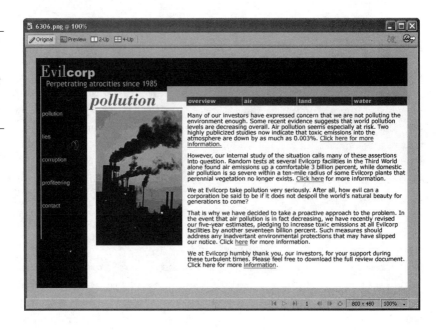

Creating ScreenTips for Hyperlinks

Occasionally, when you hover over an image with the mouse pointer on a Web page, a ScreenTip appears, giving additional information about the image. You know from Topic 34 that you, the designer, have complete control over what the ScreenTip says, because the browser displays whatever appears in the alt attribute of the img tag:

```
<img src="horse.jpg" width="100" height="50" alt="An antique red wooden rocking
horse with a brass bell on its collar">
```

Adding alt text to an image helps to make it more accessible for the visually impaired. The text describes the content of the image, allowing anyone who hears the alt text to imagine the picture without having to see it.

The same principle holds for text hyperlinks, especially hyperlinks that don't appear within a block of text. Sighted visitors simply notice the blue color of the link text and the underline, and they know what to do without having to think about it. But when you separate out a list of links in a sidebar, breadcrumb trail, or bottom-of-the-page navigation, the purpose of these links may not be clear to those who don't have the benefit of the blue, the underline, or the position of the links on the page in relation to the rest of the content. Therefore, you improve the accessibility of your site if you spell out exactly what these links do.

The anchor tag doesn't have an alt attribute for you to use in this way, but it does have a title attribute that performs the same function:

```
<p>
  <a href="../index.htm" title="Go to the home page">HOME</a> |
  <a href="../products/products.htm" title="Go to the Products page">PRODUCTS</a> |
  <a href="../services/services.htm" title="Go to the Services page">SERVICES</a> |
  <a href="../aboutus/aboutus.htm" title="Go to the About Us page">ABOUT US</a>
</p>
```

TIP

To make your ScreenTip as accessible as possible, don't just repeat the text of the link. That defeats the purpose. Instead, tell the visitor where the link goes. Don't give **Home Page** as the title of the link, in other words. **Go to the home page** is better.

When you hover over a link with the mouse pointer, the text in the title attribute appears as a ScreenTip. It's a nice touch for your sighted visitors. More importantly, accessibility tools such as screen readers include the title of the link in their output, so the visually impaired understand clearly where the links go.

TIP

In your link title, you don't need to say **Click here**, as in **Click here to go to the Product page**. Clicking is understood. Just say, **Go to the Product page**.

63

Opening a New Browser Window

When a link leads to an external site, it's common for the link to open a new browser window. The external site loads in the new window, keeping the referring page alive and well in the original window.

Some Web builders scoff at this strategy. They're usually the same people who hate popup windows with an intensity that Freud himself would find difficult to explain, which may or may not have something to do with the amount of clutter on the desktop. Given that external sites regularly go down, change URLs, or include techniques that disable the browser's Back button, opening a new browser window is not as sinister as it might at first appear. In fact, in some circles, it's common courtesy. Depositing your visitors on a File Not Found error message instead of the promised Web site seems less like a mistake when getting rid of the dud site is as simple as closing the new browser window.

Opening a new browser window is easy from any link. Just add the target attribute to the anchor tag, and set the value of this attribute to **_blank**, like this:

```
<a href="http://externalsite/" target="_blank">External site</a>
```

66

Using Named Anchors

The anchor tag is unusual in that it has two different functions in HTML. On one hand, you can use the anchor tag to link to another page:

```
<a href="anotherpage.htm">Go to another page</a>
```

On the other hand, you can use the anchor tag to set a location or **named anchor** to which to link:

```
<a name="linkhere"></a>
```

The way the anchor tag functions depends on its attributes. When the anchor tag contains the href attribute, it functions as the **source** of a link, or the element that the visitor clicks to go to another page. But when the anchor tag contains the name attribute, it functions as the **destination** of a link, or a location that appears in the browser after the visitor clicks the link.

Setting Named Anchors

To set an anchor on your page, simply drop an anchor tag in the exact location you want the browser to go. Remember to specify the name attribute instead of the href attribute so that the tag functions as a destination instead of a source.

One of the most common uses of this technique is to divide a long Web page into several sections. You see this often on FAQ pages. The top of the page contains the frequently asked questions (FAQs), which are href anchors. The answers to the questions follow, each with its own named anchor tag, like so:

```
<a name="question01"></a>
<p><strong>What is the meaning of life?</strong></p>
<p>The meaning of life is money.</p>

<a name="question02"></a>
<p><strong>What is the meaning of money?</strong></p>
<p>The meaning of money is time.</p>

<a name="question03"></a>
<p><strong>What is the meaning of time?</strong></p>
<p>The meaning of time is life.</p>
```

As Figure 66.1 shows, the named anchors themselves don't appear in the browser window. They're not visible elements. They simply provide a specific location to which you can link.

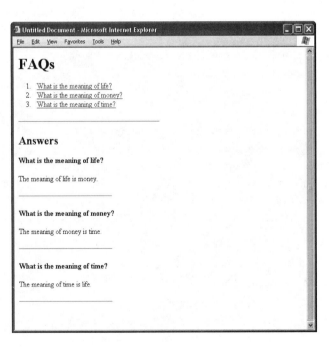

Figure 66.1

Named anchors don't appear in the browser window, but the browser definitely knows they're there. Link to one of the anchors, and the browser jumps to its precise location.

Linking to Named Anchors

To link to a named anchor, you need another anchor tag, only this one should be a source anchor, not a destination anchor. In the href attribute of the source anchor, type a number sign (#) followed by the name of the anchor to which you want to link, like this:

```
<ol>
  <li><a href="#question01">What is the meaning of life?</a></li>
  <li><a href="#question02">What is the meaning of money?</a></li>
  <li><a href="#question03">What is the meaning of time?</a></li>
</ol>
```

These anchor tags appear as regular hyperlinks in the browser. That's because they *are* regular hyperlinks. The only difference is that they go to named anchors on the same page, not to the top of some other page.

What happens if you want to link to a named anchor that exists on some other page? Not a problem. Simply tack the named-anchor nomenclature to the end of the path, like this:

IF a named anchor is invisible, how does the browser show that the visitor has jumped to one?

Normally, when the browser jumps to a named anchor, it scrolls the screen so that the anchor point is at the top.

```
<a href="../movies/movies.htm#newrelases">New Releases</a>
```

This hybrid path finds the page **movies.htm** and then jumps to the **newreleases** named anchor on this page.

TIP

It's good etiquette to include a **Back To Top** link somewhere after the named anchor. This way, the visitor can return to the source of the link quickly and easily.

You can accomplish this with another named anchor. By way of example, assume you're building a FAQ page. Right before the list of questions, insert a named anchor called top. Then, after the answer to each question, add code to this effect:

```
<a href="#top">Back to the top</a>
```

67

Creating Email Links

An **email link** isn't really a link, although it looks like one, and it uses the anchor tag. However, instead of directing the browser to another page or named anchor, it opens a blank email window. Use email links on your site as a way for your visitors to contact you.

An email link looks something like this:

```
<a href="mailto:name@emailaddress">Send me email</a>
```

The anchor tag creates the link, just as with a normal hyperlink, and it uses the href attribute, too, but the value of this attribute isn't a path. Instead, it's a special signifier called a **mailto** for obvious reasons. The text that follows the mailto is the recipient's email address. So, if you want the email to go to your

GEEKSPEAK

An **email link** opens a blank email window when clicked.

> **TIP**
>
> You can also supply a subject for the message and a carbon-copy (CC) address:
>
> ```
> <a
> href="mailto:name@emailaddress?subject=Mail&cc=another@emailaddress">Send
> me email</a>
> ```
>
> Subjects and CCs don't work with every email application, though, so don't be surprised if they don't work with yours.

personal email account, supply **mailto** in the href attribute followed by a colon (:) and your complete email address.

If you're looking for an excuse to change the color of one hyperlink on your page without affecting the default colors (see Topic 62), an email link is a good candidate. Making this link a different color helps to set it off from the regular hyperlinks on the page, which reinforces the idea that the email link has a different function.

FAQ

I engage in acts of subversion. How can email links help me?

Nobody says that the email address in an email link has to be yours. If you're feeling especially naughty, you could create an incendiary Web page, add an email link, and direct the reams of hate mail that your page is likely to generate to your least favorite political organization. But you didn't hear that in this topic.

PART VI:
Form Topics

Working with Form Widgets

Applying Styles to Text Widgets

Validating Form Input

Setting the Tab Order

Working with Fieldsets

Working with Labels

68

Working with Form Widgets

The little thingies that you click and type text into on a form have a name other than **thingies**. They're called **widgets** and occasionally also **form fields** or **form objects**. A large part of designing an effective form is being able to identify the various widgets and knowing which ones to use for what kinds of entries.

Table 68.1 runs down the list of HTML widgets, in case you need a refresher. The sections that follow take each widget in turn.

Table 68.1 **HTML Widgets**		
WIDGET	USED FOR	TAG
Button (generic)	Launching a function	`<input type="button">`
Checkbox	Selecting any number of several options	`<input type="checkbox">`
File field	Attaching an external file to the form data	`<input type="file">`
Hidden field	Storing hidden data	`<input type="hidden">`

Table 68.1 *(Continued)*

WIDGET	USED FOR	TAG
Image field	Sending the form data to the Web server	`<input type="image">`
List	Selecting any number of several options (but usually just one)	`<select size="x"></select>`
Menu	Selecting any number of several options (but usually just one)	`<select></select>`
Password field	Entering a password	`<input type="password">`
Radio button	Selecting one of several options	`<input type="radio">`
Reset button	Returning all widgets in the form to their default states	`<input type="reset">`
Submit button	Sending the form data to the Web server	`<input type="submit">`
Text area	Entering multiple lines of text	`<textarea></textarea>`
Text field	Entering a single line of text	`<input type="text">`

Working with Generic Buttons

Generic buttons (see Figure 68.1) are clickable, but they don't do anything when the visitor clicks them, unlike submit and reset buttons. You must specifically program these buttons to do what you want them to do, which is usually to launch a JavaScript function. The button's input tag takes the onClick event, where you put the name of the function that you want to launch.

Listing 68.1 View Source for Figure 68.1.

```
<form>
  <input type="button" name="totalButton"  value="Calculate Total"
onClick="doTotal();">
</form>
```

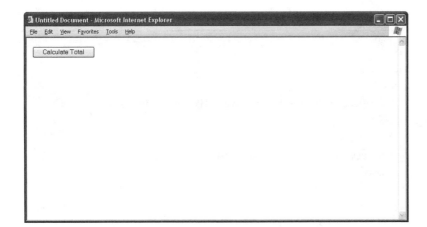

Figure 68.1

A generic button is clickable, but it doesn't do anything until you add an onClick event to its tag.

The name attribute of the button's input tag identifies the button, and the value attribute contains the label that appears on the button's face. The value of the onClick event is the name of the JavaScript function that launches when the visitor clicks the button.

Working with Checkboxes

Checkboxes are ideal for relatively short sets of options where the visitor can select one, none, all, or as many as desired, as in Figure 68.2. Don't use checkboxes for either/or situations, where the visitor needs to choose one and only one option—radio buttons work better for those.

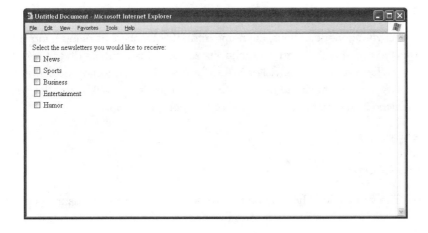

Figure 68.2

Use checkboxes when you have a short set of options where the visitor can select as many as needed (even none).

Listing 68.2 **View Source for Figure 68.2.**

```
<form>
  <table>
    <tr>
      <td>Select the newsletters you would like to receive:</td>
    </tr>
    <tr>
      <td><input type="checkbox" name="newsCheck" value="yes">
        News</td>
    </tr>
    <tr>
      <td><input type="checkbox" name="sportsCheck" value="yes">
        Sports</td>
    </tr>
    <tr>
      <td><input type="checkbox" name="businessCheck" value="yes">
        Business</td>
    </tr>
    <tr>
      <td><input type="checkbox" name="entertainmentCheck" value="yes">
        Entertainment</td>
    </tr>
    <tr>
      <td><input type="checkbox" name="humorCheck" value="yes">
        Humor</td>
    </tr>
  </table>
</form>
```

As with generic buttons, the name attribute of a checkbox's input tag supplies the name of that particular checkbox. The value attribute gives the data that the form submits if the visitor checks the checkbox in question. So, if the visitor happens to check the news, sports, and business checkboxes, the form sends the following data to the Web server upon submission:

```
newsCheck=yes
sportsCheck=yes
businessCheck=yes
```

The values don't have to be the same for every checkbox, as they are in Figure 68.1. You can supply different values for each checkbox if you like. It all

depends on what you want to send to the
Web server.

To preselect a checkbox when the
form loads, add the checked attribute to
the checkbox's input tag:

```
<input type="checkbox" name="news"
value="yes" checked>
```

As you can see, the checked attribute doesn't get a value.

Working with File Fields

File fields allow your visitors to attach computer files from their local machines
to the form submission. This way, your visitors can upload things like image
files, sounds, and text documents to the Web server. As you can see in Figure
68.3, a file field has two parts: the field itself and a Browse button.

Listing 68.3 View Source for Figure 68.3.

```
<form>
  <input type="file" name="imageFile" size="50" maxlength="70">
</form>
```

Once again, the name attribute identifies the file field. The size attribute
gives the length of the field in characters, not pixels, while the maxlength attribute determines the maximum number of characters that the field will accept. In

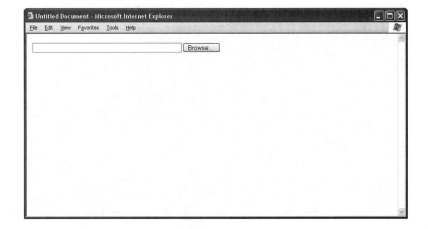

Figure 68.3
Use file fields
when you want
to allow your
visitors to
upload files
from their local
machines to
the Web server.

What happens to the uploaded file?

File fields can be tricky to handle on the server's side of things. Normally, forms of this type go directly into a database. The designer of the database needs to prepare a special column to accept file data instead of the usual text or numbers.

I don't like the Browse button. Can I change it?

Nope. You're stuck with it. HTML doesn't let you change its label or make it disappear.

the example in Figure 68.3, with a size of 50 and a maximum length of 70, the visitor sees 50 characters in the field at a time, but the field stops accepting input after 70 characters.

A valid path must appear inside the field for this widget to work correctly. That's why the file field includes a Browse button. When clicked, a dialog box opens, allowing the visitor to navigate to the exact file to upload. The browser then automatically fills in the correct path.

Working with Hidden Fields

The data in a hidden field gets submitted along with the rest of the form to the Web server, but the visitor doesn't usually know about it, since the hidden field is completely invisible on the page, as Figure 68.4 shows.

Listing 68.4 **View Source for Figure 68.4.**

```
<form>
    <input type="hidden" name="referringPage"
value="newsletter.htm">
</form>
```

Designers occasionally use hidden fields for mischief, but normally these fields are completely innocent. In the example in Figure 68.4, the hidden field

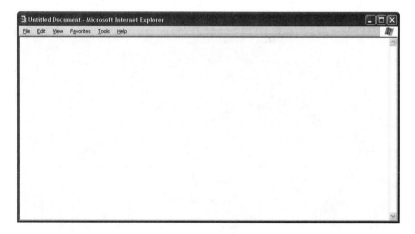

Figure 68.4

A hidden field contains form data, but the visitor can't see it, because the field is invisible.

contains the name of the page that submitted the form, which is handy to know if
your site contains multiple forms that look
more or less the same.

Even though the visitor doesn't see
the data in the hidden field, the Web
server receives it like this:

referringPage=newsletter.htm

**Can my visitors change the content of
a hidden field?**

Not directly. Because hidden fields are invisible, the
visitor can't edit or change their values. However,
JavaScript functions can update the value of a hidden
field quite easily.

Working with Image Fields

An image field is a graphical replacement for a standard HTML submit button.
The image field is clickable, and it works exactly like a submit button in that
clicking it sends the form data to the Web server. The advantage to replacing a
submit button with an image field is that you get to use whatever image file you
like to submit the form, as in Figure 68.5. You don't have to accept the standard
and generally ugly button widget that comes with your browser.

Listing 68.5 **View Source for Figure 68.5.**

```
<form>
  <input type="image" name="goButton" src="images/go.gif" width="20" height="20">
</form>
```

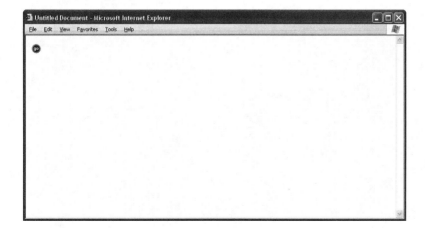

Figure 68.5

Use an image
field in place of
a standard
submit button.

The src attribute contains the path to the image field's graphic file, and the width and height attributes supply the width and height of the image, just as in the img tag.

Replacing a Reset Button

Image fields always submit form data. There's no way to change an image field so that it functions as a reset button, for example. But don't let that stop you. Just use a regular image tag. Drop anchor tags around the image to make it click-able, and then add a simple JavaScript function to duplicate the reset behavior. Here's the complete script, plus a sample link:

```
<head>
  <script language="JavaScript">

    function doReset() {
      document.formname.reset();

/* Replace formname with the value of the form tag's name attribute. */

    }

  </script>
</head>

<!-- The body of the page follows. -->

<body>

  <a href="javascript:doReset();"><img src="images/reset.gif" width="60" height="40"
alt="Click to reset the form."></a>

</body>
```

Replacing a Generic Button

Along the same lines, you can use an image to launch a JavaScript function and replace the generic button widget. Try something like this:

```
<head>
  <script language="JavaScript">
```

```
   function yourFunction() {

/* Put your JavaScript function here. */

   }

  </script>
</head>

<body>

  <a href="javascript:yourFunction();"><img src="images/button.gif" width="60"
height="40" alt="Click to launch the script."></a>

</body>
```

Working with Lists

A list displays a number of options from which the visitor can choose, as in Figure 68.5. Lists are better than radio buttons or checkboxes if the number of options is rather large, since lists make better use of space.

The size attribute of the list's select tag determines how many options are visible at once. If the list contains more options than this number, the browser adds a scrollbar to the right side of the list.

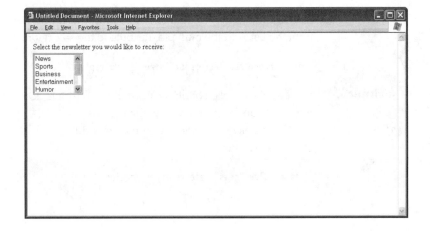

Figure 68.6

Organize a large number of choices in a list.

Listing 68.6 **View Source for Figure 68.6.**

```
<form>
  <table>
    <tr>
      <td>Select the newsletter you would like to receive:</td>
    </tr>
    <tr>
      <td><select name="newsletterList" size="5">
        <option value="news">News</option>
        <option value="sports">Sports</option>
        <option value="business">Business</option>
        <option value="entertainment">Entertainment</option>
        <option value="humor">Humor</option>
        <option value="style">Style</option>
        <option value="travel">Travel</option>
        <option value="science">Science</option>
        <option value="culture">Culture</option>
      </select></td>
    </tr>
  </table>
</form>
```

Each option in the list gets its own option tag. The value attribute of the option tag contains the data that the Web server receives when the visitor submits the form. So, if the visitor chooses to receive the Culture newsletter, the Web server gets something that looks like this:

```
newsletterList=culture
```

FAQ

How do you select multiple options from a list?

Your visitors must hold down Ctrl (Windows) or Command (Mac) to select multiple options from a list.

To allow your visitors to select more than one item from the list, add the multiple attribute to the select tag:

```
<select name="newsletterList" size="5" multiple>
```

Like the checked attribute, the multiple attribute doesn't have a value. It just appears in the tag.

To preselect an option from the list, add the selected attribute to its tag:

```
<option value="news" selected>News</option>
```

If you designed your list to accept multiple options, you may have multiple preselected options:

```
<option value="news" selected>News</option>
<option value="sports" selected>Sports</option>
<option value="business" selected>Business</option>
```

Otherwise, the browser takes one preselected option and ignores the others. Internet Explorer defaults to the first selected option, while Netscape defaults to the last.

Working with Menus

A menu is very much like a list. The markup is nearly exactly the same, and you use menus to present a large number of options, just like a list. The main difference is that the options appear in a dropdown list, as in Figure 68.7.

Listing 68.7 View Source for Figure 68.7.

```
<form>
  <table>
    <tr>
      <td>Select the newsletter you would like to receive:</td>
    </tr>
    <tr>
      <td><select name="select">
          <option value="news" selected>News</option>
          <option value="sports">Sports</option>
          <option value="business">Business</option>
          <option value="entertainment">Entertainment</option>
          <option value="humor">Humor</option>
          <option value="style">Style</option>
          <option value="travel">Travel</option>
          <option value="science">Science</option>
          <option value="culture">Culture</option>
      </select></td>
    </tr>
  </table>
</form>
```

Use a menu instead of a list if you prefer the compact look of the menu.

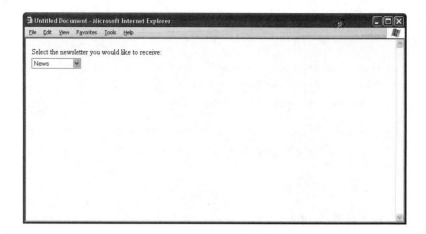

You should always preselect one option in a menu. Otherwise, the menu appears blank until the visitor opens the dropdown list.

Look very carefully in the View Source for Figure 68.7, and you see that what makes the difference between a menu and a list is the absence of the size attribute in the select tag.

Otherwise, the attributes in a menu are identical in number and function, and the data that the Web server receives looks much the same. In addition, you can add the multiple and selected attributes to the select and option tags of a menu, just as in a list, although doing this turns the menu into a list.

Can you use password fields for other kinds of input?

Certainly. You don't have to restrict password fields to passwords only. PINs, keycodes, and account numbers are all viable candidates for this type of widget.

Working with Password Fields

Password fields are like text fields, only the text inside them appears dotted out, as in Figure 68.8. You typically use these kinds of fields to accept passwords, naturally, or any other kind of input that you would rather not display literally on screen.

Listing 68.8 **View Source for Figure 68.8.**

```
<form>
  <strong>Password:</strong>
  <input type="password" name="userPassword" value="ladda">
</form>
```

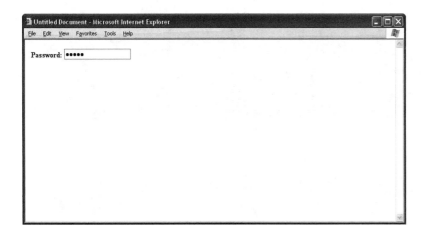

Figure 68.8

Use password fields when you don't want to display the exact text of the field on screen.

In this example, the password field has a preset value. That is, the text of the value attribute appears in the password field when the page loads. If you don't want your password field to load a preset value, simply leave this attribute out:

```
<input type="password" name="userPassword">
```

Even though the browser conceals the actual value of the password field on screen, the Web server receives the literal text inside the password field upon submission, along these lines:

```
userPassword=ladda;
```

> **TIP**
>
> As with text fields and file fields, you set the physical width of a password field with the size attribute, and the maximum number of characters that the visitor can enter with the maxlength attribute.

Working with Radio Buttons

Use radio buttons when you have a short set of mutually exclusive options, or options from which the visitor can select one and only one, as in Figure 68.9. Unlike with checkboxes, multiple options aren't allowed when you use radio buttons.

> **TIP**
>
> You can't uncheck a radio button like you can a checkbox. Therefore, always preselect one option in a list of radio buttons. This way, your visitor **must** select something—if not the default choice, then another.

Figure 68.9

Use radio buttons when you have a short set of mutually exclusive options.

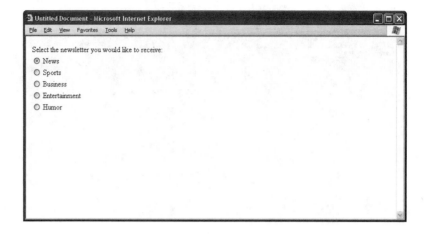

Listing 68.9 **View Source for Figure 68.9.**

```
<form>
  <table>
    <tr>
      <td>Select the newsletter you would like to receive:</td>
    </tr>
    <tr>
      <td><input type="radio" name="newsletter" value="news" checked>
        News</td>
    </tr>
    <tr>
      <td><input type="radio" name="newsletter" value="sports">
        Sports</td>
    </tr>
    <tr>
      <td><input type="radio" name="newsletter" value="business">
        Business</td>
    </tr>
    <tr>
      <td><input type="radio" name="newsletter" value="entertainment">
        Entertainment</td>
    </tr>
    <tr>
      <td><input type="radio" name="newsletter" value="humor">
        Humor</td>
    </tr>
```

```
    </tr>
   </table>
  </form>
```

Notice the checked attribute in the input tag for the News radio button. This attribute preselects the option in question when the form loads.

Normally, the names of the various widgets in your form are unique. Not so with groups of radio buttons—it's very important that all the radio buttons in the same group have the same name. Otherwise, the browser doesn't know which radio buttons belong to which group, and you don't get mutually exclusive options.

The value attribute determines the data submitted for the checked radio button. So, if your visitor chooses to receive the Humor newsletter, the form submission looks something like this:

```
newsletter=humor
```

The browser doesn't submit the other, unchecked radio buttons.

Working with Reset Buttons

Clicking a reset button (Figure 68.10) causes the browser to return all fields in the form to their default values. If a field doesn't have a default value, the browser clears the field instead.

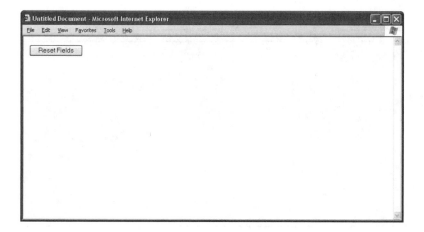

Figure 68.10

Add a reset button to allow your visitor to return the form to its default state.

Listing 68.10 **View Source for Figure 68.10.**

```
<form>
  <input type="reset" name="fieldsReset" value="Reset Fields">
</form>
```

The reset button's value attribute determines the text that appears on the button's face.

Working with Submit Buttons

Clicking a submit button (Figure 68.11) sends off the data of the form for processing. Where the form data goes appears in the form tag's action attribute, and how the form data goes appears in the form tag's method attribute.

Listing 68.11 **View Source for Figure 68.11.**

```
<form action="/forms/process.php" method="POST">
  <input type="submit" name="formSubmit" value="Submit Form">
</form>
```

In this example, clicking the submit button sends the form data via the POST method. The submission follows the root-relative path in the action attribute,

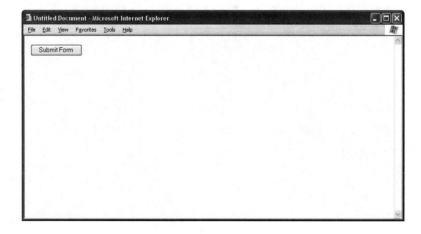

Figure 68.11

A submit button sends the form data to the Web server for processing.

winding up on a page called **process.php**, which would contain server-side code for processing the form data.

As with other buttons, the text in the submit button's value attribute appears on the button's face.

Working with Text Areas

Text areas are multiline fields for text input, as Figure 68.12 shows.

How do I process form data?

Unfortunately, you need server-side scripting to process and use form data, which is beyond the scope of this humble tome.

Don't send your submission to a client-side document like an HTML page or JavaScript file, because the browser won't know what to do with it.

Listing 68.12 **View Source for Figure 68.12.**

```
<form>
  <textarea name="typeTextHere" cols="50" rows="5">Type text here.</textarea>
</form>
```

The cols attribute of the textarea tag gives the horizontal size of the text area in characters, not pixels, while the rows attribute determines the vertical size of the text area in the number of lines. So, the example in Figure 68.12 is 50 characters wide and 5 lines tall.

The preset text of a text area appears between the textarea tags, not in a value attribute as with other widgets. If you don't want preset text, don't include any:

Figure 68.12

Use text areas for multiline text input.

```
<textarea name="typeTextHere" cols="50"
rows="5"></textarea>
```

By default, the text in a text area doesn't wrap. As the visitor types, the browser adds the new characters to the current line. Pressing Enter or Return causes a carriage return, and a new line begins.

The wrap attribute of the textarea tag changes this property. Setting this attribute to **virtual** or **physical** does the job:

```
<textarea name="typeTextHere" cols="50" rows="5" wrap="virtual"></textarea>
```

The type of wrapping affects the way the browser submits the form data. In **virtual wrapping**, the text appears to wrap in the text area, and the form submits the text as a continuous string of characters, without carriage returns (unless the visitor expressly creates them by pressing Enter or Return). In **physical wrapping**, the form submits the text exactly as it appears in the text area, complete with carriage returns at the end of each wrapped line.

Working with Text Fields

Text fields are single-line widgets for text input, as in Figure 68.13. Text fields are probably the most common widget on the Web.

The width of the text field—in characters, not pixels—appears in the size attribute. The maximum number of characters that the visitor can type into the field appears in the maxlength attribute, and the default text appears in the value field.

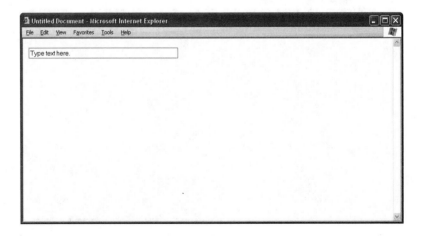

Figure 68.13

Use text fields for single-line text input.

Listing 68.13 **View Source for Figure 68.13.**

```
<form>
  <input type="text" name="typeTextHere" value="Type text here." size="50"
maxlength="80">
</form>
```

When you click inside a text field, the browser doesn't automatically select the entire string of text in the field. This is often inconvenient when your text fields contain preset values, because the visitor has to clear out the old information before typing in new information. A simple line of JavaScript remedies this problem nicely:

```
<input type="text" name="typeTextHere"
value="Type text here." size="50"
maxlength="80" onFocus="this.select();">
```

The onFocus event fires when the visitor highlights the text field, either by clicking inside it or by tabbing onto it. When the text field receives focus, the select() method selects everything in the field.

What happens if you omit the size attribute of a text field?

If you omit the size attribute, the browser uses its default width for text fields, which varies depending on the browser. If you omit the maxlength attribute, there is no limit to the number of characters that the visitor can type into the field.

TIP
You can add onFocus="this.select();" to password fields and text areas, too.

69

Applying Styles to Text Widgets

Text widgets accept CSS style rules, just as other HTML elements do. With CSS, you can change the default font of a menu, for example, or change the background color of a submit button. However, as with other HTML elements, different browsers don't always cooperate with the CSS styles you define for your text widgets, so be sure to preview your page in a variety of browsers.

FAQ

Can I use CSS styles with nontext widgets?

Yes, but don't get your hopes up. Nontext widgets such as checkboxes don't usually look the way you intend when you apply CSS styles to them.

Changing the Text Style

The various text attributes of CSS allow you to alter the appearance of the type in any widget that uses text, including text fields, text areas, buttons, menus, and lists. Table 69.1 provides a summary of common CSS text attributes if you need a refresher.

Use combinations of the attributes in Table 69.1 to work up sophisticated text widgets, as in Figure 69.1. These examples are over the top, but they show you what you can do if you have little aesthetic restraint.

412

Table 69.1 **Common CSS Attributes for the Text in Text Widgets**		
ATTRIBUTE	CONTROLS	EXAMPLE
font-family	The typeface of the text in the widget	font-family: Arial, Helvetica, sans-serif;
font-style	The style of the text in the widget	font-style: italic;
font-weight	The weight of the text in the widget	font-weight: bold;
font-size	The size of the text in the widget	font-size: 12px;
font-variant	The typeface variation of the text in the widget	font-variant: small-caps;
text-transform	The way the browser alters the casing of the text inside the widget	text-transform: lowercase;
text-decoration	The underline, overline, or line-through of the text inside the widget	text-decoration: underline;

TIP

Since different widgets often use the same tag, you're better off creating specific classes for each type of widget rather than creating one blanket style rule for the HTML widget tags.

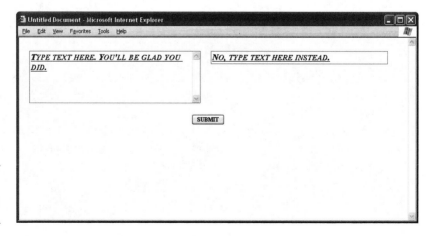

Figure 69.1

Apply CSS text attributes to alter the type in text widgets.

Listing 69.1 **View Source for Figure 69.1.**

```
<head>
  <style type="text/css">

    .textfields {
      font-family: "Times New Roman", Times, serif;
      font-style: italic;
      font-weight: bold;
      font-size: 18px;
      font-variant: small-caps;
      text-decoration: underline;
    }

    .buttons {
      font-family: "Times New Roman", Times, serif;
      font-size: 12px;
      font-weight: bold;
      text-transform: uppercase;
    }

  </style>
</head>

<body>

  <form>
    <table cellpadding="10">
      <tr valign="top">
        <td>
          <textarea cols="50" rows="5" class="textfields">Type text here. You'll be
glad you did.</textarea>
        </td>
        <td>
          <input type="text" class="textfields" size="50" value="No, type text here
instead.">
        </td>
      </tr>
      <tr>
        <td colspan="2" align="center">
          <input type="submit" value="Submit" class="buttons"></td>
      </tr>
```

414

```
      </table>
    </form>

</body>
```

Changing the Colors and the Border

The color and background-color CSS attributes allow you to modify the foreground and background colors of a text widget, as in Figure 69.2. You can also modify the borders of buttons with the border-color, border-width, and border-style attributes.

Listing 69.2 **View Source for Figure 69.2.**

```
<head>
  <style type="text/css">

    .listsmenus {
      color: #FFFFFF;
      background-color: #000000;
    }

    .buttons {
      background-color: #000000;
      color: #FFFFFF;
      border-color: #999999;
      border-width: 6px;
      border-style: double;
      font-weight: bold;
    }

  </style>
</head>

<body>

  <form>
    <table cellpadding="10">
      <tr valign="top">
```

```
      <td><select name="select" size="5" class="listsmenus">
          <option value="1" selected>List Option 1</option>
          <option value="2">List Option 2</option>
          <option value="3">List Option 3</option>
          <option value="4">List Option 4</option>
          <option value="5">List Option 5</option>
        </select></td>
      <td><select name="select" class="listsmenus">
          <option value="1" selected>Menu Option 1</option>
          <option value="2">Menu Option 2</option>
          <option value="3">Menu Option 3</option>
          <option value="4">Menu Option 4</option>
          <option value="5">Menu Option 5</option>
        </select></td>
    </tr>
    <tr>
      <td colspan="2" align="center"><input type="submit" class="buttons"
value="Submit"></td>
    </tr>
  </table>
  </form>


</body>
```

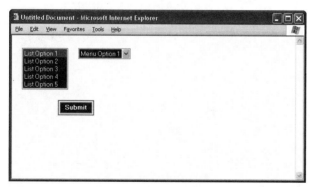

Figure 69.2

Use the color and background-color attributes to change the foreground and background colors of a text widget.

Validating Form Input

E ven though you need server-side coding to process form data, you can use good old client-side scripting to review the visitor's submission before it goes to the Web server. This process is called **validation**, and it's a very good idea for most types of forms.

A validation pass helps to prevent errors, both intentional and accidental, from confusing or crashing the server-side code that eventually receives the form data. Say your form asks visitors to supply an email address so that the server-side form handler can send out a confirmation email. Obviously, you need the visitor to supply an email address, or the server-side code won't work right. If someone out there gets clever and tries to leave the field blank or types in something other than an email address, the validation script catches it and asks for a correction. Of course, the visitor could still supply an invalid email address, but at least the validation script screens out a good chunk of potentially bad data.

Any validation script requires close coordination with the structure of the form. And since no two forms are alike, there's no such thing as an all-purpose, one-size-fits-all validation script. For this reason, the Toolkits in this topic aren't like the others in this book, in that you don't just copy the code to your Web site. You start with the Validation Script Skeleton instead, and then you pick from the rest of the Toolkits, adding the validation features that you need for your particular form.

Validation Script Skeleton

This Toolkit contains the skeleton for a form validation script. By itself, it doesn't validate anything—you need to add other blocks of code for that. The other Toolkits in this topic give you the actual validation routines. Pick and choose the ones you need, and add them to this framework.

```
<script language="JavaScript">

/* If you're adding this script to an external JavaScript file, you
don't need the script tags at the beginning and end of this listing. If
you're embedding the script on a Web page, make sure it's the same page
that contains the form. */

  function validateForm() {

/* Add components from the other Toolkits here. */

    return true;

/* Assuming the form data passes all validation checks, the above com-
mand gives the go-ahead for the browser to submit the form to the Web
server. */

  }

</script>
```

You need one more thing besides this framework for the validation function: a form that runs the script upon submission. Add the onSubmit event to the form tag, like so:

```
<form name="formname" action="formaction" method="formmethod"
onSubmit="return validateForm();">
```

Of course, you should insert the appropriate values in the name, action, and method attributes for your particular form.

Checking for an Email Address

Add this block of code to the validation script to check that the visitor has entered an email address in a text field.

```
var email = new String(document.formname.textfieldname.value);

/* In the line of code above, insert the name of the form and the name
of the text field that contains the email address. This statement cre-
ates a variable called email to hold whatever the visitor typed in the
field. */

if (email.indexOf("@") == -1) {
```

```
/* The statement above checks to see if the field contains an at-sign
(@). If it doesn't, the validation script assumes that whatever the
visitor typed isn't an email address. */

  alert("You must supply a valid email address.");

/* The statement above displays an error message in a popup window. */

  document.formname.textfieldname.select();

/* The statement above selects the email field of the form. */

  return false;

/* The statement above cancels the form submission. */

}
```

Checking Required Text Fields

Add this block of code to the validation script to check that the visitor has filled out all required text fields. This Toolkit also works with password fields and text areas.

```
var field01 = new String(document.formname.requiredfield01.value);
var field02 = new String(document.formname.requiredfield02.value);
var field03 = new String(document.formname.requiredfield03.value);
var field04 = new String(document.formname.requiredfield04.value);
var field05 = new String(document.formname.requiredfield05.value);

/* The above statements create variables for each of the required text
fields in your form. If you have fewer than five, omit the lines you
don't need. If you have six or more, just add lines to the script,
using these as a template. */

var pass = true;

/* The line above creates a Boolean (true/false) variable called pass
and sets it to true. */

/* The if/then blocks below check to see if the visitor has filled out
each required text field. If the script comes across a missed field,
pass equals false. You need one if/then block per required text field,
so adjust these according to your particular form, removing unneeded
blocks or adding extra ones. */

if (field01.length == 0) {
  pass = false;
}

if (field02.length == 0) {
  pass = false;
}
```

```
if (field03.length == 0) {
  pass = false;
}

if (field04.length == 0) {
  pass = false;
}

if (field05.length == 0) {
  pass = false;
}

/* The following block of code tests the value of the pass variable. If
pass equals false, which is to say if at least one of the required text
fields is blank, then the browser displays an error message and stops
the submission of the form. */

if (pass == false) {
    alert("You must fill out all required fields.");
    return false;
}
```

TOOL. KIT.

Checking Required Lists and Menus

Add this block of code to the validation script to check that the visitor has filled out all required lists and menus.

The code assumes that your list or menu begins with a preselected default option like this:

```
<option selected>Choose an option...</option>
```

You can change the **Choose an option...** text between the option tags to match your specific form. Just make sure you also change the text as it appears in the following code:

```
var list01 = document.formname.requiredlist01;
var list01Text = list01.options[list01.selectedIndex].text;

var list02 = document.formname.requiredlist02;
var list02Text = list02.options[list02.selectedIndex].text;

var list03 = document.formname.requiredlist03;
var list03Text = list03.options[list03.selectedIndex].text;

var list04 = document.formname.requiredlist04;
var list04Text = list04.options[list04.selectedIndex].text;

var list05 = document.formname.requiredlist05;
var list05Text = list05.options[list05.selectedIndex].text;

/* The code above creates new variables for the required lists and
menus in your form and gets the text of the selected option in each. If
```

you have fewer than five lists or menus, delete the lines that you don't need. If you have six or more, add new lines.

The line below creates a new variable called pass and sets its value to true. */

```
var pass = true;
```

/* The if/then blocks that follow make sure that none of your required lists or menus still show the default option. If at least one list or menu does, the value of pass becomes false. You need one if/then block per required list or menu, so delete the blocks you don't need, or add similar blocks if you need more than five. */

```
if (list01Text == "Choose an option...") {
  pass = false;
}

if (list02Text == "Choose an option...") {
  pass = false;
}

if (list03Text == "Choose an option...") {
  pass = false;
}

if (list04Text == "Choose an option...") {
  pass = false;
}

if (list05Text == "Choose an option...") {
  pass = false;
}
```

/* The if/then block below checks the value of pass. If false, the form doesn't submit. */

```
if (pass == false) {
  alert("You must fill out all required fields.");
    return false;
}
```

TOOL KIT

Checking for Alphanumeric Characters Only

Add this block of code to the validation script to check that the visitor has entered only alphanumeric characters in a text field, text area, or password field.

```
var field = new String(document.formname.fieldname.value);
```

/* The code above creates a new variable for the value of the field in question. Replace formname with the name of the form and fieldname with the name of the field that you want to check.

The line below creates the variable called pass and sets its value to true. */

```
var pass = true;
```

/* The next block of text creates a for/next loop. The script looks at each character in the field and decides if this character is a letter or number. If not, the value of pass becomes false. */

```
for (var x = 0; x < field.length; x++) {

  if (field.charCodeAt(x) < 48 ||
      (field.charCodeAt(x) > 57 && field.charCodeAt(x) < 65) ||
      (field.charCodeAt(x) > 90 && field.charCodeAt(x) < 97) ||
      field.charCodeAt(x) > 122) {
               pass = false;
      }
  }
```

/* Now, if pass equals false, the browser displays an error message, deletes the value of the offending field, and automatically selects this field so that the visitor can try again. */

```
if (pass == false) {
  alert("Your entry contains characters other than letters and num-
bers.");
  document.formname.fieldname.value = "";
  document.formname.fieldname.select();
    return false;
}
```

TOOL KIT.

Checking for Matching Password Fields

Add this block of code to the validation script to check that the visitor has matching password fields. You know the routine: One field asks for a password, and the next field asks the visitor to retype the password. This script also works with text fields and text areas.

```
var password = new String(document.formname.passwordname.value);
var retype = new String(document.formname.retypename.value);
```

/* The code above creates new variables for the values of the password field and the retype field. Replace formname with the name of the form, replace password name with the name of the password field, and replace retypename with the name of the field where the visitor retypes the password. */

```
if (password.valueOf() != retype.valueOf()) {
  alert("Your password fields don't match.");
    document.formname.retypename.value = "";
  document.formname.passwordname.select();
  return false;
}
```

```
/* The if/then block above compares the value of password with the
value of retype. If they don't match, the browser displays an error
message, clears the value of the retype field, selects the password
field, and stops submission. */
```

TOOL KIT

Verifying an "I Agree" Checkbox

Add this block of code to the validation script to verify that the visitor has checked an "I Agree" checkbox, like when the visitor has to agree to the terms of service or your privacy policy or what have you.

```
if (document.formname.checkboxname.checked == false) {
  alert("You must agree to proceed.");
  return false;
}
```

```
/* The if/then block above looks to see if the checkbox is checked. If
not, the browser displays an alert message and stops submission.
Replace formname with the name of the form, and replace checkboxname
with the name of the "I Agree" checkbox. */
```

Setting the Tab Order

Not everybody on the Web browses with a mouse. Some people can't because of physical disabilities. Others just prefer using the keyboard. As you may know, you can press the Tab key to step through the interactive elements on a page such as links and form widgets.

TIP

You can also use the tabindex attribute in anchor tags for links.

By default, the browser chooses the order of the tab stops by the appearance of the corresponding tags in the HTML. However, when you lay out your form in a table, the browser might not understand the proper order of the widgets, since the widget tags don't always appear in the code in the logical sequence that they show up on screen.

To keep your form flowing naturally and logically when the visitor steps through it with the Tab key, you can specify the exact order of the widgets with their tabindex attributes.

Take the form in Figure 71.1. Its widgets don't use the tabindex attribute, leaving the browser to determine their correct tab order.

TIP

If you set the tabindex attribute for one tag, set this attribute for all the widgets and links on your page. Otherwise, the browser might not get the order right.

Figure 71.1

This form's widgets don't use the tabindex attribute. The browser determines their tab order.

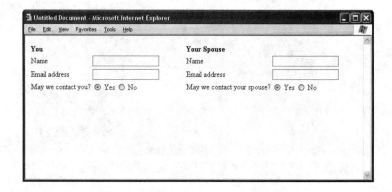

Listing 71.1 **View Source for Figure 71.1.**

```
<form>
  <table>
    <tr>
      <td colspan="2"><strong>You</strong></td>
      <td width="50" rowspan="4"> </td>
      <td colspan="2"><strong>Your Spouse</strong></td>
    </tr>
    <tr>
      <td>Name</td>
      <td><input type="text" name="yourName"></td>
      <td>Name</td>
      <td><input type="text" name="spouseName"></td>
    </tr>
    <tr>
      <td>Email address</td>
      <td><input type="text" name="yourEmail"></td>
      <td>Email address</td>
      <td><input type="text" name="spouseEmail"></td>
    </tr>
    <tr>
      <td>May we contact you?</td>
      <td><input type="radio" name="contactYou" value="yes" checked>
        Yes
        <input type="radio" name="contactYou" value="no">
        No</td>
      <td>May we contact your spouse?</td>
      <td><input type="radio" name="contactSpouse" value="yes" checked>
```

```
          Yes
          <input type="radio" name="contactSpouse" value="no">
          No</td>
      </tr>
    </table>
</form>
```

If the browser determines the tab order for this form, it works its way from
the top of the HTML listing to the bottom. So, it chooses the yourName field first,
followed by the spouseName field, followed by the yourEmail field, followed by
the spouseEmail field, and so on. But this isn't the best tab order for the form. It
would be better if the visitor could fill out all the personal information first
before moving on to the spouse.

Enter the tabindex attribute:

```
<form>
  <table>
    <tr>
      <td colspan="2"><strong>You</strong></td>
      <td width="50" rowspan="4"> </td>
      <td colspan="2"><strong>Your Spouse</strong></td>
    </tr>
    <tr>
      <td>Name</td>
      <td><input type="text" name="yourName" tabindex="1"></td>
      <td>Name</td>
      <td><input type="text" name="spouseName" tabindex="5"></td>
    </tr>
    <tr>
      <td>Email address</td>
      <td><input type="text" name="yourEmail" tabindex="2"></td>
      <td>Email address</td>
      <td><input type="text" name="spouseEmail" tabindex="6"></td>
    </tr>
    <tr>
      <td>May we contact you?</td>
      <td><input type="radio" name="contactYou" value="yes" checked tabindex="3">
      Yes
      <input type="radio" name="contactYou" value="no" tabindex="4">
      No</td>
      <td>May we contact your spouse?</td>
      <td><input type="radio" name="contactSpouse" value="yes" checked tabindex="7">
```

```
        Yes
        <input type="radio" name="contactSpouse" value="no" tabindex="8">
        No</td>
    </tr>
  </table>
</form>
```

TIP

If you have more than one form on the same page, don't go back to **tabindex="1"** for the first widget in the next form. Pick up the counting where you left off.

Notice that each widget gets the tabindex attribute. The value of this attribute determines its place in the tab order, from lowest to highest. So, taking the tabindex values in turn, the form logically proceeds from yourName to yourEmail to contactYou yes to contactYou no, and then it jumps over to the spouse's column and hits the corresponding fields in the same order.

FAQ

What happens when two or more tags have the same tabindex value?

The browser orders them according to which is closer to the top of the HTML code.

Working with Fieldsets

A **fieldset** is a group of logically related widgets. The members of a fieldset don't have to be the same type of widget. In fact, each widget can be different. As long as the widgets appear next to each other in the HTML listing, you can group them together as a fieldset, as in Figure 72.1.

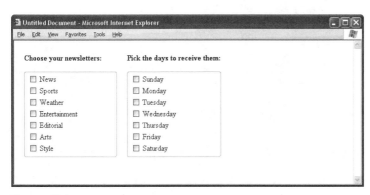

Figure 72.1

This form has two logical divisions or fieldsets.

Listing 72.1 **View Source for Figure 72.1.**

```
<form>
  <table cellpadding="10">
    <tr valign="top">
      <td width="50%">
        <p><strong>Choose your newsletters:</strong></p>

<!-- First fieldset begins -->

        <fieldset>
          <table>
            <tr>
              <td>
                <input name="news" type="checkbox" value="yes">
                News
              </td>
            </tr>
            <tr>
              <td>
                <input name="sports" type="checkbox" value="yes">
                Sports
              </td>
            </tr>
            <tr>
              <td>
                <input name="weather" type="checkbox" value="yes">
                Weather
              </td>
            </tr>
            <tr>
              <td>
                <input name="ent" type="checkbox" value="yes">
                Entertainment
              </td>
            </tr>
            <tr>
              <td>
                <input name="ed" type="checkbox" value="yes">
                Editorial
              </td>
            </tr>
```

```
      <tr>
        <td>
          <input name="arts" type="checkbox" value="yes">
          Arts
        </td>
      </tr>
      <tr>
        <td>
          <input name="style" type="checkbox" value="yes">
          Style
        </td>
      </tr>
    </table>
  </fieldset>

<!-- First fieldset ends -->

    </td>
    <td width="50%">
      <p><strong>Pick the days to receive them:</strong></p>

<!-- Second fieldset begins -->

      <fieldset>
        <table>
          <tr>
            <td>
              <input name="sun" type="checkbox" value="yes">
              Sunday
            </td>
          </tr>
          <tr>
            <td>
              <input name="mon" type="checkbox" value="yes">
              Monday
            </td>
          </tr>
          <tr>
            <td>
              <input name="tues" type="checkbox" value="yes">
              Tuesday
            </td>
```

432

```
        </tr>
        <tr>
         <td>
           <input name="wed" type="checkbox" value="yes">
           Wednesday
         </td>
        </tr>
        <tr>
         <td>
           <input name="thurs" type="checkbox" value="yes">
           Thursday
         </td>
        </tr>
        <tr>
         <td>
           <input name="fri" type="checkbox" value="yes">
           Friday
         </td>
        </tr>
        <tr>
         <td>
           <input name="sat" type="checkbox" value="yes">
           Saturday
         </td>
        </tr>
       </table>
      </fieldset>

<!-- Second fieldset ends -->

      </td>
     </tr>
    </table>
</form>
```

As you can see, the browser draws a thin, rectangular border around the widgets in the fieldset. You can even embed a short string of text into the border with the legend tag, as Figure 72.2 shows.

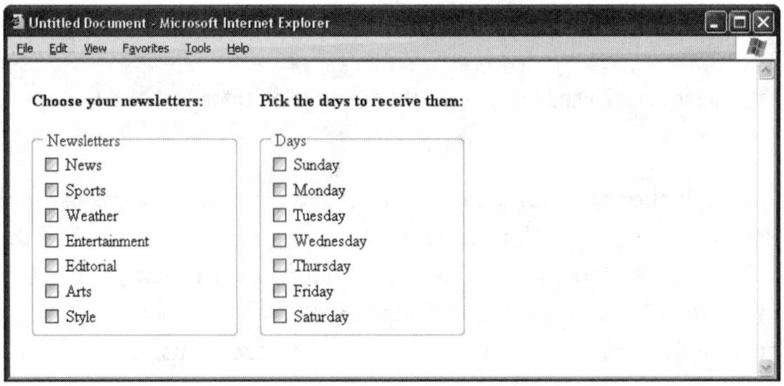

Figure 72.2

Use the legend tag to embed a short string of text within the rectangular border.

Listing 72.2 **View Source for Figure 72.2.**

```
<form>

<!-- Layout table begins -->

  <p><strong>Choose your newsletters:</strong></p>
  <fieldset>
    <legend>Newsletters</legend>

<!-- Widgets go here -->

  </fieldset>

<!-- More layout table -->

  <p><strong>Pick the days to receive them:</strong></p>
  <fieldset>
    <legend>Days</legend>

<!-- More widgets -->

  </fieldset>

<!-- Layout table ends -->

</form>
```

By default, the text color of the legend is blue in Internet Explorer and black in Netscape. Blue is an unfortunate color choice here, since it's also the standard color of unvisited hyperlinks. A blue legend can trick your visitors into clicking, even without the telltale underline.

Fortunately, CSS lets you redefine the legend tag to display whatever color you like:

```
<style type="text/css">

  legend {
    color: #000000;
  }

</style>
```

Why not make the legend bold while you're at it:

```
<style type="text/css">

  legend {
    color: #000000;
    font-weight: bold;
  }

</style>
```

Can I create CSS styles for fieldsets?
Sure, but watch out. Remember that, in CSS, a child tag almost always inherits the styles of its parent. This is certainly one of those cases. All the child tags of the fieldset, including the legend, the widgets, and the text, inherit the fieldset's styles.

See the results of this style in Figure 72.3.

You can also use CSS to modify the appearance of the border around the fieldset. The border-color, border-style, and border-width attributes perform nicely in this regard. Use the color attribute in your style rule to change the color of the text inside the fieldset, and use the background-color attribute to create a colored region behind the fieldset, as in Figure 72.4.

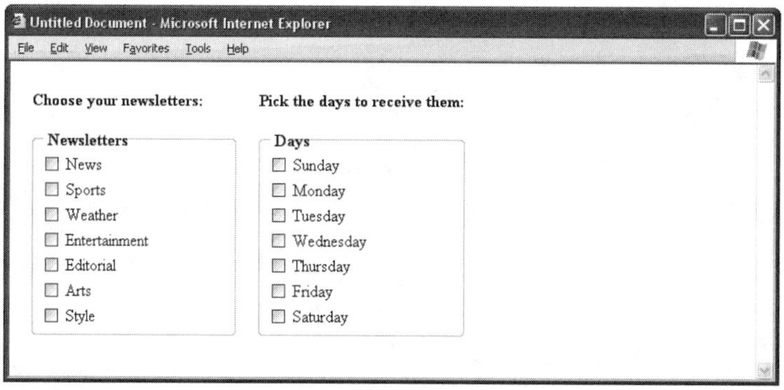

Figure 72.3
Use CSS to
modify the
appearance of
your fieldset's
legends.

Listing 72.3 **View Source for Figure 72.4.**

```
<head>

  <style type="text/css">

    fieldset {
      border-style: dashed;
      border-width: 4px;
      border-color: #FF0000;
      color: #FF0000;
      background-color: #FFCCCC;
    }

  </style>
</head>

<!-- Body content goes here -->
```

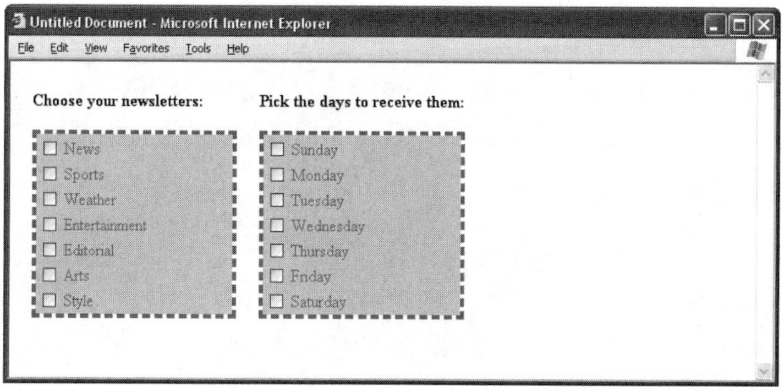

Figure 72.4
You can create
a style rule for
the fieldset tag,
too.

73

Working with Labels

n the spirit of good markup and to satisfy the standards police like the World Wide Web Consortium (W3C), you may be wondering how to mark up the labels of your form. The widgets have their own tags, so no worries there. And you probably lay out your form in a table structure, which has its own set of tags. But what about the text inside the form that describes what your visitors should type into the fields? In other words, what about the **labels**?

You might be tempted to use the familiar text tags for the job, like paragraph tags or some species of heading. The problem is, your tags should accurately identify the type of elements they mark up. A label in a form isn't really a paragraph. It isn't a heading, either, in the sense that HTML defines a heading rather strictly as a headline or marker for a section of the page.

This conundrum isn't nearly as difficult as such a dramatic lead-in implies. HTML provides a little-known text tag especially for form labels: the label tag, conveniently enough. See it in action in Figure 73.1.

> **GEEKSPEAK**
> A label in a form is a piece of text that describes what the visitor should type into the corresponding field.

438

Figure 73.1

*This form uses
label tags to
mark up the
text labels of
the checkboxes.*

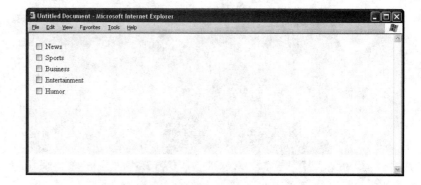

Listing 73.1 **View Source for Figure 73.1.**

```
<form>
  <table>
    <tr>
      <td><label>
        <input type="checkbox" name="news" value="yes">
        News</label></td>
    </tr>
    <tr>
      <td><label>
        <input type="checkbox" name="sports" value="yes">
        Sports</label></td>
    </tr>
    <tr>
      <td><label>
        <input type="checkbox" name="business" value="yes">
        Business</label></td>
    </tr>
    <tr>
      <td><label>
        <input type="checkbox" name="entertainment" value="yes">
        Entertainment</label></td>
    </tr>
    <tr>
      <td><label>
        <input type="checkbox" name="humor" value="yes">
        Humor</label></td>
    </tr>
  </table>
</form>
```

As you can see, the browser doesn't render labels in any special style. The labels look like ordinary text. Why bother with the extra markup? There are at least three good reasons.

First, the more accurate your markup, the more accessible your Web page becomes. If you have something on the page that you can identify as a label, you should mark it up as such. This way, when someone visits your site with nonstandard browsing equipment such as a screen reader or text-to-speech converter, your site translates more accurately.

Second, when you use label tags, your markup spells out the precise relationships of the elements in the form. You create a connection between the text and the widget that doesn't exist otherwise. Sure, for those with perfect vision, it's clear to see which piece of text corresponds to which label. But having the relationships spelled out goes a long way toward making your work intelligible to those who don't have the benefit of a visual display.

TIP

When you nest the widget tag inside its label tag, the widget inherits whatever CSS styles you apply to the label. If you don't want this to happen, don't nest the widget inside the label. Keep their markup separate, and use the id and for attributes to create the association between them.

Third, you can whip up a CSS style for label tags and create a custom appearance for these elements. You don't need to create a special class of paragraph or heading.

End of commercial. Notice that the label tag nests the input tag of its checkbox:

```
<label>
  <input type="checkbox" name="humor" value="yes">
  Humor
</label>
```

This is one way for the browser to associate the label with its widget. But what if your labels and widgets appear in different columns of a table, like this:

```
<form>
  <table>
    <tr>
      <td><input type="checkbox" name="humor" value="yes"></td>
      <td>Humor</td>
    </tr>
```

```
    </table>
</form>
```

This markup makes it impossible for you to nest the input tag inside the label tag, since you have a couple of table-cell tags in the way. In cases like these, the label tag goes around the text. Then, to create the association between the elements, use a pair of attributes instead: the id attribute and the for attribute:

```
<form>
  <table>
    <tr>
      <td>
        <input type="checkbox" name="humor" id="humor" value="yes">
      </td>
      <td>
        <label for="humor">Humor</label>
      </td>
    </tr>
  </table>
</form>
```

> **TIP**
>
> Use unique IDs for each element on your page. Don't give the same ID to two or more elements.

PART VII:
Tricks Topics

74

Embedding Media

The term **media** is one of those technical catchall buzzwords like **content** and **functionality** that is so general as to be practically meaningless, so the best you're going to get is a nonspecific definition. Essentially, **media** on the Web are sound files, movie files, Flash animations, SVG (Scalable Vector Graphics) files, Acrobat documents, and anything that isn't an image, HTML, CSS, client-side script, or server-side script. Table 74.1 lists many common media types.

There are a couple of ways to tell if something is probably a media file. First, media are usually external files. That is, a media file is usually separate from the HTML document that displays or presents the media. But not always. For example, you can write SVG code directly into an HTML page.

More tellingly, media files usually require features that aren't built into the typical browser. For example, by itself, Microsoft Internet Explorer can't display Acrobat files. The visitor needs to install a special piece of software called a **plug-in** that expands the browser's capabilities, giving it what it needs to display Acrobat. This rule of thumb doesn't always hold true, however. Microsoft Internet Explorer now comes standard with Macromedia's Flash Player plug-in for viewing Flash animations. The typical nontechnical computer user probably has no idea that what makes those funny cartoons come to life on the Web

Table 74.1 **Common Media Types**

MEDIA TYPE	USES	FILE EXTENSION
Adobe Acrobat (Portable Document Format)	Rich text documents and forms	PDF
Apple Audio Interchange Format	Sounds	AIFF, AIF
Apple QuickTime	Streaming audio and video	MOV
Macromedia Flash	Animations, movies, interactive presentations, and games	SWF
Macromedia Shockwave	Robust animations, movies, interactive presentations, and games	DCR
Microsoft Wave	Sounds	WAV
Microsoft Windows Media	Streaming audio and video	WMA, WMV
MIDI (Musical Instrument Digital Interface)	Songs, tunes	MID
RealMedia	Streaming audio and video	RM
Scalable Vector Graphics	Line art, animations	SVG
Sun Audio Format	Sounds	AU

isn't really their browser but a separate application by a non-Microsoft software company that works hand in hand with their browser.

So much for what media usually are or aren't. The easiest way to get one of these things into your Web page is to use the embed tag. But in doing so, be warned: The embed tag isn't a genuine HTML tag. It has never been a part of any specification of HTML. Instead, it's unofficial markup that all the major browsers have more or less adopted.

Standards police, such as the World Wide Web Consortium (W3C) prefer to think that the embed tag doesn't exist. But the official, W3C-approved, per-spec alternative, the object tag, simply doesn't work as well as it should across platforms and browsers. In fact, most designers have better luck getting their CSS styles to function properly than to get the object tag to present a media file. And when the object tag doesn't work, it *really* doesn't work. It creates all kinds of strange problems, up to and including actually crashing the browser.

All things being equal, it's always better to use proper markup. However, in the case of media, all things are not equal at all. The object tag doesn't do the job, so don't waste your time with it. Go with the nonstandard embed tag instead.

To see the embed tag in action, have a look at Figure 74.1.

Listing 74.1 **View Source for Figure 74.1.**

```
<body>
  <p>Enjoy this Flash move!</p>
  <embed src="movie.swf" width="550" height="400"></embed>
</body>
```

As you can see from the View Source of Figure 74.1, the embed tag appears in the code exactly where you want the media file to appear, just like an img tag. Another similarity is the src attribute, which directs the browser to the location of the media file. Also, the width and height attributes determine the physical size of the media file on your page. So, in some ways, you can think of the embed tag as an img tag for media files.

For better results, the embed tag uses some attributes that the img tag doesn't. Assume that your visitor's browser doesn't have the Flash Player plug-in—a highly unlikely scenario, since virtually every computer on the Web displays Flash movies. But just imagine for a moment that the impossible happens. Without the plug-in, the browser doesn't know how to present the SWF file, and you get the Web equivalent of an uncomfortable silence. Therefore, it's common

TIP

The embed tag also shares the align attribute with the img tag. But the embed tag's align attribute doesn't work like the img tag's, especially in the horizontal direction, so you're better off aligning media files with trickery. Drop div tags around the embed tag, and set the div's align attribute to position the media file:

```
<div align="center">
  <embed src="movie.swf" width="550"
height="400"></embed>
</div>
```

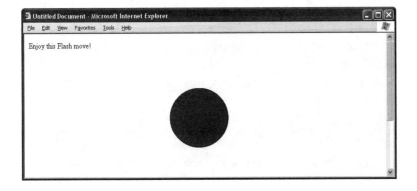

Figure 74.1

Use the embed tag to refer to an external media file.

courtesy to add the pluginspage attribute, which directs the browser to a Web page where the visitor can download and install the necessary plug-in and view the media file:

```
<embed src="movie.swf" width="550" height="400"
    pluginspage="http://www.macromedia.com/go/getflashplayer">
</embed>
```

TIP

The width and height attributes of a sound file determine the size of the plug-in's control bar (with buttons for stop, play, fast forward, volume, and the like). If you don't want the control bar to appear at all, set the embed tag's hidden attribute to **true**.

Depending on the type of media file, there may be other attributes that you can specify in the embed tag. For instance, the Flash Player plug-in accepts three quality settings: low, medium, and high. You may set a default choice with the quality attribute:

```
<embed src="movie.swf" width="550" height="400" quality="high"
    pluginspage="http://www.macromedia.com/go/getflashplayer">
</embed>
```

TIP

For the plug-in page, when in doubt, just link to the home page of the plug-in maker's Web site; for example, **http://www.adobe.com/** or **http://www.macromedia.com/**. From there, the download page is usually pretty easy to find.

Likewise, if you don't want the Flash movie to start automatically when the browser loads the page, or if you don't want playback to loop, you can set the play and loop attributes:

```
<embed src="movie.swf" width="550" height="400" quality="high"
    play="false" loop="false"
    pluginspage="http://www.macromedia.com/go/getflashplayer">
</embed>
```

Table 74.2 lists common embed-tag attributes for controlling various kinds of media files. These attributes don't always work as described for certain media types in certain browsers, so be ready for a little trial and error.

Table 74.2 **Common Attributes of the Embed Tag**

ATTRIBUTE	CONTROLS	POSSIBLE VALUES	NOTES
autoplay	Whether the media file automatically plays when the browser loads the page	true, false	Not for Flash movies
height	The vertical size of the media file in pixels	Any numeric	None
hidden	Whether the media file's control panel appears on the Web page	true, false	Usually for sound files
loop	Whether the media file plays over and over again	true, false	None
play	For Flash movies; whether the media file automatically plays when the browser loads the page	true, false	For Flash movies
playcount	The number of times the media file plays	Any numeric	Internet Explorer only*
quality	The visual clarity of the media file	low, medium, high	For Flash movies
volume	The volume level of the media file's audio	1–100	None
width	The horizontal size in pixels of the media file	Any numeric	None

* The loop attribute in Netscape performs the same function when you set its value to a number instead of **true** or **false**. However, Flash movies do not seem to respond to numbered loop attributes in Netscape.

FAQ

How do I know which attributes work with my media?

Short answer: You don't always. Documentation on the subject is sketchy, too, so determining the special attributes that control the media file often requires some trial and error. For instance, while a Flash movie uses the play attribute to turn autoplay on and off, sound files use the autoplay attribute for the same function. Ideally, find a Web page that embeds the same type of media, and view the source code to see what's going on.

75

Automatically Refreshing the Page

ormally, the visitor needs to click the browser's Refresh button to reload the current Web page. But there's an easy way for you, the designer, to build an automatic refresh cycle into your page, so that the browser reloads the current document without the visitor's interaction. This trick comes in handy if your page contains time-sensitive or **real-time** information, like the current weather conditions, stock quotes, or inventory levels.

GEEKSPEAK

Information is said to be real-time if it reflects the current, up-to-the-second state, whether it's the number of units of product in a warehouse, the price of a share of stock, or the national debt.

Say you have a Web page that generates and displays lucky-number lottery picks for your visitors, as in Figure 75.1. A simple JavaScript function called doLucky() handles the picks.

Now say that you want to avoid a lawsuit, and you decide to change your page so that the browser displays the visitor's lucky numbers for the next three seconds only, thinking that your visitors will have a harder time proving fraud if your lucky-number sets are only good for three seconds each. Essentially, you have a real-time situation here. To keep your page accurate, you need to refresh it every three seconds.

450

Figure 75.1

This Web page calls a simple JavaScript function three times to generate the visitor's lucky numbers for the day.

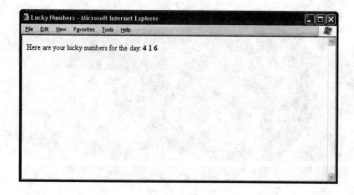

Listing 75.1 **View Source for Figure 75.1.**

```html
<html>
  <head>
    <title>Lucky Numbers</title>
    <script language="JavaScript">

/* This function picks a random number between 0 and 9 and writes it to the page. */

        function doLucky() {
          var x = Math.round(Math.random() * 9);
          document.write(x);
        }

    </script>
  </head>
  <body>

<!-- The following paragraph calls the doLucky() function three times to write three
random numbers to the page. -->

    <p>Here are your lucky numbers for the day: <strong>
        <script language="JavaScript">doLucky();</script>
        <script language="JavaScript">doLucky();</script>
        <script language="JavaScript">doLucky();</script>
        </strong></p>
  </body>
</html>
```

The easiest way to do this is to insert a special meta tag in the head section of your page. Meta tags indicate information in an HTML document that isn't for the browser to display. These tags have a variety of functions. Most often, they include keywords or descriptions of the page for the benefit of search engines. But you can also use a particular type of meta tag to enable the refresh behavior, as in Figure 75.2.

Listing 75.2 View Source for Figure 75.2.

```html
<html>
  <head>
    <title>Lucky Numbers</title>
    <meta http-equiv="refresh" content="3,#">
    <script language="JavaScript">

/* The doLucky() function goes here. */

    </script>
  </head>
  <body>
    <p>Here are your lucky numbers for the next three seconds:
      <strong>
      <script language="JavaScript">doLucky();</script>
      <script language="JavaScript">doLucky();</script>
      <script language="JavaScript">doLucky();</script>
      </strong></p>
  </body>
</html>
```

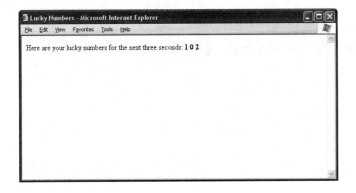

Figure 75.2

Use a meta tag to make the browser reload the page every three seconds.

Just as the type attribute of an input tag determines the kind of form widget that the browser displays, the http-equiv attribute of a meta tag works the magic. Different values in the http-equiv attribute create different kinds of meta tags. By setting the http-equiv attribute to **refresh**, you turn the meta tag into an automatic page refresher.

How often the browser refreshes the page depends on the value of the content attribute. In the View Source for Figure 75.2, the meta tag looks like this:

```
<meta http-equiv="refresh" content="3,#">
```

The **3** in the content attribute indicates a refresh cycle of three seconds. In other words, the browser reloads the page every three seconds. The **#** in the content attribute is browser shorthand that stands for the current page. You've used this notation before to create self-referential links. So, to express the value of the content attribute in plain language, you get something like, "Every three seconds, reload the current page."

There's no rule that says the page has to reload every three seconds. For a longer refresh cycle, increase the number of seconds:

```
<meta http-equiv="refresh" content="60,#">
```

This meta tag causes the page to reload every minute.

76

Automatically Redirecting the Browser

n Topic 75, you saw how to use a meta tag to set an automatic refresh cycle. The syntax of the meta tag looked like this:

```
<meta http-equiv="refresh" content="x,#">
```

where **x** represents the number of seconds before the browser refreshes the page, and **#** is browser shorthand for the current document.

Just as you're free to change the value of **x**, you're free to change the Web page that the browser reloads. Simply supply a different URL in place of the number sign.

In effect, this trick creates a page that automatically redirects the browser to a new location after a specified number of seconds. These kinds of pages are handy to have. Say you just redesigned and reorganized your site, and some old nav categories no longer exist in the new, improved version. But visitors to your site might have bookmarks to the old pages. Instead of frustrating your audience when they try to load a nonexistent document, pop a replacement page like the kind in Figure 76.1 to the location of your old, obsolete page. Very classy.

If I use a refresh meta tag to do a redirect, doesn't the redirect behavior happen again and again?

Not necessarily. After the browser jumps to the new page, the previous page's meta tag no longer applies. If the new page doesn't have a redirect on it, the browser stays put. Of course, if the new page does have a redirect on it, then the browser waits the required number of seconds and jumps again.

Figure 76.1

Use a page like this to redirect your visitors to a new location.

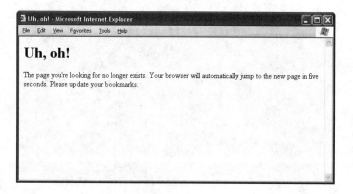

Listing 76.1 **View Source for Figure 76.1.**

```html
<html>
  <head>
    <title>Uh, oh!</title>
    <meta http-equiv="refresh" content="5, http://newpage.htm">
  </head>
  <body>
    <h1>Uh, oh!</h1>
    <p>The page you're looking for no longer exists. Your browser will automatically jump to the new page in five seconds. Please update your bookmarks.</p>
  </body>
</html>
```

What kinds of paths can I use for a meta tag's URL?

The URL in the meta tag can be any type of path: absolute, document-relative, or root-relative.

The meta tag in the View Source for Figure 76.1 works just like the one at the beginning of this topic. The **5** in the content attribute indicates a five-second pause, and the URL tells the browser where to jump after the five seconds.

Five seconds is probably way too long a wait for most of your visitors. Still, you want to give the few who actually read your content a fair chance to see what the page says before the browser jumps away, in which case five seconds is probably way too short. How do you satisfy both types of Web surfers?

Easy. Crank up the redirect delay to about ten to fifteen seconds, and include a direct link to the new page, as in Figure 76.2.

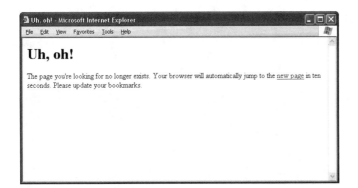

To make the redirect go faster for impatient visitors, include a direct link to the correct page.

Listing 76.2 **View Source for Figure 76.2.**

```html
<html>
  <head>
    <title>Uh, oh!</title>
    <meta http-equiv="refresh" content="10, http://newpage.htm">
  </head>
  <body>
    <h1>Uh, oh!</h1>
    <p>The page you're looking for no longer exists. Your browser will automatically
jump to the <a href="http://newpage.htm">new page</a> in ten seconds. Please update
your bookmarks.</p>
  </body>
</html>
```

TIP

Click Here links are never good, yet they seem to crop up in redirect pages a lot. When you include a direct link to the new page, choose the text of the link from the wording of the paragraph, or create a special link that gives the name of the new page.

77

Displaying Random Content

common problem of many Web sites is that, while the main sections of the site get plenty of tender loving care and lots of content updates, the peripheral sections suffer from a kind of neglect. Don't feel bad. Your resources are probably limited, and you need to prioritize. Your product listings need to be accurate, and your news needs to be fresh. Under the deadline crunch, changing your About Us page places pretty low on your list.

One way to spice up an otherwise neglected Web page is to let the browser do it for you with a random content generator. Take your About Us page. Instead of having the same image file load every time the visitor goes to this page, you can ask the browser to choose from one of three images, or five images, or ten images, or a hundred images.

Random content doesn't have to be an image. You can randomize literally anything: the background color of the page, the typeface, the type style, the exact wording of a paragraph, and so on. This topic offers several Toolkits to give you an idea of the possibilities.

Random Image Generator

This Toolkit picks a random image from a predefined set and displays it on the page. The code comes in two parts. The first part is the JavaScript function that actually chooses the random image. The second part is the line of code that appears in the body of your Web page. You place it in the HTML where you want the random image to appear.

Can I use this Toolkit as a poor person's ad server?

Sure. You can shuffle among several possible ad banners for the top of your page. The browser picks a random ad each time the page loads.

Here's the JavaScript function:

```
<script language="JavaScript">

/* If you're adding this script to an external JS file, you don't need
the script tags at the beginning and ending of this code. If you're
embedding this script inside an HTML document, keep the script tags,
and put the entire thing in the head section of the page. */

function doRandomImage() {

/* The following line chooses a random number between 1 and 5. Feel
free to alter the code to match the precise number of random images in
your set. The formula goes like this: Math.round(Math.random() * [number
of images - 1]) + 1. So, to choose from ten possible images, the code
becomes Math.round(Math.random() * 9) + 1. Likewise, to choose from two
possible images, the code is Math.round(Math.random() * 1) + 1. */

  var x = Math.round(Math.random() * 4) + 1;

/* The following line initializes the image variable, which will con-
tain the HTML code that displays the image. */

  var image;

/* The following if/then blocks test the value of x and set the value
of the image variable accordingly. You need one if/then block per pos-
sible image. So, if you have ten possible images, you need ten if/then
blocks. But if you have only three possible images, you only need three
if/thens. */

  if (x == 1) {
    image = "<img src=\"src01\" width=\"width01\" height=\"height01\"
alt=\"alt01\">";
  }
```

```
   /* Replace src01 with the path to the first random image. Likewise,
replace width01, height01, and alt01 with the width, height, and alt text
of this image. The random images may be different sizes, but your page
looks better when all random images share the same physical dimensions.

Notice that you precede internal quotation marks with the back slash
(\). This is the escape character. It tells the browser that the quota-
tion mark is part of the variable's value. */

   if (x == 2) {
      image = "<img src=\"src02\" width=\"width02\" height=\"height02\"
alt=\"alt02\">";
   }

   if (x == 3) {
      image = "<img src=\"src03\" width=\"width03\" height=\"height03\"
alt=\"alt03\">";
   }

   if (x == 4) {
      image = "<img src=\"src04\" width=\"width04\" height=\"height04\"
alt=\"alt04\">";
   }

   if (x == 5) {
      image = "<img src=\"src05\" width=\"width05\" height=\"height05\"
alt=\"alt05\">";
   }

   /* In the following line, the browser writes the HTML code in the image
variable to the Web page. */

   document.write(image);

}

</script>
```

That was the function. Now you need the code that calls it. Place the following bit of HTML exactly where you want the random image to appear:

```
<script language="JavaScript">doRandomImage();</script>
```

TIP

If the random image is clickable and the link always goes to the same place, no matter, the image, nest the HTML that calls the function inside anchor tags:

```
<a href="targetpath"><script
language="JavaScript">doRandomImage();</script></a>
```

However, if the link's destination depends on which random image the browser displays, build the anchor tag into the value of the image variable in the doRandomImage() function:

```
if (x == 1) {
  image = "<a href=\"targetpath01\"><img src=\"src01\" width=\"width01\"
height=\"height01\" alt=\"alt01\"></a>"
}
```

TOOL KIT

Random Quote Generator

This Toolkit picks a random quote and displays it on the page. Like the previous Toolkit, there are two components: the JavaScript function itself and the call to the function from the page.

The JavaScript function follows:

```
<script language="JavaScript">

/* If you're adding this script to an external JS file, you don't need
the script tags at the beginning and ending of this code. If you're
embedding this script inside an HTML document, keep the script tags,
and put the entire thing in the head section of the page. */

function doRandomQuote() {

/* The following line chooses a random number between 1 and 5. Feel
free to alter the code to match the precise number of random quotes in
your set. The formula goes like this: Math.round(Math.random() *
[number of images - 1]) + 1. */

  var x = Math.round(Math.random() * 4) + 1;

/* The following line initializes the quote variable, which will
contain the text of the quote. */

  var quote;

/* The following line initializes the tag variable. Set its value to
whatever type of tag you want to use to mark up the quote: p,
blockquote, h1, whatever. */

  var tag = "blockquote";

/* The following line initializes the source variable. Its value will
equals the name of the person who said the quote, along with the name
of the book, speech, or article where it was said. */
```

```
  var source;

/* The following line initializes the code variable, which will contain
the block of HTML code that displays the quote. */

  var code;

/* The following if/then blocks test the value of x and set the value
of the quote variable accordingly. You need one if/then block per
quote.

If you don't want to display a source, use this line instead: source =
""; */

  if (x == 1) {
    quote = "Quote 1 goes here.";
    source = "Source Line 1 goes here.";
  }

  if (x == 2) {
    quote = "Quote 2 goes here.";
    source = "Source Line 2 goes here.";
  }

  if (x == 3) {
    quote = "Quote 3 goes here.";
    source = "Source Line 3 goes here.";
  }

  if (x == 4) {
    quote = "Quote 4 goes here.";
    source = "Source Line 4 goes here.";
  }

  if (x == 5) {
    quote = "Quote 5 goes here.";
    source = "Source Line 5 goes here.";
  }

/* Now the browser starts to build up the HTML to write to the page. */

  code = "<" + tag + ">";

/* If you don't want to display a left quotation mark, remove the
following line. */

  code += "&#8220;";

/* Next comes the quote text. */

  code += quote;

/* If you don't want to display a right quotation mark, remove the
following line. */

  code += "&#8221;";
```

```
/* The following line adds a cite tag for the source. Even if you don't
have a source, keep this line anyway. */

  code += "<cite>";

/* This if/then block checks to see if the source variable is defined.
If so, it adds a dash between the quote text and the source text.

If you never want to display a dash between the quote text and the
source text, remove this block. Or, if you want to display a character
other than a dash, replace the dash code (&#8212) with the character of
your choice, such as a colon (:). */

  if (source.length != 0) {
    code += "&#8212;";
  }

/* The following line adds the source, closes the cite tag, and closes
the main markup tag. */

  code += (source + "</cite></" + tag + ">");

/* In the following line, the browser writes the entire code string to
the Web page. */

  document.write(code);

}

</script>
```

To call this function, place the following HTML exactly where you want the quote
to appear on the page:

```
<script language="JavaScript">doRandomQuote();</script>
```

TIP

For added visual interest, create a special CSS class style for your random
quotes. Then, in the doRandomQuote() function, replace the following line:

```
code = "<" + tag + ">"
```

with:

```
code = "<" + tag + " class=\"classname\">"
```

TOOL KIT

Generating Random Page Properties

For a real switch, this Toolkit picks a random style rule from a style sheet and applies it to the body tag of your page. Your random style rules can contain virtually anything, including background colors, link colors, typefaces, and type styles.

There are three parts to this Toolkit. The first is the set of style rules from which the browser picks. The second is the JavaScript function that picks the style, and the third is the line of HTML that writes the correct body tag to your page.

Here are the style rules:

```
<style type="text/css">

/* If your style rules appear in an external CSS file, you don't need
the style tags. If you're embedding the style rules inside the HTML
file, keep the style tags, and place the entire block of CSS in the
head section of the page.

You may include as few or as many style rules as you like, with whatever
style definitions you care to add to them. The following blocks of code
create three different style rules. Note that each is a special class
style of the body tag. */

  body.style01 {

    background-color: #000000;
    color: #FFFFFF;
    font-family: Arial, Helvetica, sans-serif;

  }

  body.style02 {

    background-color: #FFFF00;
    color: #FF0000;
    font-family: "Times New Roman", Times, serif;

  }

  body.style03 {

    background-color: #FFFFFF;
    color: #000000;
    font-family: "Courier New", Courier, mono;

  }

</style>
```

Here comes the JavaScript function:

```
<script language="JavaScript">

/* If you're adding this script to an external JS file, you don't need
the script tags at the beginning and ending of this code. If you're
```

embedding this script inside an HTML document, keep the script tags, and put the entire thing in the head section of the page, either before or after the style sheet. */

```
function doRandomProperties() {

/* The following line chooses a random number between 1 and 2. Feel
free to alter the code to match the number of style rules in your set.
The formula goes like this: Math.round(Math.random() * [number of style
rules - 1]) + 1. */

  var x = Math.round(Math.random() * 2) + 1;

/* The following line initializes the style variable, which will
contain the name of the class style that the browser uses. */

  var style;

/* The following if/then blocks test the value of x and set the value
of the style variable accordingly. You need one if/then block per style
rule. */

  if (x == 1) {
    style = "style01";
  }

  if (x == 2) {
    style = "style02";
  }

  if (x == 3) {
    style = "style03";
  }

/* In the following line, the browser writes a body tag to the Web
page. Note again the use of the escape character (\) to signify when a
quotation mark belongs to the HTML code instead of the JavaScript
statement. */

  document.write("<body class=\"" + style + "\">");

}

</script>
```

To call this function, immediately after the opening body tag of your page, add the following line of HTML:

```
<script language="JavaScript">doRandomProperties();</script>
```

All told, the body section of your page looks something like this:

```
<body>
  <script language="JavaScript">doRandomProperties();</script>

  <!-- Content of the page goes here -->

</body>
```

Doesn't this technique give you two body tags?

Very perceptive. Your Web page does indeed end up with two opening body tags: the original that appears in the HTML code, and the one that doRandomProperties() writes. The coding police can't condone this practice, since a Web page should have one and only one opening body tag. But it works.

You may be wondering why you don't just replace the original body tag with the doRandomProperties() function call. You can do this if you like, but you probably shouldn't. Browsing devices that don't support JavaScript may have a hard time interpreting the HTML without a hard-coded body tag in there.

Displaying a Browser Alert

ne of the great holy grails of Web design is to build a perfectly transparent site—a site that works in every conceivable browsing device on every possible platform without sacrificing the interactive features and compelling visual design that Web audiences have come to expect.

It's a holy grail for a very good reason: You're not likely to achieve it in this lifetime. Browsers are simply too varied, and platforms are too incompatible. Computing technology as a whole is far too proprietary, and trade secrets, market shares, licensing programs, corporations, IPOs, and good old-fashioned greed-based economies ensure that it will remain this way.

In light of this, Web designers learn to manage their expectations. They shoot for target audiences instead, designing for the browsers that most of their visitors prefer to use. They also engage in a little Machiavellian encouragement, subtly persuading the holdouts and sticks-in-the-mud in the peripheries of their audience to update to the latest browser versions. It's hard to imagine that anyone gets any enjoyment at all from browsing the Web on Microsoft Internet Explorer 4.0 or Netscape Navigator 3.0 (back when it was called Navigator instead of just Netscape), yet some people refuse to upgrade their equipment.

Until the day of the Revolution, when greedy software companies collapse alongside the rest of the postindustrial infrastructure, and fully transparent sites become a practical reality, you might consider posting a browser alert on your home page.

TIP

To avoid annoying your visitors too much, it's usually best to keep the browser alert on your home page. Don't add it to every page of your site.

FAQ

It seems like you shouldn't have to slog through a bunch of data that you don't need just to get the browser's make and model. Aren't there more precise navigator properties in JavaScript?

Yes, JavaScript offers more precise navigator properties, such as appCodeName, appName, and appVersion, but these often return misleading or incorrect results. The most accurate information appears in the userAgent property. Unfortunately, userAgent also gives you a lot of junk that you don't need for a browser-alert function, so you have to screen out the extraneous data before you can make an accurate comparison between the visitor's browser version and your site's target version.

A browser alert does two things. First, it gives a heads-up to visitors with antiquated software that your site might not work the way you're describing and the way they're expecting. It's the polite thing to do. Second, a browser alert implies to those who see it that it's way past time for them to update to the latest version of their favorite free browser. It encourages this course of action by annoyance, generating a popup window. People with older browsers tend to correlate to those who can't stand popups.

The Toolkit in this topic gives you a complete, ready-to-run browser-alert function that checks the make and model of the visitor's browser, compares the version number to your site's recommended version, and displays an alert message for those visitors whose browsers don't make the cut.

The function begins by grabbing the userAgent property of JavaScript's navigator object. The userAgent property contains a long string of information about the visitor's browser. Check out this property by creating the following HTML document and loading it into different browsers:

```html
<html>
  <head>
    <title>userAgent Test</title>
  </head>
  <body>
    <script language="JavaScript">
      document.write(navigator.userAgent);
    </script>
  </body>
</html>
```

Microsoft Internet Explorer version 6.0 for Windows returns the following results:

```
Mozilla/4.0 (compatible; MSIE 6.0; Windows NT 5.1; .NET CLR 1.0.3705)
```

while Netscape 7.1 for Windows gives the following:

```
Mozilla/5.0 (Windows; U; Windows NT 5.1; en-US; rv:1.4) Gecko/20030624
Netscape/7.1 (ax)
```

and Opera version 7.23 displays:

```
Mozilla/4.0 (compatible; MSIE 6.0; Windows NT 5.1) Opera 7.23 [en]
```

The browser-alert function examines this property to determine which version of which browser the visitor is using. As you can see, you get a lot more than just the browser name and version number in the userAgent property, so the function has to screen out the extraneous information, going from this:

```
Mozilla/4.0 (compatible; MSIE 6.0; Windows NT 5.1) Opera 7.23 [en]
```

to this:

```
Opera 7.23
```

The comments in the Toolkit take you through each step of the process.

TOOL KIT.

Browser Alert

To use this browser alert, copy the following code into the head section of your HTML document, or remove the script tags and place the function in an external JavaScript file.

```javascript
<script language="JavaScript">

/* You don't need the script tags at the top and bottom of this listing
if you're putting the function in a separate JavaScript file. */

  function doBrowserCheck() {

/* The following block of code initializes some variables.

The userBrowser variable holds the content of the navigator object's
userAgent property, which gives the name and version of the visitor's
browser, among other things.

The pass variable is a Boolean (true/false) switch. When pass equals
true, the visitor's browser meets the site's minimum requirements. At
the start, the function assumes that the value of this variable is true.

The versionStart and versionEnd variables will hold the starting and
ending positions of the version number inside the userBrowser string.
Eventually, you extract this portion of the string to compare with the
target version for your site. */

    var userBrowser = navigator.userAgent;
    var pass = true;
    var versionStart;
    var versionEnd;
```

/* The next three blocks of code give the target versions of three
browsers: Internet Explorer, Netscape, and Opera. The current target
versions are 5.5, 6.0, and 5.0, respectively. You may adjust these
values as you require for your site.

The versionMSIE, versionNetscape, and versionOpera variables will
contain the version numbers that you extract from the userBrowser
string. */

```
    var targetMSIE = 5.5;
    var versionMSIE;

    var targetNetscape = 6;
    var versionNetscape;

    var targetOpera = 5;
    var versionOpera;
```

/* The following if/then block checks for Microsoft Internet Explorer.
*/

```
    if (userBrowser.indexOf("MSIE") != -1 &&
userBrowser.indexOf("Opera") == -1) {
```

/* The line above scans the contents of the userBrowser variable,
looking for the text "MSIE." If userBrowser contains "MSIE" and does
not simultaneously contain "Opera" (since Opera's userAgent property
also includes the text "MSIE"), the function concludes that the
visitor is using Microsoft Internet Explorer. */

```
    versionStart = userBrowser.indexOf("MSIE") + 5;
```

/* The line above finds the start position of the version number inside
the userBrowser string, which is five characters to the right of the M
in "MSIE." */

```
    versionEnd = userBrowser.indexOf(";", versionStart);
```

/* The line above finds the end position of the version number inside
the userBrowser string, which is the semicolon character. */

```
    versionMSIE = userBrowser.substring(versionStart, versionEnd);
```

/* The line above extracts the version number from the userBrowser
string and places it in the versionMSIE variable. */

```
    if (versionMSIE < targetMSIE) {
      pass = false;
    }
  }
```

/* The if/then block above compares the visitor's version of Internet
Explorer with your target version. If the visitor's version number is
less than the target version, the variable pass becomes false.

The following if/then block checks for Netscape. */

```
    if (userBrowser.indexOf("Netscape") != -1) {
```

/* The lines below grab the start and ending position of the version
number inside the userBrowser string (nine characters to the right of
the N in "Netscape" to the next spacebar) and extract the version
number into the versionNetscape variable. */

```
        versionStart = userBrowser.indexOf("Netscape") + 9;
        versionEnd = userBrowser.indexOf(" ", versionStart);
        versionNetscape = userBrowser.substring(versionStart,
versionEnd);
```

/* Once again, if the visitor's Netscape version is lower than the
target version, pass equals false. */

```
        if (versionNetscape < targetNetscape) {
          pass = false;
        }
    }
```

/* The following if/then block checks for Opera. */

```
    if (userBrowser.indexOf("Opera") != -1) {
```

/* Get the version number by extracting it from the userBrowser
variable. The start position is six characters from the O in "Opera,"
and the end position is the next spacebar. */

```
        versionStart = userBrowser.indexOf("Opera") + 6;
        versionEnd = userBrowser.indexOf(" ", versionStart);
        versionOpera = userBrowser.substring(versionStart, versionEnd);
```

/* If the visitor's version of Opera is lower than the target version,
pass equals false. */

```
        if (versionOpera < targetOpera) {
          pass = false;
        }
    }
```

/* The following if/then block checks to see if pass is false. If so,
the browser displays a popup message. Feel free to change the wording
as you require, but remember to be polite, and try to phrase your
request so as to emphasize how a free browser upgrade will personally
benefit the visitor. */

```
    if (!pass) {
        alert("To improve your Web experience, this site uses advanced
JavaScript and CSS techniques. Older browsers like yours may not
support these features. For best results, please update your browser
to the latest version.");
    }

  }

</script>
```

472

> **TIP**
>
> You don't have to display an alert message. Add your own JavaScript commands to the **if (!pass)** block to determine what happens when the visitor's browser doesn't meet the required version.

To launch this script, add the onLoad event to the body tag of your HTML document:

```
<body onLoad="doBrowserCheck();">
```

This way, when the browser loads the page, it automatically runs the doBrowserCheck() function.

79

Displaying a "You Are Now Leaving" Popup

ere's a little trick that you might find useful: displaying a "You Are Now Leaving" popup when the visitor clicks an external link.

As a site designer, you go to great pains to establish the placeness of your Web site. You want it to feel like a logical, unified physical space, like a house with many rooms. While your visitors remain on your site, a consistent graphic design from page to page to page promotes this sense of place nicely. But the pages of a Web site aren't exactly like the rooms of a house. For one thing, your visitors can leave from any room, not just through the ones with the front and back doors, and, once they leave, they can go literally anywhere. This is the legendary nonlinearity of the Web.

When your external links are recognizable as such, the jarring teleportation from one house to another across the world is less disorienting. Your visitors are less likely to feel like they're lost. But when the peculiars of your site make it difficult to separate external links from internal links, you might consider giving your visitors a fair warning. Tell them that they're now leaving your site when they click an external link. Give them the opportunity to cancel if they don't want to leave.

A simple JavaScript function, like the one in this topic's Toolkit, does the job.

473

474

"You Are Now Leaving" Popup

TOOL KIT

Add this short JavaScript function to any page that contains an external link.

```
<script language="JavaScript">

/* If you're adding this function to an external JavaScript file, you
don't need the script tags. */

  function doYouAreNowLeaving(url) {

/* The entire function consists of a single if/then block. The browser
displays a confirm popup, which contains OK and Cancel buttons. (Feel
free to change the wording of the message.) If the visitor clicks OK,
the browser goes to the URL that it receives from the link that calls
the script. If the visitor clicks Cancel, the script simply ends, and
the browser remains on the current page. */

    if (confirm("You are now leaving the current site. Click OK to pro-
ceed.")) {
        location.href = url;
    }
  }

</script>
```

To make the function work, you must format your external links differently than your internal links. External links need to look like this:

```
<a href="javascript:doYouAreNowLeaving(src);">External Link Text Goes
Here</a>
```

Replace src with the full Web address (including the **http://www** part) of the external site, and of course add your own link text.

If you don't like using JavaScript links because of compatibility problems with older browsers, the following link format works also:

```
<a href="#" onClick="doYouAreNowLeaving(src);">External Link Text Goes
Here</a>
```

Again, replace src with the full Web address of the external site.

TIP

To open the external link in a new browser window, don't add **target="_blank"** to the link's anchor tag. It won't work in this particular scenario, since the link technically goes to a JavaScript, not to a Web site. Instead, change the following line in the doYouAreNowLeaving(url) function:

```
    location.href = url;
```

to:

```
    open(url);
```

PART VIII:
Basic Training Topics

Creating HTML Documents

eveloping a Web site means creating HTML documents. **HTML** stands for **Hypertext Markup Language**—it's the computer language that describes the content of a Web page.

HTML documents are actually just text files. You don't need any software more advanced than a text editor to create them. Where do you get a text editor? You have one already, even if you don't realize it. Microsoft systems come with a program called Notepad, which you launch by choosing Start → All Programs → Accessories → Notepad from the Windows desktop. Older Mac systems come with the text editor SimpleText, while newer Mac systems come with TextEdit. All three of these programs perform more or less the same function, in that they allow you to write and save text files.

What separates HTML documents from other kinds of text files is the inclusion of **tags**, or HTML keywords that identify the structure of the text inside the file. **Structure** is technical jargon—it means, quite simply, what kind of element the text happens to be, such as a paragraph, a heading, or the name of an image file. You can say that an HTML tag identifies a piece of text as a specific element on your Web page.

GEEKSPEAK

HTML stands for Hypertext Markup Language. This is the computer language that describes the content of a Web page.

GEEKSPEAK

Tags are HTML keywords that identify the structure of the text inside the HTML file. The **structure** of the text is simply what kind of element the text happens to be: a paragraph, a heading, the name of an image, and so on.

478

FAQ

My text editor is lame. Do I have to use it?

No. You probably also have a word-processing application such as Microsoft Word on your computer. Word processors are text editors, too, although they have many advanced features that you don't really need for creating HTML files. If you prefer working in the word processor, by all means, use it to create HTML pages. Just don't run out and buy one expressly for HTML editing.

Say your HTML file contains a line of text:

```
Take my wife. Please.
```

The HTML tags tell the browser what kind of text it is. To make the text a paragraph, add the paragraph tag, like so:

```
<p>Take my wife. Please.</p>
```

The paragraph tag, like most HTML tags, comes in two parts: the opening tag (<p>), which marks the beginning of the paragraph, and the closing tag (</p>), which marks the end of the paragraph. When the browser sees the paragraph tag, it understands that the text inside it is supposed to be a paragraph, and it displays the text in its built-in paragraph style, as in Figure 80.1.

It stands to reason, then, that if you change the tag, you change the structure of the text. And if you change the structure of the text, maybe the browser displays the text differently. Replace the paragraph tag with the first-level-heading tag:

```
<h1>Take my wife. Please.</h1>
```

Figure 80.1

Mark up a piece of text as a paragraph, and the browser displays the text in paragraph style.

Untitled Document - Microsoft Internet Explorer

File Edit View Favorites Tools Help

Take my wife. Please.

and the browser displays the text as a first-level heading instead of a paragraph, as in Figure 80.2.

TIP

When you save your HTML file, don't use the standard .txt extension for text files. Use the extension for HTML documents instead: .htm.

No matter how advanced, complex, or sophisticated your HTML document becomes, the tags work the same way. They identify the structure of the text, which the browser interprets according to its built-in styles.

HTML documents have two distinct sections:

1. The head section, which contains specific information about the HTML file such as the title of the page. Scripts and style sheets also appear in this section. The browser doesn't display the head section inside the document window.

2. The body section, which contains the content of the page. The browser displays the body section inside the document window.

You mark off the sections with the head and body tags, like so:

```
<head>
  <!-- The head section goes here. -->
</head>
```

FAQ

I don't like the way the browser displays a insert any element name here . Who do I complain to?

The maker of the browser. But why not take matters into your own hands? If you don't like the way the browser displays a certain element, you can redefine the element's appearance with Cascading Style Sheets (CSS). See Part IV for details.

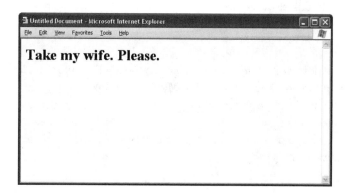

Figure 80.2

Change the paragraph tag to a heading tag, and the browser changes the appearance of the text.

```
<body>
  <!-- The body section goes here. -->
</body>
```

Go back to the earlier example with the bad punch line. Since you want the browser to display this text inside the document window, it goes inside the body section of the page:

```
<head>
  <!-- The head section goes here. -->
</head>
<body>
  <p>Take my wife. Please.</p>
</body>
```

To add more content to the page, add more text to the body section:

```
<head>
  <!-- The head section goes here. -->
</head>
<body>
  My Favorite Jokes
  We could talk about women.
  <p>Take my wife. Please.</p>
</body>
```

Don't forget to identify the new content with the proper tags:

```
<head>
  <!-- The head section goes here. -->
</head>
<body>
  <h1>My Favorite Jokes</h1>
  <p>We could talk about women.</p>
  <p>Take my wife. Please.</p>
</body>
```

You're now well on your way to creating the My Favorite Jokes Web page. Notice that the heading of the page—**My Favorite Jokes**—appears inside the body section of the page, which means that the browser displays this text inside the document window. If you want to make **My Favorite Jokes** the official title of your page as well, you need to add this text to the head section of the page, between title tags:

```
<head>
   <title>My Favorite Jokes</title>
</head>
<body>
   <h1>My Favorite Jokes</h1>
   <p>We could talk about women.</p>
   <p>Take my wife. Please.</p>
</body>
```

The title of your page doesn't have to match the heading. You can title the page anything you like:

```
<head>
   <title>My Humor Site: The Jokes Page</title>
</head>
<body>
   <h1>My Favorite Jokes</h1>
   <p>We could talk about women.</p>
   <p>Take my wife. Please.</p>
</body>
```

As a finishing touch, put the entire page inside opening and closing html tags. These tags are just a courtesy to the browser, to let it know that the page is an HTML document:

```
<html>
   <head>
      <title>My Humor Site: The Jokes Page</title>
   </head>
   <body>
      <h1>My Favorite Jokes</h1>
      <p>We could talk about women.</p>
      <p>Take my wife. Please.</p>
   </body>
</html>
```

The entire document, from top to bottom, looks something like Figure 80.3 in a browser. So it's not much to look at. Who cares? The important thing is that you're learning how to write HTML code. Many Web designers got their start this way.

Figure 80.3

Your completed My Favorite Jokes page looks like this in a browser.

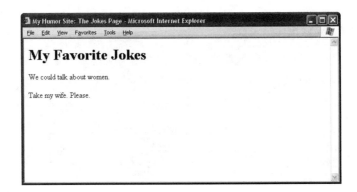

Organizing Your Web Site

While a Web page is a single HTML document, a **Web site** is a collection of related HTML documents, plus all the extra files, such as images and movies, that appear on the Web pages. A common question for beginning Web designers is how to organize and store the various files that make up the site.

The answer is pretty straightforward: Just use the folders of your computer's operating system.

Most Web designers begin a new project by creating a folder that will hold all the site's files. This is called the **local folder** or **local root folder**. Think of it as a convenience: It's handy to keep all the site files in one place. You don't want them scattered across your hard drive. But having a local root folder is important for technical reasons, too. When you upload your site to the Web, you want the locations of the files on your personal computer to match their locations on the Web server as closely as possible. If this kind of parallel organization doesn't exist, you may have trouble getting the links among the various pages to work correctly. So make sure you start off on the right foot and create a local root folder.

Inside the local root folder, there's additional organization that creates the structure of the site. Be careful here—structure in this sense isn't the same as the structure of an HTML document. The **structure** of a Web site is the way in which you organize the files into categories and subcategories. It doesn't have anything to do with HTML tags or marking up a text file.

GEEKSPEAK

A **Web site** is a collection of related HTML documents, plus all the images, movies, and other files that appear on the site's pages.

GEEKSPEAK

A **local folder** or **local root folder** is the folder on your personal computer that holds all the files for a Web site.

GEEKSPEAK

The **structure** of a Web site is the way in which you organize the files into categories and subcategories.

Use folders and subfolders to create your site's structure. To do the job right, you need a little think time up front. Imagine to the best of your ability the categories of information that will appear on your site. If you're building a personal site, your categories might look like this:

- My Hobbies
- My Favorite Books
- My Favorite Jokes
- About Me

The general rule of thumb states that you should create a folder inside your local root folder for each of the main categories of your site. In the preceding example, you need four folders inside the local root folder: one for each of the four categories. Don't put the folders one inside the other. Instead, set up your structure so that, when you double-click the local root folder to open it, you see all four folders inside—on the same **level**, to borrow the technical jargon.

What should you name your folders? Anything will do, but make the names short (eight characters or less, if possible). Use the underscore (_) in place of a spacebar, and stick to the standard alphanumeric characters. That means no special typographical symbols or punctuation marks. For the structure of your home site, you might try folder names like this:

- hobbies
- books
- jokes
- about_me (or **aboutme**, or just **about**)

Now, watch what happens. When you begin creating the pages for your site, you can guess pretty easily where they belong. You put the pages about your hobbies in the hobbies folder. You put the pages about your favorite jokes in the jokes folder. It's as simple as that.

If you need to divide a main category into subcategories, no problem. Create subfolders:

- hobbies
  - sports
  - movies
  - computers
  - games

- books
- jokes
- about_me

The extra structure gives you a more precise filing system. Now you know exactly where all your pages about movies go, for example.

You need one more folder for your site—the images folder:

- hobbies
  - sports
  - movies
  - computers
  - games
- books
- jokes
- about_me
- images

As you can see, it goes at the top level of your structure, directly inside the local root folder. Use the images folder to store all the graphics for the various pages of your site.

It may be tempting to store the image files in the respective folders of the pages that use the images. At first glance, this strategy seems to make sense. You can certainly set up your site like that, but you probably shouldn't. Once your Web site starts growing, you don't want to have to try to remember which folder contains which particular image. Better just to keep all the graphics in the same folder. This way, you'll always know where to look to find an image file.

Finally, you need a home page for your site, the one that loads when the visitor types your Web address into the browser. The home page's HTML document goes inside the local root folder, next to the folders for your main categories. Don't put the home page in its own folder. It should be at the same level as the category folders. Also, make sure your home page has the filename **index.htm**. If you give it another name, the browser might not understand that it's supposed to be the home page.

To sum up, here's what a typical site structure looks like:

- Local root folder
  - Home page document (**index.htm**)
  - Main category folder
    - Main category document
    - Subcategory folder
      - Subcategory document
  - Image folder
    - Image files
    - Movie files
    - Sound files
    - Other files

TOOL KIT | **Standard HTML Document Template**

This Toolkit gives the standard structure of an HTML document. Use it as a template for testing the examples in this book or creating your own Web pages from scratch.

```
<html>
  <head>
    <title>Title goes here</title>

    <!-- Meta tags go here -->

    <!-- JavaScripts go here, between script tags -->

    <!-- Style sheets go here, between style tags -->

  </head>
<body>

    <!-- The body of the page goes here. -->

</body>
</html>
```

81

Adding Keywords and Page Descriptions

When search engines such as Google and Alta Vista catalog your site, they examine the content of your pages and catalog the particular words and phrases that seem to crop up regularly. When a visitor to google.com or altavista.com searches under, say, **shoelaces**, there's a good chance that your site appears among the results if you use the word **shoelaces** on your pages.

What happens if your site is all about shoelaces, but you don't really find yourself using the word that often in the actual running text? This isn't as unlikely a scenario as it might seem. How many times does the work **book** appear on amazon.com? Not as often as you might think.

One way to help search engines catalog your site more accurately is to provide keywords and page descriptions on every page. **Keywords** are subject headings for the page, while a **page description** is a short, one-paragraph summary of its content.

Your keywords and page descriptions don't display in the browser, so they don't affect the appearance of your pages. That's fine, because you're not adding this information for looks. You're making it as easy as possible for potential visitors to find your site.

Use meta tags for the job. **Meta tags** are special HTML tags that contain general information about the page. These tags go in the head section of an HTML document, along with the page title and any embedded scripts or style sheets.

The following block of code shows typical markup for the keywords and description of a page:

```
<head>
  <title>Shoelaces Etc. Home</title>
  <meta name="keywords" content="shoelaces, sneakers, running shoes, tennis shoes,
dress shoes, laced shoes, laces, knots, shopping">
  <meta name="description" content="The home page of the world's first full-service,
24-hour shopping shoelace experience, featuring  warehouse selection and pricing for
all the top names in high-quality shoelaces, including designer labels and value
brands."
</head>
```

In both cases, the meta tag is the same. There isn't a separate keywords tag, in other words, and a separate description tag. Both use the same general meta tag. What distinguishes these types of tags is the name attribute. To create a meta tag for keywords, set the value of the name attribute to **keywords**. To create a meta tag for the page description, set the value to **description**. The value of the content attribute becomes either the list of keywords or the description of the page.

Exactly how search engines work depends on the search engine, and the actual procedures are well-kept company secrets. But, in general, the process works something like this. The search engine's **robot** or Web-sniffing program visits your site and looks at your pages. It compares the keywords and descriptions with the actual content of your pages. If it seems to the robot that your keywords and page descriptions are accurate, it takes them into account when cataloguing your site. However, if the robot suspects that the keywords and descriptions don't match your site's content, it may penalize your site in the search engine's listing. For this reason, be very honest about supplying accurate keywords and descriptions. If you list keywords like **shoelaces**, **laces**, and **knots**, make sure your site doesn't cater to...well, other types of bonds.

GEEKSPEAK
Meta tags are special HTML tags that contain general information about a page.

TIP
When you come up with a list of keywords, try to think of the words and phrases that your visitors will type into their search engines.

GEEKSPEAK
A **robot** is a special piece of software that catalogs or **sniffs** (or **spiders**) your site for a search engine.

82

Blocking Parts of Your Site from Search Engines

It may seem counterintuitive to want to restrict search engines from any part of your site. You probably take great pains to get your site listed on as many search engines as possible. But follow the logic here: Maybe you want to control exactly how a visitor finds your site. You would rather new visitors come in by the front page, say, instead of some page three levels deep. Or maybe you don't want visitors to come in on a page that is supposed to be a popup window, where you may not offer the full range of navigation choices. The more you think about it, the more restricting certain areas from search engines makes good sense.

There's a relatively easy and reliable way to communicate your indexing preferences to **robots**, the software programs that search engines send out to catalog your site. You add a special text file called **robots.txt** to the top level of your remote site, right inside the remote root folder. The robots.txt file tells visiting search engines to ignore the specific directories or files that you list.

Here's the catch: For this to work, the robots have to follow the Robots Exclusion Standard, which is a little-known corollary to Asimov's Three Laws of Robotics. The Robots Exclusion Standard simply states that a robot must obey the instructions in robot.txt. But this standard isn't a law. It's more like good manners. The people who design robots for search engines don't have to program their creations to abide by the standard, and there are indeed renegade robots running amok on the Web, just as in *I, Robot*. Nevertheless, the robots for all the major search engines operate according to the guidelines.

A simple robots.txt file looks something like this:

```
User-agent: *
Disallow: /popups/
Disallow: popup.htm
Disallow: /images/
Disallow: /js/
Disallow: /css/
```

The Disallow lines tell the robot which directories or files are off limits. In the preceding example, the popups, images, js, and css directories are blocked, as is the file called **popup.htm**.

The User-agent line indicates to which robot the Disallow lines apply. Giving the asterisk (*) as the value of User-agent means that the Disallow instructions apply to all robots. You may specify individual robots, too, and give different levels of access to each:

```
User-agent: googlebot
Disallow: /popups/
Disallow: popup.htm

User-agent: Roverdog
Disallow: /popups/
Disallow: popup.htm
Disallow: /images/
Disallow: /js/
Disallow: /css/
```

In this scenario, google's googlebot can't look at the popups directory or the popup.htm file, while Roverdog can't get at the images, js, or css directories in addition to the popups folder and the popup.htm file.

The values in the Disallow lines are root-relative paths, by the way. So, if you want to hide a subfolder but not the top-level folder, make sure you give the entire path to the subfolder:

```
User-agent: Roverdog
Disallow: /swf/sourcefiles/
```

If you want to hide absolutely everything (in this case, from all robots), use:

```
User-agent: *
Disallow: /
```

The following example keeps google out but permits all other robots:

```
User-agent: googlebot
Disallow: /
```

If you want to make everything on your site available to all robots, use:

```
User-agent: *
Disallow:
```

And if you want to permit only one robot (in this case, google's), use:

```
User-agent: googlebot
Disallow:

User-agent: *
Disallow: /
```

Now go back to the example at the beginning of this topic, where you want to try to force new visitors to come in through the front page. Say your site has five top-level directories: products, services, aboutus, images, and apps, along with an HTML file called **contact.htm**. Your robots.txt file looks like this:

```
User-agent: *
Disallow: /products/
Disallow: /services/
Disallow: /aboutus/
Disallow: /images/
Disallow: /apps/
Disallow: contact.htm
```

Put this file in the top-level directory of your remote site, and search engines will only index your home page (index.htm).

TIP

The asterisk character in robots.txt is not a wildcard. For example, you can't disallow *.gif to bar search engines from all GIF image files—for that, you have to put all your GIFs in a folder and then disallow that folder. The asterisk only works in the User-agent line, and only then as shorthand for **all robots**.

TIP

For more information about robots.txt and to look up the names of the various robots out there, see www.robotstxt.org/.

Testing Your Site

You don't have to be connected to the Web to test a Web site. In fact, you don't have to have Web service at all. Web browsers work perfectly well reading HTML files stored on your personal computer.

Testing your site from your personal or **local** files makes good sense. You don't have to be online to test your site, for one thing, and you can make whatever changes you like to your pages without affecting the published version of your site. Your changes don't take effect until you upload the modified pages to the Web server. For this reason, testing locally helps you to improve quality control. You don't have to post buggy or poorly coded pages for the entire world to see. Instead, you iron out the kinks offline and upload your pages after everything is working properly.

To test your site offline, launch a Web browser. Go to the File menu, and choose the Open command. (In Netscape, the command is Open File.) A dialog box appears, asking you to choose the file to open. Browse to your local root folder, and select the home page for your site. The page loads, but remember that it's the local version, not the **remote** version, or the one on the Web.

It's a good idea to download the latest versions of many different browsers for testing purposes. Even if you're strictly an Internet Explorer person or a diehard Netscape fan in your personal life, as a Web designer, you need to think like your visitors. You never know what browser someone will use to visit your site. Since different browsers display the same Web page differently—and the differences can be considerable—you want to be on top of any potential problems before you upload the page to the Web.

What kinds of links work when I test my site offline?

Document-relative links work just fine when you test the local version of your site. However, absolute links require a Web connection, and root-relative links only work on a Web server. See Topic 61 for a discussion about the various types of link paths.

The most common browser by far is Microsoft Internet Explorer for Windows. Whatever you do, make sure your site works well in this browser. Trailing a distant second is the Netscape browser for Windows. While you can probably get away with designing an effective site solely on the basis of how it looks and works in the Microsoft browser, most designers don't consider their sites finished until the pages look right in both IE and Netscape. In Europe, the Opera browser for Windows is quite popular, so sites with a large international audience are wise to take Opera into account.

Visit www.netscape.com/ to download your free copy of the Netscape browser, and go to www.opera.com/ to download your free copy of Opera.

What about Mac browsers? What about Linux browsers? What about alternative Windows browsers?

As cruel as it may sound, there simply aren't enough non-Windows, non-Microsoft, non-Netscape machines on the Web to make a statistical difference. If you're building a general-purpose site, don't feel compelled to test your site in a Macintosh browser, for instance. If you have access to a Mac browser, by all means, test. But don't think that you need to buy a Mac just to make sure that your site works properly in Mac browsers.

Netscape and Opera are the biggie alternatives to the Microsoft browser, but they aren't the only ones. Alternative browsers—most notably the open-source darling Mozilla, the post-browser-wars form that the Netscape project has taken—appeal to the lifestyles and philosophies of an all-too-small user base of early adopters, original Web heads, and boundary pushers.

If the Web had never exploded into the mainstream as it did, you would be designing sites for browsers such as these. But, as fate (or, more predictably, commerce) would have it, the Web became a popular medium, and the vast majority of its users know no more about its technical workings than TV viewers know about how television works. These days, it takes a serious and dedicated Web connoisseur to look for any experience beyond the Microsoft one. Of course, Mozilla came by way of Time Warner, the corporate owners of the Netscape brand, so if you crave a truly alternative Web experience, you may need to look elsewhere.

Regardless of who used to own what and which empire sued which conglomerate over which technology that neither invented, the fact remains: Your site will gain the respect of the true tech heads if it works with alternative browsers. Unfortunately, once again, the realities of the Web as it exists today make it so that general-purpose sites need not concern themselves with anything but IE. But check out www.mozilla.org/ anyway.

84

Choosing a Web Host

You don't need a Web host to develop and design a site. You can do it all from your personal computer. However, if you want to publish your site for the world to see, you need some Web server space. Fortunately, server space is abundant and inexpensive. This topic helps you sort through your options.

Finding a Web Host

A **Web host** owns (or rents) the computer that serves the files of your Web site to your visitors, usually in exchange for a monthly fee. You don't have to cancel your current Internet account to hire a Web host. In fact, many Web hosts don't offer Internet service provider (ISP) service. Those that do need to be local, or it isn't worth it for you. The great thing about your neighborhood ISP is that it's in your neighborhood, and it gives you a local dial-up number. You don't want to have to dial in to Albuquerque whenever you want to browse the Web (unless, of course, you live in Albuquerque).

There's a good chance you already have a Web host, even if you don't know it. Many standard Internet accounts come with a healthy amount of server space for personal Web pages. So, the first step in choosing a Web host is to contact your ISP. Find out how much server space comes with your

FAQ

I want to use my Web site for commercial purposes. Can I host my site on the personal Web space that comes with my Internet service?

Why would you want to? For one thing, your ISP usually assigns you a generic Web address, which doesn't make your business look very professional. For another, you don't need the typical lags in response time that you find on the servers of large ISPs. Plus, commercial sites are probably against your ISP's terms of service, and you don't need the hassle of them closing down your site along with your personal email account and Internet connection.

account. If the answer is none, you might want to inform your customer service representative that many of their direct competitors offer this benefit to their subscribers for a lot less than you're currently paying.

If you'd prefer not to use your personal server space for your site, just go to your favorite search engine, and look up **Web hosting** to begin your research. Don't be surprised if your results number in the millions. There are many, many, many Web hosts out there. You can't possibly research them all. You need to narrow your options—and fast. A good way to start is with the names that you recognize: Yahoo!, Earthlink, Netfirms, perhaps also your phone or cable company. If they don't have what you need or want, work your way down the list.

By and large, with Web hosting, you get what you pay for. True bargains are few and far between. Keep this in mind when you come across hosts that offer "free" service. Free hosts generally don't give you as many account options (or as good) as the pay-by-the-month outfits, and forget about customer service. In addition, you have to remember high-school economics. These people remain in business by making a profit. They have to get money somehow. And that somehow is off you. Free Web hosts typically load your site with advertisements, advertisements that you can't control, turn off, modify, or move. Conversely, the angry visitor emails complaining about your shameless, ubiquitous advertising go right to your in-box. Your free Web host lets you handle these. They're all yours.

TIP

Before you sign on with a Web host, check them out. Look up their name under your favorite search engine, and see what turns up. Look for reviews, too. Many of the better Web hosts have lots of positive press. If your check-up search is strangely silent about your host of choice, think twice.

TIP

If an offer sounds to good to be true, it probably is. Buyer beware!

Every Web site is different, of course, and only you can make the choice about the right Web host for your particular site. That said, in general, here are a few qualities of good Web hosts:

- **Reasonable monthly charge.** Shop around, and see what the competitors are offering. Expect to pay between $10 and $25 a month for a typical personal or small business site. Pay less, and your Web host probably makes up the difference by giving you terrible customer support or tacking advertisements onto your site. Pay more, and you're probably buying services and features that you don't need.

- **Domain name registration (preferably free).** Many of the better Web hosts offer to register your Web site's domain name for you. Some even front you the yearly $35 registration service charge. Keep an eye out for these hosts. They're worth it, even if they tack on a setup charge (as long as it's less than $35).

- **Reasonable (or no) setup charge.** Some Web hosts tack on a special, one-time service charge to set up your account. Others do not. Many perfectly reputable and reliable Web hosts charge setup fees. Many do not. Those that don't charge setup fees often make up their money elsewhere, so read the fine print. If you go for a fee-charging service, don't pay more than $35, or you're probably being soaked. And if you can catch a fee-charging Web host during one of its "fee waived" promotional periods, do it.

- **Upgrade plans.** Your site is successful. It grows. You want your Web host to grow with you. Ideally, your host should offer several levels of service at reasonable price points. Start with the cheapest plan and work your way up.

- **Reliable customer service (preferably by phone).** You need customer service. Period. And don't fall for the usual 24/7 customer-service sales pitch. Any fool with an email account can advertise 24/7 customer service. But is the fool actually reading the email—ah, that's the rub. You want a toll-free phone number for customer support. If you don't have 24/7 access to a live human being by telephone, then you don't have 24/7 customer support. It's far better to go with a Web host who offers toll-free phone support during normal business hours than a host who offers 24/7 support by email.

Considering Features

Web hosts offer a variety of features. It's hard to know what you need and what you don't. Here are some important factors to consider:

- **Server space.** Exactly how much server space do you need? You can figure this out pretty easily. Find out the combined file size of your Web site by examining the properties of its local root folder. If your site is 5 MB, then you need at least 5 MB of server space. Generally, you don't need huge amounts of server space, unless your site includes lots of heavy multimedia files, such as MP3s.

- **Bandwidth limits.** Your Web host measures **bandwidth**, or the amount of data its computers push to the visitors of your site over a period of time. Typically, you get a monthly limit, and, if you exceed your cap, your host charges you extra. A good data-transfer baseline for a typical personal or small-business Web site is 1 GB. Roughly speaking, one gigabyte of data transfer equals 20,000 page views—that's one person viewing one page of your site 20,000 times, or 5,000 people viewing one page of your site four times, or 20,000 people viewing one page of your site one time. It's hard to know exactly how much bandwidth you need, so start low. If you exceed your limit regularly, consider upgrading your plan. Keep in mind: If you offer a total of 1 GB of MP3s on your site, you can exceed 1 GB of bandwidth very quickly.

> **GEEKSPEAK**
>
> Bandwidth is the amount of site data that your Web host transfers every month.

- **POP3 email accounts.** You may or may not want extra email accounts for your site. But if you want them, go for a Web host that provides them. Generally, you want POP3 email instead of Web-based email. POP3 email works with client software such as Microsoft Outlook and Eudora, which let you jump on the Internet quickly, download your mail, and answer it offline. Web-based email requires you to be online to write and receive messages. Many Web hosts count the amount of email that you send and receive over their servers as part of your overall transfer limit, so be sure to take this factor into account.

- **Streaming audio/video and other media.** If you want to host streaming audio or video files on your site, or even if you want to display Flash animations and other common media types, your Web host needs to be set up to do this. You don't need special service to host Web images such as JPEG, GIF, and PNG.

- **FrontPage extensions.** Heaven forbid, but if your Web site uses the stupid special effects that come with Microsoft FrontPage, you should find a Web host that *doesn't* offer FrontPage extensions. This way, the dumb things won't work, and the quality of your site will improve dramatically.

- **CGI, server-side scripting, and database access.** If your site uses server-side technology to connect to a database, you need a Web host who is set up to do this. You don't have to worry about this level of service if your site sticks to the client side: HTML, JavaScript, and CSS. All the projects in this book are client-side only.

- **Site reports.** You want a host that gives you access to the data that the Web server collects about the visitors to your site. You want to see where they're from, what browsers they're using, what pages they visit most often, and which sections of the site they seem to be missing. You don't want this information for evil purposes. You want it to help you improve your site. Definitely check into what kind of site reporting tools the host offers.

TIP

One feature that you definitely don't need is a shopping cart application, "free" or otherwise. Shopping carts that come with Web hosting plans are generic, overpriced, feature-poor, difficult to customize, and next to impossible to integrate into your site. If you're serious about launching a Web-based retail storefront, you need to hire a programming team to develop a shopping cart application for you.

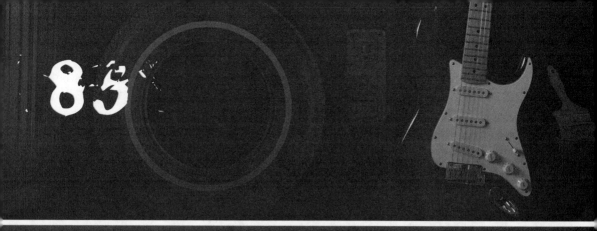

Uploading Your Site

You have a Web site. You have Web server space. Now all you need to do is upload your site to the server.

To do this, get yourself a free FTP program. **FTP** stands for **File Transfer Protocol**—it's the method that computers use to pass data files back and forth on the Internet. An FTP program allows you to connect to your Web host (the remote computer) from your personal machine (the local computer). Once connected, you simply indicate which files you want to move to the server, and the FTP program uploads them. You can also download files from the server to your personal machine. Two of the most popular and absolutely free FTP programs are WS_FTP and CuteFTP, both readily available on the Web. Search for them with your favorite search engine. Then download and install, and you're ready to go.

To connect to your Web server through an FTP program, you need to know a few technical details:

1. **The host address.** This is the URL to which you upload. Many times, the host address is the same as your domain name, but not always. Check with your Web host to be sure.

2. **Your user ID.** This is the username that your Web host assigned to you.

3. **Your password.** This is the password of your hosting account.

Depending on your Web host, you might need to provide some other information, too. When in doubt, contact customer support.

After you connect for the first time, you must create the remote **structure** of your site—the hierarchy of folders where you store your files. The remote structure should match the local structure as closely as possible. For example, if you have five folders in your site's local root folder, you need to create five identical folders on your remote site. Your FTP program has buttons or commands for creating folders or **directories**, as they're called technically.

Once you have created the remote structure, start uploading files. Copy them from their local folders to their corresponding remote folders through your FTP program. Note that uploading files doesn't remove them from your personal computer. Instead, the process creates identical copies on the Web server.

When the files on the remote server match those on the local computer, your site is **synchronized**. But when you edit your local site, adding new content or modifying existing pages, your site becomes **out of sync**. Why? Because the local and remote files don't match anymore. When you save your edits to the home page on your personal machine, your computer doesn't automatically update the home page on the Web server. Remember, the remote file is a separate document. To get your site back into sync, log back on to the Web server through your FTP program, and replace the out-of-date remote files with their updated local counterparts.

For the most part, the files on the remote server are for reading only. You usually can't open and edit them on the remote computer. As an alternative, just download the files that you want to edit. (Be sure to download them somewhere other than your local root folder, or you could overwrite the local files of the same name.) Make your changes, and upload the modified files back to the remote machine.

86

Validating Your Source Code

The World Wide Web Consortium (W3C) is so ape over on-spec coding that they offer to validate Web pages for free. If you want to see how well your site conforms to current standards and recommendations, this service might be of interest to you. Not only does the W3C's validator point out every last coding mistake or *faux pas* on a Web page, it gives you a lengthy report as to why, and it offers ways to correct the problems.

> **TIP**
> If you feel bad about receiving poor marks, just send the W3C's validator to the home page of a popular site such as Amazon or eBay.

To validate a Web page, go to http://validator.w3.org/. Enter the URL of the Web page that you want to validate, or attach an offline document and send it in. Good luck! If your page validates successfully, the W3C encourages you to display their official badge proudly by adding the following code, usually at the bottom of your page:

```
<p>
  <a href="http://validator.w3.org/check/referer">
    <img src="http://www.w3.org/Icons/valid-xhtml10" alt="Valid XHTML 1.0!"
height="31" width="88" />
  </a>
</p>
```

To improve your page's chances, try these tips:

- Use lowercase letters for tag and attribute names.
- Put quotes around attribute values.
- Some attributes, like checked and selected, don't have values. Give them values equal to their attribute name, like this:

```
<input type="checkbox" checked="checked" />
```

- Observe proper nesting. That is, close nested tags in the reverse order that you open them. The first opened should be the last closed.
- If a tag doesn't have a closing version, like the img, br, and hr tags, include a slash before the closing angle bracket, like this:

```
<img src="image.jpg" width="200" height="100" alt="An image" />
```

- Nest lists within li elements, like this:

```
<ol>
  <li>List item 1</li>
  <li>List item 2</li>
  <li>
    <ol>
      <li>Nested list item 1</li>
      <li>Nested list item 2</li>
    </ol>
  </li>
</ol>
```

- Don't embed scripts or style sheets. Link to external JavaScript or CSS files instead.
- If you must embed scripts or style sheets, remove any comments that hide the code from incompatible browsers.

Glossary

absolute path. A path to a file that provides its full and complete Web address. The great thing about absolute paths is they're always the same, no matter where they appear on your site. You can move a link with an absolute path to any level of your site without having to change the path's format. The drawback to absolute paths is that they don't work offline. You have to be online to follow a link with an absolute path. For this reason, most designers reserve absolute paths for external links only, using document-relative or root-relative paths for internal links.

accessibility. A virtue of Web design that requires a site to make its content available to all visitors, regardless of disability. To make your site as accessible as possible, give text equivalents for all purely visual elements such as images, and observe proper markup conventions.

active link. A link that the visitor is currently clicking or highlighting.

affordance. A visual clue that hints at a design element's function. For example, the beveled, 3D design of a standard HTML button suggests the idea of clickability, since it stands out from the flat, 2D topography of the rest of the page.

antialiasing. A technique for creating the appearance of smooth, flowing curves by inserting subtly blended pixels along a curved edge. Also, the process that Noel from *Felicity* underwent when his then-wife, Jennifer Garner of *Alias*, dumped him.

attaching. Linking an external JavaScript or CSS file to an HTML document. Compare with **embedding**.

attribute. A setting of a tag or CSS property that further defines the tag or property.

below the fold. The areas of a Web page that appear off the boundaries of the screen. The visitor has to scroll to see content below the fold. Never put the main navigation for your site below the fold!

block. The rectangular area in which an HTML element sits. Normally, a block is transparent, although you can tint it by adding a color attribute to its tag or style definition.

branding. A design technique that borrows elements from an organization's marketing material: logos, corporate colors, slogans, lifestyle associations, and so on.

breadcrumb trail. A navigation element that helps your visitors figure out where they are in the site hierarchy by showing the current page's relationship to the rest of the surrounding structure.

button states. The different appearances that a graphical button takes on depending on how the visitor interacts with it. For example, in a typical rollover, the button has two states: the default state, and the way it looks when the visitor hovers over it with the mouse pointer.

Cascading Style Sheets (CSS). A client-side technology for describing the style or appearance of HTML elements. CSS greatly expands the design potential of the Web, particularly with regard to typography, but browsers are notorious for spotty support. Even the most recent browsers chop up CSS in the most annoying and unpredictable ways, so be sure to test your CSS-enhanced site in a variety of browsers.

cellpadding. The amount of interior whitespace between the borders of a table cell and its content. In layout tables, this attribute is usually set to 0.

cellspacing. The amount of exterior whitespace between individual table cells. In layout tables, this attribute is usually set to 0.

child selector. A style selector that identifies all HTML tags of a particular type that have as their immediate parent a tag of another type, such as all paragraphs that are the immediate children of table cells.

class. A custom-made style selector that doesn't necessarily apply to any particular HTML tag or sequence of tags.

colspan. The number of vertical columns that a table cell straddles. Colspans are fine for data tables, but avoid them when you create layout tables! Use nested tables instead. Compare with **rowspan**.

compression. The process of making an image file lighter in file size by losing a portion of the visual information. Too much compression gets rid of too much information, and image quality deteriorates noticeably.

contextual selector. A style selector that identifies all HTML tags of a particular type that appear somewhere within the tag of another type, such as all strong tags that appear inside an ordered list.

data table. An HTML table that presents rows and columns of data as per HTML specs. Compare with **layout table**.

dateline. A short piece of text that gives the current date. Drop a dateline on a Web page to make its content seem fresher than it might actually be.

descender. The portion of a letter or typographical character that dips below the baseline of a line of type, like the stem of the lowercase letter **p**.

destination. In a link, the page that loads when the visitor clicks the source element.

div element. The more technical name for a CSS **layer**. Div stands for **division**, and that's exactly what it is—a division of your page.

document-relative path. A path to a file based on the current location of the browser. Links with document-relative paths work offline, but their format depends entirely on the level of the site at which they appear. If you move the link to a different level, the path no longer works. Document-relative paths are for internal links only. You can't use these paths for external links.

drop cap. An oversized capital letter that usually appears at the beginning of a chapter. It hangs below the baseline of the text, and the surrounding lines of type wrap around it.

Dynamic HTML (DHTML). Dynamic HyperText Markup Language, or the combination of HTML, JavaScript, and Cascading Style Sheets (CSS) for sophisticated, interactive Web sites.

email link. A link that opens a blank email window when clicked.

embedding. Including code such as CSS or JavaScript inside the head section of an HTML document between style or script tags. Compare with **attaching**.

end sign. A bullet or typographical character that appears at the end of a story or article. It is also a prophecy that Armageddon is nigh.

expando layout. A layout that automatically resizes to match the width of the browser window. This is the same thing as a **liquid layout**.

external link. A link to a file outside the current site. You must use absolute paths for external links. Compare with **internal link**.

fieldset. A group of logically related widgets.

File Transfer Protocol (FTP). The method that computers use to transfer data files back and forth on the Internet.

fixed-width layout. A design layout that uses absolute pixel measurements to determine the horizontal size of the page. Fixed-width layouts always display at the same width, regardless of the size of the screen or browser window.

floating. Pushing an element (usually an image) to the left or right of a block of text so that the text wraps around it.

form field, form object. More respectable names for **widgets**, or the thingies that you click or type text into on a form.

formatting tag. An HTML tag that describes the presentation of a block of content without identifying the content's structure.

hanging indent. A paragraph style where the first line of type pushes out to the left, not in to the right.

hotspot. A clickable region in an image map.

hover state. The status of a link when the visitor mouses over it. You don't get this link state in regular HTML. Define the hover state with CSS instead.

Hypertext Markup Language (HTML). A computer language that describes the content of a Web page.

ID selector. A style selector that applies to one and only one element per page.

image map. A clickable image with one or more **hotspots**, or clickable regions.

inline image. An image that appears inside a block of HTML text.

inline link. A link that appears inside the running text of a page.

internal link. A link to a file within the current Web site. You can use absolute, document-relative, or root-relative paths for internal links. Compare with **external link**.

JavaScript. A client-side technology for adding logical functions and mathematical calculations to a Web page.

jump menu. A quick index to the most common pages on your site that appears in a dropdown menu.

justified. A paragraph style where all the lines of text have the same length. The browser inserts whitespace between words and characters to pad out shorter lines. Compare with **ragged**.

keywords. Terms that describe the content of a Web page for the benefit of search engines. Put keywords for your page in a meta tag.

label (button). The text on a button.

label (form). The text that describes the function of a widget.

layer. A CSS-based box of content on a Web page. Layers aren't flat, like table cells, so you can stack them one atop another and position them anywhere on screen. Another name for a layer is a **div element**.

layout table. An HTML table that forms the structure of a page layout. HTML specs discourage layout tables. Compare with **data table**.

level. The position of a folder or file in the hierarchy of the site structure.

link state. The status of a hyperlink. Normally, there are three link states: **unvisited**, **visited**, and **active**, each with its own color. CSS adds a fourth: the **hover** state.

liquid layout. A layout that automatically resizes to match the width of the browser window. This is the same thing as an **expando layout**.

local. Pertaining to your personal computer.

local file. A computer document on your personal computer.

local folder, local root folder. The folder on your personal computer in which you store all the files of a site.

media. Components of a Web site that don't fall into the image, HTML, CSS, client-side scripting, or server-side scripting categories. Common types of media are sound files, movie files, Flash animations, SVG files, and Acrobat documents.

meta tag. A special HTML tag that contains general information about a Web page, such as keywords, the page description, and the refresh rate. The browser doesn't display the content of meta tags in the document window.

monospace. A typeface such as Courier New that displays all characters with the same amount of spacing between them for a typewriter-like effect.

named anchor. A location on a Web page to which you can link.

nav bar (navigation bar). A common Web interface element that presents links to the main content categories of the site.

nested div, nested layer. A div element that appears inside another div element.

nested table. A table that appears inside the table cell of another table.

optimizing. Reducing the file size of an image for faster downloading while maintaining image quality.

out of sync. The state of a Web site when its local files don't match its remote files.

palette. An image file's built-in color chart. GIFs and PNGs have palettes of up to 256 colors, while JPEGs don't have palettes and therefore aren't limited to 256 colors.

path. The set of directions that tells the browser how to get to a certain file.

phrase element. An HTML element that defines the structure of a segment of text within a larger element such as a paragraph. The em, strong, cite, and dfn tags are phrase elements, among others.

physical wrapping. A type of word wrapping in a text area where the browser submits the text with the extra line breaks that wrapping creates. Compare with **virtual wrapping**.

popup menu. A list of menu choices that appears when you hover over an item in the main navigation. You typically create popup menus with DHTML div elements.

popup window. A separate, often smaller browser window or JavaScript alert box that the main browser window opens. If the popup is a browser window, a predetermined page loads inside it.

presentation. The appearance of a Web page in a browser. HTML isn't supposed to get into presentation issues; the browser is supposed to handle that aspect. But traditionally, HTML has provided **formatting tags**, which allow designers to control the presentation of content without identifying its structure. Cascading Style Sheets (CSS) allow HTML to become a purely structural language once again.

pseudo-class. A special add-on to the anchor-tag selector that tells the browser to which link state the style rule applies.

pseudo-element. A special add-on to an HTML tag selector that identifies a particular section of the text inside the element, such as the first line or the first letter.

ragged. A paragraph style where the lines of type are their natural lengths, without extra spacing between the letters or words. Compare with **justified**.

ragged center. A paragraph style where the browser centers lines of type horizontally, leaving both sides uneven.

ragged left. A paragraph style where the lines of type line up on the right and leave the left sides uneven.

ragged right. A paragraph style where the lines of type line up on the left and leave the right sides uneven.

real-time. The designation of something—usually information—when it is up-to-the-second accurate.

remote. Pertaining to a computer to which your local machine connects over a network.

remote file. A computer document on the Web server.

remote folder, remote root folder. The folder or directory on the Web server that holds all the files for a site.

resolution. The size of the pixels in an image file: the higher the resolution, the smaller the pixels and the sharper the image but the larger the file size.

robot. Search-engine software that visits a Web site to catalog its content.

rollover graphic. An image file that seems to change when the visitor mouses over it. What actually happens is that a JavaScript function swaps in a separate image file.

root. The uppermost level of a site.

root-relative path. A path to a file based on the current Web site. As with absolute paths, root-relative paths always have the same format, no matter where they appear on your site. As with document-relative paths, you use root-relative paths for internal links only, not external links. But root-relative paths only work on a Web server. For this reason, most designers prefer to use document-relative paths for internal links.

rowspan. The number of horizontal rows that table cell straddles. Rowspans are fine for data tables, but avoid them when you create layout tables! Use nested tables instead. Compare with **colspan**.

rule. An interior border in a table. Rules retain their standard thickness, no matter the size of the table's border attribute.

sans serif. A typeface such as Arial that doesn't have little decorations on the ends of the letters. Compare with **serif**.

serif. A typeface such as Times New Roman that has little decorations on the ends of the letters. Compare with **sans serif**.

sibling selector. A style selector that identifies all HTML tags of a particular type that follow a tag of another type but aren't the children of this tag, like all paragraphs that follow first-level heads.

slicing. A technique for creating layout tables in graphics applications such as Fireworks and Photoshop. First, you design the layout in the graphics editor, and then you cut the layout into divisions or slices based on the different sections of the page. When you export the slices as individual graphics files, you also get an HTML table that reassembles the pieces in a Web browser.

source. In a link, the element that the visitor clicks to go to another page.

span. A segment of content identified by span tags in an HTML document.

structure (in HTML). The technical description of which pieces of content are what kinds of things on Web page. You use HTML tags to indicate structure, which the browser displays according to its built-in styles or designer-defined Cascading Style Sheets.

structure (Web site). The way in which you organize the hierarchy of categories and subcategories of a site.

style definition. The set of CSS attributes and values that describe how the browser should display a specific element.

style rule. A single set of presentation instructions for the browser in CSS. A style rule consists of a **style selector** and a **style definition**.

style selector. The CSS indicator that tells the browser to which element a style rule applies.

style sheet. A block of CSS code that appears between style tags in an HTML page or in a separate CSS file. A style sheet consists of one or more **style rules**.

synchronized. The state of a Web site when its local files exactly match its remote files.

text equivalents. Textual descriptions of nontextual content for use in screen readers and other accessibility tools. Providing alt text for images is adding text equivalents.

tag. An HTML keyword that identifies the structure of a piece of content.

tiling. Repeating an image to fill a given area.

timestamp. A short piece of text that gives the current time.

Universal Resource Locator (URL). The exact address of a file on the Web.

unvisited link. A link to a page that the browser doesn't remember visiting.

validating (form input). Checking the visitor's input in a form for mistakes. Validating a form helps to prevent bad data from crashing the server-side application that processes the form submission.

validating (page). Checking the source code of a Web page for standards compliance.

virtual wrapping. A type of word wrapping in a text area where the form submits the text without the extra line breaks that wrapping creates. Compare with **physical wrapping**.

visited link. A link to a page that the browser remembers visiting.

visual weight. How heavy a design element appears to be. In general, larger elements tend to look heavier than smaller ones.

Web host. A company or individual who provides the server for your Web site.

Web page. A single HTML document, plus its images, media files, scripts, and style sheets.

Web site. A collection of related HTML documents, plus the accompanying images, media files, scripts, and style sheets.

widget. One of the little thingies that you click or type text into on a form. Widgets are also called **form fields** and **form objects**.

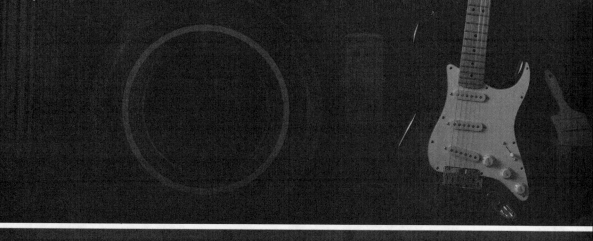

Index

C

capitalize text-transform CSS attribute, 249, 250
Capitalizing text, 247, 249–250
caption HTML tag, 319, 321
Carbon-copy email addresses, 327
Cascading Style Sheets (CSS), 232–240
  adding to Web pages with HTML style attribute, 240–241
  adding to Web pages with style sheets, 232–240
  attaching external, 86–87, 89
  browser support of, 232
  changing appearance of text elements with, 251–258
  changing default color for link states with, 369–371
  changing text style in text widgets with, 411–414
  coloring and formatting divs in, 155–162
  correct HTML markup and, 221, 224, 227
  defining class styles for, 259–263
  div elements and. See Divs (divisions), CSS
  embedding, 85–86, 89, 237–238
  example of, 233
  fixed-width layouts using. See Fixed-width CSS layouts
  floating inline images with, 185–188
  hiding code of from older browsers, 238
  hyperlink styles in, 352–355
  importing, 238–240
  inheritance (cascading) in, 235–237
  liquid (expando) layouts and, 121–125
  list formatting attributes supplied by, 295–301
  margin control with, 165–166, 275–276
  multicolumn layouts using, 137–139
  popup menus and, 68
  pseudo-elements, 341–345
  replacing HTML formatting with style definitions, 243–245
  rollover hyperlinks with, 359–361
  setting fieldset borders and legends with, 434–435
  spacing control with, 275–280
  as structural and graphical language, 231–232
  style definitions and, 232
  style rules and, 232
  style selectors and. See Style selectors, CSS
  table border styles and attributes supplied by, 333–335
  text formatting attributes supplied by, 247–250
  type justification and, 281–283
  type size and, 269–272, 273
  typefaces and, 265–268
  Web page background images and, 215–218
  writing, 232–237
Categories, site hierarchies and, 3–8
cellpadding HTML attribute, 134, 328–330
Cells, table
  background colors for, 149–153
  background images in, 207–209
  spacing of, 134, 328–330
cellspacing HTML attribute, 134, 328–330
Checkboxes, 391, 393–395, 423
Child elements, 235–237
Child selectors, 254–255
Citations, HTML tag for, 228
cite HTML tag, 228
Classes
  defining CSS, 259–263
  IDs for, 347–348
clear:both CSS style definition, 188
Click Here links, 377–378, 455
Clickable images, 19–20. See also Buttons
  accessibility and, 42–43
  affordances and, 18–23
  creating, 17
  grouping, 10–13, 18
  icons and symbols, 20–23
  removing borders from, 17–18
Client-side scripting, 407, 498–499

528

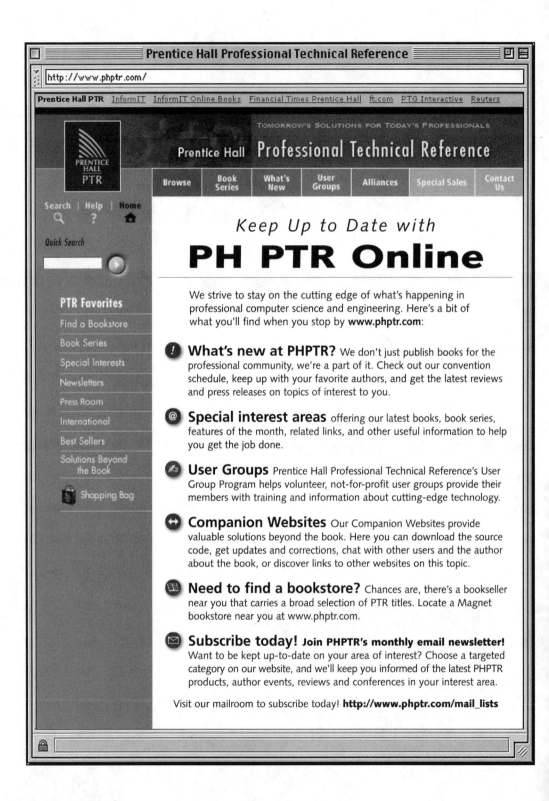